CULTURES IN ORGANIZATIONS
Three Perspectives

JOANNE MARTIN

New York   Oxford
OXFORD UNIVERSITY PRESS
1992

Oxford University Press

Oxford   New York   Toronto
Delhi   Bombay   Calcutta   Madras   Karachi
Kuala Lumpur   Singapore   Hong Kong   Tokyo
Nairobi   Dar es Salaam   Cape Town
Melbourne   Auckland

and associated companies in
Berlin   Ibadan

Copyright © 1992 by Oxford University Press, Inc.

Published by Oxford University Press, Inc.,
198 Madison Avenue, New York, New York 10016-4314

Oxford is a registered trademark of Oxford University Press

Library of Congress Cataloging-in-Publication Data
Martin, Joanne
Cultures in organizations : three perspectives /
by Joanne Martin.
p.   cm.   Includes bibliographical references and index.
ISBN 0–19–507163–8 ISBN 0–19–507164–6 (pbk.)
1. Corporate culture.
HD58.7.M374   1992   302.3'5—dc20   92–6607

Quotations from *Organizational Culture,* edited by P. Frost, L. Moore,
M. Louis, C. Lundberg, and J. Martin,
are reprinted by permission of Sage Publications, Inc.

Quotations from *Reframing Organizational Culture,* edited by P. Frost,
L. Moore, M. Louis, C. Lunberg, and J. Martin,
are reprinted by permission of Sage Publications, Inc.

Quotations from *Sexual/Textual Politics,* by Toril Moi,
are reprinted by permission of Methuen and Co.

9 8 7 6

Printed in the United States of America
on acid-free paper

Preface

The last decade has brought a renaissance of interest in cultural phenomena in organizations. In addition to the proliferation of popular books on the topic, scholars from a variety of disciplines (including anthropology, psychology, sociology, and organizational behavior) have produced a range of theoretical and empirical studies. Perhaps because of the epistemological, methodological, and political orientations that distinguish these disciplines, this literature remains theoretically unintegrated—in a state of conceptual chaos. This is not theoretical hairsplitting, a problem of importance only to ivory-tower scholars. Without some sense of theoretical consolidation, practitioners will find it difficult to draw on organizational culture research as a source of useful ideas.

Researchers cannot agree about some fundamental issues: What is culture in an organizational context? Are cultures necessarily characterized by conflicts and contradictions? Is ambiguity an indicator of the absence of culture, or is it the essence of any adequate contemporary cultural portrait? How do cultures change? To what extent can, and should, the cultural change process be influenced by those who hold power and those who dissent? How how can we write about cultures in a way that acknowledges the complexities and uncertainties inherent in any such study?

Given this conceptual chaos, it is no wonder that researchers adopt simplifying theoretical perspectives, fail to appreciate (or even read) research conducted within other perspectives, and argue about incommensurabilities. This book consolidates a diverse array of theoretical and empirical studies into an analytic framework that clarifies and challenges the assumptions that have guided studies of cultures in organizations. Without this kind of theoretical framework, organizational culture research may become, to cite some metaphors offered by critics, an intellectual dead end, a ghetto for softheads, or last year's fad.

This book delineates three competing perspectives that researchers use to understand cultures in organizations. It offers a way out of the conceptual chaos caused by conflicts among these three perspectives. This resolution acknowledges and tries to bridge incommensurabilities, without denying their importance, while offering insights unavailable to any single perspective. The book also brings an integrative, interdisciplinary perspective to the study of cultures in organizations, exploring links to major developments (such as environmental dependence and postmodernism) within and outside of organizational theory. By delineating and trying to bridge these different approaches to the understanding of cultures in organizations, this text offers a breadth that might be otherwise unavailable.

The book's abstract, theoretical focus is leavened with the analysis of many specific examples. In order to ground the abstract concepts that are the focus of the three-perspective framework, each theoretical perspective is illustrated with a qualitative case study of the cultures at the OZ Company—a large, multinational electronics corporation. The book alternates between presentations of the OZCO material and theoretical discussions that draw on quantitative and qualitative studies conducted by a variety of scholars in a variety of organizational settings, including Peace Corps/Africa, university settings, small nonprofit organizations, and a number of large and small private-sector companies. The inclusion of summaries and excerpts of this research gives the book's theoretical arguments a solid empirical base. It also, hopefully, makes it more interesting to read.

The book is written for an audience composed primarily of faculty and students in various kinds of management and organizational study departments. These would include organizational behavior, policy and strategy, and some psychology and sociology groups located both in traditional social science disciplines and in professional schools that focus on business, education, and public administration. In addition, the audience might include faculty and students in other departments that are beginning to include consideration of cultures in organizations, such as political science, anthropology, accounting, and information systems. Some managers might also—hopefully—be interested.

The book could serve as a text in organizational courses (broadly defined) at the graduate or advanced undergraduate level and could also be used in more specialized courses that include cultural issues. It can serve as a main text or as one of two or three major texts in a course. M.B.A. and undergraduate courses might find it helpful to begin by reading the four short chapters that focus on the OZCO case material (Chapters 2, 3, 5, and 7) before proceeding to a theoretical analysis. More advanced or theoretically oriented courses might wish to focus on the chapters which outline the three-perspective framework (Chapters 4, 6, 8, and 9). Whatever way it is read, it is my hope that this book will stimulate and structure a lively dialogue among researchers, faculty, students, and managers.

Stanford, Calif.   J. M.
February 1992

Acknowledgments

This book has been a long time in gestation, and my debts are many. I would particularly like to thank those who were kind enough to give me page-by-page comments on this entire manuscript. I owe the biggest debt to Debra Meyerson, who worked with me on the OZCO case, the Fragmentation perspective, and the development of a three-perspective view of cultural change. Her wit, gentle persistence, and intelligence have been a joy. Her comments on the first draft of this book were insightful enough to add quite a few months to the process of revision. Paul DiMaggio warned me of the perils of postmodernism and accentuated issues of power and conflict. Peter Frost thinned the ranks of unnecessary apologies and unclear ideas, adding an innovative twist whenever possible. Ed Schein was the finest of critics—disagreeing with me vehemently, cogently, and openly. In addition, I have had help and advice regarding the three-perspective framework from many colleagues, not all of whom approve of it, including Herb Addison, Howard Aldrich, Steve Barley, Jan Beyer, John S. Brown, Marta Calas, John Carroll, Richard Daft, Lex Donaldson, Richard Dunford, Peter Frost, Pasquale Gagliardi, Sylvia Gherardi, Michael Owen Jones, Meryl Louis, Craig Lundberg, Anne Miner, Larry Moore, Bill Ouchi, Chick Perrow, Lou Pondy, Majken Schultz, Linda Smircich, Harry Trice, Andy Van de Ven, and John Van Maanen.

I have learned much from the students who have worked with me on cultural research, especially Cathy Anterasian, Michael Boehm, Martha Feldman, Wendy Harrod, Mary Jo Hatch, Tom Kosnik, Debra Meyerson, Kerry Patterson, Melanie Powers, Caren Siehl, Sim Sitkin, and Alan Wilkins. In addition, some of my organizational colleagues at Stanford have over the years tried (and some of them would say, failed) to educate me: Jim Baron, Rod Kramer, Linda Ginzel, Hal Leavitt, John Meyer, Jim March, Don Palmer, Jeff Pfeffer, Jerry Porras, Dick Scott, Bob Sutton, and Gene Webb. Feminist and postmodern theories are also woven into this text, something that would never have happened without the intellectual company of the faculty associated with Stanford's Institute for Women and Gender, particularly Barbara Babcock, Laura Carstensen, Reginia Gagnier, Elizabeth Hansot, Nan Keohane, Diane Middlebrook, Deborah Rhode, and Susan Okin. Aromie Noe gave invaluable, painstaking help with references and quotation verification and Elsie Young provided expert secretarial help. Thank you, all.

I wrote this book with considerable support, financial and otherwise, from the Graduate School of Business at Stanford University, in particular the James and Doris McNamara Faculty Fellowship. In addition, the Australian Graduate School of Management, University of New South Wales, and the Department of Psychology, Sydney University, gave me visiting scholar appointments during my sabbatical year. During that time, I wrote the penultimate draft of this manuscript at a desk overlooking Gibson's Beach in Sydney.

The biggest thank you, however, goes to my family: my husband, Beau (A.) Sheil, and my son, Beau (M.) Sheil. They have let me write when they thought I should be sailing boats on Sydney Harbor, or otherwise enjoying their fine company. The younger Beau has brought smiles and a keen sense of what is important into my life. He has also monitored my progress with a checklist and has raced to see whether he could finish his book before I did (he won). Beau the elder (he prefers the word *mature*) has been the foundation of my life for years now, providing love, welcome distraction, and unwavering support through easy times and hard. He has also specialized in providing the emotional and technical assistance required to get me through three generations of word-processing software. To the two Beaus, this book is dedicated.

Contents

Cultures in Organizations

Seeing Cultures from Different Points of View

What does it mean to say that an organization has a culture or cultures? It is the purpose of this book to give an extended answer to that question. However, it would be useful to get an intuitive sense, at the beginning, of what culture can mean in organizations.

It is a rare person who has not had experience with a variety of organizations—schools, clubs, teams, charities, as well as the government bureaucracies and business organizations—that are the primary focus of this book. *As individuals come into contact with organizations, they come into contact with dress norms, stories people tell about what goes on, the organization's formal rules and procedures, its informal codes of behavior, rituals, tasks, pay systems, jargon, and jokes only understood by insiders, and so on. These elements are some of the manifestations of organizational culture. When cultural members interpret the meanings of these manifestations, their perceptions, memories, beliefs, experiences, and values will vary, so interpretations will differ—even of the same phenomenon. The patterns or configurations of these interpretations, and the ways they are enacted, constitute culture.* The word *patterns*, like the word *cultures* in the title of this book, is plural. This book is about differences in perspective.

RESEARCH DILEMMA

The recent proliferation of organizational culture research has produced considerable controversy. Many have hailed this as a long-overdue source of innovative thinking about organizations. Others criticize it as "old wine in new skins," an intellectual ghetto unrelated to mainstream organizational research, a metaphor without a theory, a "dead end" dominated by managerial concerns, or a fad that, at great expense to organizations, has failed to keep its seductive promises of improved morale, loyalty, harmony, productivity, and—ultimately—profitability.

Given the abundance of studies now available, it seems reasonable to expect that organizational culture researchers could, if they wish, answer these critics by summarizing what has been learned so far. This has not happened, and for good reasons. Organizational culture researchers disagree vehemently about fundamental issues, such as

1. Is culture a source of harmony, an effect of irreducible conflicts of interest, or a reflection of the inescapable ambiguities that pervade contemporary organizational life?
2. Must culture be something internally consistent, integrative, and shared? Or can it be inconsistent and expressive of difference? Or can it incorporate confusion, ignorance, paradox, and fragmentation?
3. What are the boundaries around culture(s) in organizations? Are boundaries essential?
4. How do cultures change?

Objectives of This Book

The primary objective of this text is to examine how these questions are answered by three social scientific perspectives that have come to dominate organizational culture research. This book shows the internal coherence of each perspective, explores its unstated assumptions, and suggests why it has emerged in a particular form. The book also delineates the insights offered by each perspective, the range and depth of which demonstrate that organizational culture research can no longer be dismissed as a fad, old wine, an intellectual ghetto, or a dead end.

This is, however, an area of inquiry that lacks a common definition of its central concept (culture) and has no theoretical paradigm that cultural researchers share. Thus a second goal of this book is to suggest why this is an understandable and perhaps even a desirable state of affairs. The blindspots and distortions associated with each of the three perspectives are complementary. Often one perspective's blindspot is another's focus, so that one's ''strength'' is another's ''weakness.'' There are good reasons why the differences among the perspectives exist. The objective of studying organizational culture, like any other area of organizational research, is to help us understand organizational life more fully. *When any single organization is viewed from all three perspectives, a greater understanding emerges than if it were viewed from any single perspective. If any cultural context is studied in enough depth, some things will be consistent, clear, and generate organization-wide consensus. Simultaneously, other aspects of the culture will coalesce within subcultural boundaries and still other elements of the culture will be fragmented, in a state of constant flux, and infused with confusion, doubt, and paradox.* For this reason, it is useful to understand the differences among the perspectives and to use a multiperspective approach or, at least, acknowledge what is excluded when only one perspective is used.

Understanding the differences among the three perspectives necessarily entails taking a meta-theoretical stance. (To move from a theoretical to a meta-theoretical position entails moving to a higher level of abstraction that encompasses previous theoretical positions.) The meta-theory offered in this book does not define culture as a variable that is embedded in a model of causes and effects.

This meta-theory is also not an integrative assimilation that undermines the differences among these three theoretical perspectives. This book's meta-theory explores each perspective from within, leaving its integrity undisturbed by pressures toward merger. It explores unstated assumptions in order to explain why disagreements among these perspectives are so deep, vehement, and productive. What is to be learned from culture research is, in part, the usefulness of preserving the differences among these social scientific perspectives and deepening, rather than eradicating, the conflicts among them.

A third objective of this book is to be critical of this meta-theoretical approach, by acknowledging and exploring its oversimplifications and oversights. A postmodern approach (to be defined in later chapters) is used to illuminate what this meta-theory distorts and excludes. The postmodern approach suggests other ways of examining cultures that reflect, more fully, the complexities of working in organizations as well as the unavoidable difficulties of building a theory of culture.

Organizational research has often been criticized for its managerial bias and, more recently, for the ways it reflects the vested interests of whites and of men. All too often the views of lower-ranking employees, women, and/or minorities have not been sought, deeply understood, or fully incorporated into theories of organization. The fourth goal of this book is to ensure that, in the domain of organizational culture, these voices influence the kinds of theoretical conclusions that are drawn. A multiperspective approach to understanding cultures in organizations draws attention to the viewpoints of cultural members, particularly those who are women and/or minorities and those who hold blue-collar and clerical positions. Once the voices of these people are heard, the idea that any organization has a single culture, understood in the same way by all its members, seems oversimplified.

The three social scientific perspectives are theoretical viewpoints developed by organizational culture researchers. These must be conceptually distinguished from the perspectives of cultural members, which also vary. Although these two kinds of perspectives are conceptually distinct, social scientific theories are empirically derived from the perspectives of cultural members. In order to get a sense of how these two kinds of cultural perspectives can coincide and vary, two sets of examples are given below. The first consists of a set of quotations, illustrating differences in perspective among cultural members who are employees of a large corporation. The second is a hypothetical argument among advocates of the three social scientific perspectives.

SEEING CULTURES DIFFERENTLY

Perspectives of Cultural Members at OZCO

OZCO is a pseudonym for a real corporation. It is one of the Fortune 500, a firm that employs over 80,000 employees worldwide. The company has been the focus of several major cultural studies and has been mentioned frequently in a wide range of other texts.[1] Generally, these are glowing reports that any company would be proud of. The firm is described as being a haven of consensus, "family feeling," and contentment in an industry (high technology) that has been wracked by economic difficulties and a turbulent environment.

The "conversation" below is composed of quotations excerpted from transcripts and field notes of interviews conducted with OZCO employees.[2] (The sampling procedure and methodology of this study is described more fully in Chapter 2.) The conversation is hypothetical only in that employees were talking to researchers, rather than to each other. These quotations were selected because they all refer to OZCO's reputation for having a "family feeling" of closeness among its employees. The first employee, Denise, works in OZCO's headquarters, an open office where low partitions separate desks, and there are few walls or doors:

> People get involved in each other's personal lives simply because they overhear each other on the phone. There is no privacy, so a family atmosphere is fostered. (Denise, product marketing)

> OZCO is like a family. . . . Even in the nicest, friendliest family you are going to find some reward and punishment mechanisms. You expect that even if it is hidden, there are high level discussions about this subtle control strategy. Even though I've had some high level organizational dealings, I haven't seen evidence of this. The parents don't seem to talk about them. This good homey feeling is pretty deep; I haven't seen that fade away. The battling is more like two brothers battling than competitive strangers. I keep thinking that there have to be things going on that I'm not seeing, but I don't think so. (Stuart, marketing engineer)

> Along with this very nice, humanitarian theme goes the midwestern mommy and daddy: daddy makes the decisions and takes care of the family and mommy does the supplementary stuff. (Sally, human resources consultant)

> I guess I hired on with the company just by their reputation. . . . They treated their employees very well and it had a type of family atmosphere, and that once you were hired on at OZCO, you were almost like one of the family and you never got thrown out of the company. They treated you very well. They cared about you—that sort of thing. And I must admit, I don't hear that today. Yes, I think you hear good things about OZCO, but not in the same way: that you are an individual, that you are cared about, [that] type of thing. I think basically that if you're here at OZCO and you do a good job you will be rewarded. But, you don't have that feeling of closeness. (Aida, personnel clerk)

> I'm beginning to wonder if they really care. I don't know. Well, the thing is, from my experiences and from other peoples' experiences that I know of, when you try and take [problems] high up, it seems to be—everybody seems to try and hush you up and pass it by you and say, "Yes, we'll look into it." And then you start hearing all the different stories that everybody is telling and it never gets told as it really is. (Ron, operations staff)

Although these employees are all discussing some aspect of "family feeling," they are focusing on different aspects of what a family means and are coming to different conclusions about OZCO. Both Stuart and Denise are saying that the company is like a family, but Stuart is discussing parents and fights between brothers, while Denise is talking about a lack of privacy. Sally focuses on the gender relations of a family, while Ron and Aida worry about the absence of family closeness. These quotations illustrate the importance of allowing for differences in the meanings people attach to cultural manifestations: there is no single, objectively correct view of the "family feeling" at OZCO. Different cultural members have different opinions.

These quotations raise a number of questions that are crucial for the study of culture. For example, did OZCO used to have a widely shared feeling of family closeness that has disappeared as the company has grown? How representative is this sample of cultural members? Is there a shared feeling of closeness in the higher ranks of the company, or among the engineers, that is lacking among clerical workers or custodial staff? Do all members of a given rank or job have similar reactions or are there major variations within some of these groupings? Are any of these groupings a subculture; how would a researcher decide? Given differences in the perspectives of cultural members, what kinds of conclusions about culture can legitimately be drawn? Do these differences of opinion mean that OZCO has a culture characterized by fragmentation, with no clear, stable consensus within or across groups? Or does OZCO lack a culture? Or, at some deeper level not evident in these quotations, are there assumptions about OZCO that all these employees share?

To complicate matters further, what cultural members say or do can also depend on who is observing. For example, employees may be unwilling to speak or act freely in front of a researcher who has a different educational background, or who is a member of a different occupational or demographic group (class, race, ethnicity, or gender, for example). In the presence of a white man in a suit, whose research is known to have the approval of management, some cultural members may be more guarded (or confrontative) in their behavior. And a researcher's own background may affect that researcher's choice of what to attend to, what is remembered, or what interpretations are seen as plausible. As a result, different researchers studying the same context might carefully and honestly report what they see, yet come to quite different, empirically based conclusions.

As a result of difficulties such as these, organizational researchers have developed radically different approaches to studying culture. Some define culture in different ways and study quite different phenomena; other researchers define culture in nearly identical ways (usually as consensus about shared values or assumptions), but from the evidence they present, it is clear that they do not have the same understanding of the meaning of the term. Some are generalists, writing as if any aspect of organizational life were part of culture, while others attempt to define culture more narrowly, in order to distinguish it from related concepts, such as norms, climate, or values.

Practical Implications of Different Points of View

These differences of opinion are not theoretical hairsplitting with relevance only for ivory-tower scholars. Corporations have spent considerable amounts of money in response to seductive promises of easy cultural change. Some managers have sought to replicate the strong cultures of successful companies, while others have tried to "engineer" commitment to a philosophy of management, in the hopes of increasing loyalty, productivity, or profitability. Some founders have sought to create a culture cast in their own image, to perpetuate their own personal values and achieve an organizational form of immortality. Usually practitioners respond to easy solutions and quick fixes with well-deserved skepticism, but organizational culture has sometimes seemed to be immune from such skepticism. For some corporations, this has been an expensive mistake. Now, many dismiss culture as yesterday's fad.

This seesaw between credulity and disillusionment has caused a considerable waste of money, time, and emotional effort. Practitioners need to know enough about theory and research to judge—with skepticism—what researchers are focusing on and what they are ignoring or distorting. Otherwise, it is impossible to make a knowledgeable decision about whether a particular kind of research will have useful applications in a particular context. Furthermore, the three social scientific perspectives come to different conclusions about how cultures change, making implications for managing cultural transitions difficult to decipher. For all these reasons, practitioners cannot afford to dismiss the theoretical disagreements discussed in this book as irrelevant hairsplitting.

Social Scientific Differences of Opinion

Before offering formal definitions of the social scientific perspectives that have come to dominate organizational culture research, it is instructive to listen to an argument among hypothetical proponents of these positions (labeled *Integration, Differentiation,* and *Fragmentation*). The main theoretical points of difference will emerge from the dialogue, and some sense of the differing world views behind the perspectives will become evident. Although fierce arguments like the one that follows really do occur, these three voices are amalgamations of opinions, drawn from a variety of sources. They do not represent real people, and they are not referring to the opinions of the OZCO employees quoted earlier.

Integration: Well, I think we would all agree that culture is what people share—the social glue that binds organizational members together.

Differentiation: No. That is exactly the kind of homogenizing assumption that makes an Integration perspective problematic. You cannot assume that such consensus exists. Even if employees tell you they agree with top managers' views or with your own interpretations, if you look at their behavior you will see a much more differentiated vision of culture. Organizations are full of conflicts of interest among groups of people. Engineering and marketing, for example, often have very different cultures.

Integration: But aren't you agreeing with me that culture implies consensus? Aren't you just drawing the boundary of the culture around a smaller collectivity: the subculture?

Differentiation: No. When I consider a higher level of analysis and look at the whole organization, subcultural differentiation permits me to see conflict, as well as harmony. Without a Differentiation viewpoint, power dynamics are masked.

Integration: But there are some fundamental convictions that everyone in a group shares, however you want to define that group.

Differentiation. This is more than just a question of where you draw the boundaries around a culture or subculture. The Integration perspective ignores inconsistencies within cultural boundaries. Even if you restrict your attention just to managers, as you sometimes do, there is always the possibility that managers may, for good reasons, say one thing and do the opposite. If you fail to attend to inconsistencies, you can fail to penetrate the surface rhetoric; when you get only the "official view," you may miss the essence of a culture.

Fragmentation: Don't both of you assume that culture is the absence of ambiguity, that culture is that which seems clear? Even from a Differentiation perspective, the inconsistencies and conflicts that you describe are clear, in the sense that opposites are juxtaposed: for example, engineers want one thing and marketing wants the antithesis, or managers say one thing and do another. Doesn't this emphasis on culture as clarity leave out most of contemporary life? Clear consensus is hardly the hallmark of our society. Clear, dichotomous conflicts are also rare. From a Fragmentation perspective, the confusions, paradoxes, and unknowns that we encounter every day are salient and inescapable. Many conflicts are more like irreconcilable tensions, difficult to articulate, often paradoxical, rarely resolvable. Given the lives we lead, isn't ambiguity the essence of any adequate cultural description?

Integration: Ambiguity is not culture; it is the absence of a culture. We must define culture in terms of clarity, consistency, and consensus. If we allow the core concept of culture to include the Differentiation or Fragmentation perspectives, we have lost the ability to distinguish culture from other domains of organizational research, such as climate, norms, roles, or values. Organizations can differ in the extent to which they have a culture.

Fragmentation: Isn't the Integration perspective assuming we should consider culture as yet another variable, to be used to account for variance unexplained by other variables studied in organizational research? Why can't some of us, at least, consider culture not as a variable, but as a metaphor for all of organizational life? Theorists have examined organizations as if they were machines or organic systems—maybe we'll learn something different if we assume they *are* cultures?

Integration: That's the kind of vague and fuzzy thinking that gives culture research a bad name. What does it really mean to say that organizations are cultures? What, then, isn't culture? How does that help us understand organizations—or cultures?

Fragmentation: But the Integration perspective's theoretical and empirical claims of clarity may not be justified. Organizations, environments, and group boundaries are constantly changing. Individuals have fragmented, fluctuating self-concepts. One moment a person thinks of himself or herself as belonging to one subculture, and a minute later another subcultural membership becomes salient. People fluctuate in this way because they are faced with inescapable contradictions, as well as things they do not understand. Good cultural research should capture these complexities, rather than exclude them from the definition of culture.

Integration: You sound like a belly-gazing academic, paralyzed by complexity. If we focus on ambiguity and fragmentation, how can leaders expect to manage organizational culture? How can you explain the fact that organizations engage in coordinated action, often in a very rapid manner? Some cultural changes are leader-controlled and organization-wide. For example, don't successful organizations often have cultures congruent with the values of their founders? What can you say that would help leaders adjust their cultures to improve problems of morale or quality control? Have you no interest at all in helping managers create or modify cultures so that employees' organizational lives will be more satisfying and more productive?

Differentiation: But the Integration perspective assumes that value homogeneity is possible and, sometimes, that it has desirable effects, such as enhancing productivity or morale. In addition, this work focuses primarily on what leaders want and do. Integration studies often do not ask how lower-ranking employees feel about cultural interventions that attempt to interfere with their personal values or require more work without more pay. What about those blacks or women who might not be comfortable with values and norms chosen by high-ranking managers who are, mostly, white men? If you advocate value homogeneity that reflects the views of top managers, aren't you are assuming that the interests of managers are the same as the interests of members of these other groups? Instead, you should see change as a struggle among groups, with varying degrees of power to impose and resist change. You should place more emphasis on the interests, viewpoints, and goals of subordinated groups, as well as managers.

Fragmentation: What worries me is that the Integration perspective is valuing homogeneity at a time when organizations are experiencing, and learning to value, unprecedented diversity. Demographic research indicates this will continue. As women and minorities begin to move into different kinds of occupations and higher levels of the hierarchy, as they are already starting to do, individual identities will become even more complex. For example, a black woman engineer may find her self-concept fragmented in unprecedented ways as she moves through a day or up a hierarchy. Or a rapidly growing start-up company may have no stable job descriptions or even product lines, as vice presidents and receptionists join in packing boxes in order to meet a shipping deadline. In such contexts, old models of conflict between labor and management, men and women, blacks and whites, will become less useful as traditional divisions between groups erode, fluctuate, or become more complicated. Organizational theories that focus on homogeneity and clarity or clearly delineated conflicts between stable and well-defined groups will not provide adequate explanations for observed phenomena. We need the complexity inherent in the Fragmentation perspective if our theories of culture are going to have relevance to contemporary organizational life. Unless cultural researchers are willing to grapple with these complexities, they cannot presume that their work can be useful to practitioners.

The Costs of These Social Scientific Disagreements

When organizational culture researchers interact with advocates of opposing points of view, arguments like the preceding one actually do occur. Professional reputations, promotion reviews, and publication decisions are sometimes at stake. The utility and ethics of cultural change interventions are being questioned. No wonder, then, that the struggle is so intense. The vehemence with which these social scientific perspectives are defended, however, creates costs— to organizational culture research, to research in other domains of organizational theory, and to practitioners interested in understanding and perhaps applying the results of this work. And these costs are not trivial.

For organizational culture researchers, it becomes difficult to engage in constructive discourse across viewpoints. One culture researcher's assumptions are, to a researcher working from a different perspective, evidence of epistemological naiveté, methodological sloppiness, or inexcusable political bias. As a result, organizational culture researchers often fail to appreciate, acknowledge, or even read research representative of other viewpoints. Without this minimal level of intellectual cross-fertilization, effort is wasted and opportunities to learn are missed. The result is conceptual chaos. Organizational culture researchers duplicate and contradict each other's unread work and argue about incommensurabilities without acknowledging (or sometimes even realizing) this is what they are doing. Under these conditions, it is impossible to determine what has been learned from the recent proliferation of interest in cultural phenomena.

For researchers outside the cultural domain, the vehemence of this clash makes it difficult to understand whether cultural research can make any unique contribution to the rest of organizational theory. These researchers ask, for example: Why call it culture? Why not just talk about harmony, conflict, or ambiguity in organizations? Why do culture researchers seldom acknowledge their intellectual ancestors or integrate what they do into mainstream organizational theory or other related areas of cultural inquiry? Is culture a "kitchen sink" for all the variance unexplained by the usual variables, such as structure, norms, technology, size, and so on? If not, what, then, is culture?

BLURRING CATEGORIES AND DECONSTRUCTING META-THEORIES

Given the high costs of this vehement conflict—to practice as well as to research—it is not surprising that some people have begun to ask for a resolution: a definitive, integrative assessment of what has been learned from the proliferation of culture research. One traditional response would be to classify cultural studies into clearly defined, mutually exclusive categories. The weaknesses of each category could then be analyzed, probably judging one type of research to be better—that is, more "accurate"—than the others. As a culmination of this traditional theory-building process, a meta-theory of organizational culture could then be offered, encompassing and presumably surpassing all previous contributions. (Not surprisingly, critics of this traditional approach to theory building refer to meta-theories as "totalitarian" efforts to dominate or assimilate the work of predecessors.) Of course, soon someone else would come along with an even-more-grand meta-theory, thereby encompassing and surpassing this first attempt to build a meta-theory—perpetuating this process in the name of intellectual progress.

This book approaches the theory-building process in a style that has some of these characteristics, but differs in important ways. It outlines a theoretical framework that clarifies the assumptions, contributions, and blindspots of the three social scientific approaches to the study of culture—without permitting one approach to absorb or distort another. The next section of this chapter explains the advantages of this framework and how it differs from more traditional approaches to theory-building.

Introducing the Three Perspectives

This book examines the commonalities and fundamental conflicts in culture research by distinguishing and then analyzing three social scientific perspectives: the Integration, Differentiation, and Fragmentation views.[3]

Studies conducted from an *Integration* perspective have three defining characteristics: all cultural manifestations mentioned are interpreted as consistently reinforcing the same themes, all members of the organization are said to share in an organization-wide consensus, and the culture is described as a realm where all is clear. Ambiguity is excluded.

In contrast, research conducted from a *Differentiation* perspective describes cultural manifestations as sometimes inconsistent (for example, when managers say one thing and do another). Consensus occurs only within the boundaries of subcultures, which often conflict with each other. Ambiguity is channeled, so that it does not intrude on the clarity which exists within these subcultural boundaries.

Studies conducted from a *Fragmentation* perspective focus on ambiguity as the essence of organizational culture. Consensus and dissensus are issue-specific and constantly fluctuating. No stable organization-wide or subcultural consensus exists. Clear consistencies and clear inconsistencies are rare.

These three social scientific perspectives are summarized in Table 1-1 and represented (in partial and idiosyncratic ways) in the second of the two culture arguments earlier.

Why These Perspectives Are Subjective

Many cultural researchers assume or assert that a particular perspective represents an accurate reflection of an objectively observed reality, rather than subjectively construed conceptual judgments. Thus some companies are said to have more consistency, organization-wide consensus, and clarity than others. Or a company is seen as passing, in stages, from having an Integrated culture to having a Differentiated or Fragmented culture. Furthermore, some researchers would argue that when enough high quality cultural research has been done, it will be possible to declare a winner in the war of the three perspectives, in the sense that one of the three (or some variant or combination of the three) will be shown to be the single most accurate way to describe the majority of organizational cultures. These conclusions reify cultures as having an objective reality that can be accurately assessed as fitting one of the social scientific perspectives more than the others.

In contrast, this book argues that *a social scientific perspective is an interpretive framework that is subjectively imposed on the process of collecting and analyzing cultural data. A social scientific perspective is not considered here to*

Table 1-1 Defining characteristics of the three perspectives

Perspective	Integration	Differentiation	Fragmentation
Orientation to consensus	Organization-wide consensus	Subcultural consensus	Multiplicity of views (no consensus)
Relation among manifestations	Consistency	Inconsistency	Complexity (not clearly consistent or inconsistent)
Orientation to ambiguity	Exclude it	Channel it outside subcultures	Focus on it
Metaphors	Clearing in jungle, monolith, hologram	Islands of clarity in sea of ambiguity	Web, jungle

Adapted from Martin and Meyerson (1988), Table 1; Meyerson and Martin (1987), Figure 3; and Frost, Moore, Louis, Lundberg, and Martin (1991), Table 1.1.

be an objective description of empirical facts. This is not because researchers are careless, dishonest, or otherwise inadequate social scientists. It is because different researchers, studying the same cultural members and the same organizational events with equal care, skill, and honesty may evaluate, recall, and interpret what happens differently. This is so, in part, because who a researcher is, or is seen to be, may affect what cultural members say and do. In addition, different researchers have different preconceptions, sensitivities, and skills. For example, an African-American researcher with personal experience of subtle forms of racial prejudice, in contrast to a white researcher less conscious of race, may elicit or offer a different interpretation of the meaning of an inter-racial interaction.

Because of these issues, it is essential to realize that when a study concludes, for example, that all members of a culture share a particular value, this is a subjective judgment. Whether that judgment is based on quantitative or qualitative data, the measurement, collection, and interpretation of that data are affected by subjective factors. The three social scientific perspectives, then, should be thought of as subjectively perceived "ideal types," rather than objective descriptions of particular cultural realities. Culture is not reified—out there—to be *accurately* observed.[4]

Once these social scientific perspectives are conceptualized as subjective, it becomes easier to see their shortcomings and imagine them changing. An example from another area might clarify this contention. There is nothing "natural" about categorizing people by the color of their skin. For instance, why do race classifications focus on skin color, rather than the color of a person's eyes? In the United States, why is color so often conceptualized as a dichotomy (black or white)? Once race is seen as a subjective, socially constructed category, different ways of seeing racial relations become possible. A "fact of nature" becomes a social relationship of domination and oppression that might be viewed quite differently and changed.[5] In a similar way, once the three social scientific perspectives are seen as subjective and socially constructed, it becomes possible to envision other ways of conceptualizing what cultures are and how they change.

Why the Use of These Categories Is Problematic

The three social scientific perspectives are categories and as such are usually based on dichotomous reasoning. Almost always, one end of the dichotomy comes to be seen as inferior to the other, as in black:white and emotion:reason.[6] Continua offer a more subtle, gradated version of this kind of reasoning, as one end of a continuum is usually similarly devalued. Linear thinking, such as stage theories, are a variant of this system because they assume some sort of progressive movement (perhaps with allowance for regression) toward an endpoint that is considered a superior state. Hegelian thesis-antithesis-synthesis is a more sophisticated variant of linear thinking. In each of these types of categorization schemes, there is a temptation to see the categories as differentially valuable. One reason categories are problematic, then, is that they tend to become hierarchies. Therefore, the three social scientific perspectives are not to be understood as a kind of dichotomy, continuum, or linear movement of stages.

Categories have other shortcomings, most significant—their failure to capture some information of importance. Since categories implicitly exclude consideration of dissimilarities within (and similarities across) category boundaries, some phenomena may fit mostly, but not entirely, within a category. Other phenomena straddle category boundaries, making boundaries permeable. In addition, category definitions and memberships can change over time. To summarize, people and things seldom fit categories in any easy way and much of importance is always ignored whenever categories are used.

A single study usually places a primary emphasis on one of the three perspectives, perhaps because it helps the work be concise and coherent enough to be published, read, and understood. Some researchers adopt a single perspective in all of their culture studies, perhaps because it reflects their personal values or gives their work continuity. Other researchers, over the course of their careers, do research that wanders in and out of these three perspectives, perhaps in response to changing beliefs about cultural phenomena, different kinds of data, or even the demands of particular reviewers. In addition, particular studies often straddle the boundaries among these perspectives, giving minor levels of attention to secondary or tertiary points of view.

The danger inherent in describing the three perspectives is that these categories will be misused. The boundaries of the three social scientific perspectives are permeable and a goal of this book is to make them more so. Thus attempts to acknowledge the limitations of a perspective, or to cross perspective boundaries, should be encouraged. If these efforts are ignored, and only a category label for a study or a researcher is remembered, the three-perspective framework would be reifying the nature of the phenomena being classified and the differences among the categories themselves. The three social scientific perspectives should not be used to "pigeonhole" the life work of researchers or to oversimplify the characteristics of a piece of research or a sequence of studies that tries to represent, fully, more than one of these points of view. Therefore, *the three social scientific perspectives are used in this book to describe the primary emphasis of a single study, with the understanding that secondary emphases within that study or other studies by the same researcher might be more congruent with another perspective.*

To complicate matters further, cultural members sometimes speak or act in ways that are congruent with a social scientific perspective. For example, sometimes cultural members focus on what is agreed on, what arouses conflicts between groups, or what is ambiguous. Sporadic, partial congruence between the social scientific perspectives and the viewpoints of cultural members is not surprising. The three social scientific perspectives were derived inductively; they describe many of the important differences among large numbers of empirical studies of organizational culture. Thus each social scientific perspective has an extensive empirical foundation that is based on the viewpoints of members of a wide variety of organizational cultures.

Nevertheless, what cultural members do or say sometimes does not fit within these three social scientific perspectives. In addition, cultural members often switch rapidly from one perspective to another, even in the course of a single utterance. Perhaps because cultural members are not trying to leave a coherent, publishable written record of their perceptions, they feel freer to sacrifice conceptual consistency if it is necessary in order to capture the complexity of what they want to say.

To summarize the argument made in this section, the three social scientific perspectives are empirically derived categories. These perspectives capture some of the major conceptual (but not methodological or epistemological) dimensions of agreement and disagreement among studies of cultural members. Most of this book focuses on what these perspectives include. Perhaps its most important objective, however, is to show how working within any one of the three perspectives forces a researcher to ignore and distort cultural phenomena. To study a cultural context from all three of these perspectives broadens and deepens understanding. But because of the problematic nature of categories, even a three-perspective framework (like any other meta-theory) must distort the viewpoints it encompasses and reduce the complexities of individuals, ideas, and actions— both those that are included and those that are excluded.

Paradigms or Preparadigmatic Debates?

Are these perspectives really paradigms? In this book this question is answered with a resounding "no." Unless the reasons for this refusal are understood, the content and structure of this book will not make sense. Kuhn defines a *paradigm* as a constellation of shared convictions that facilitates the development of an intellectual movement into an institutionalized part of a mainstream of "normal" scientific inquiry.[7] In early publications, Meyerson and I referred to the three perspectives, all too casually, as "paradigms."[8] Others have referred to the three-perspective framework itself as a transition point in the development of cultural studies from an intellectual movement to a paradigm—that is, an institutionalized component of mainstream organizational science. Gagliardi discusses the ambivalence inherent in such a transition.[9] He characterizes the three-perspective framework as an attempt to articulate a paradigm that speaks to "needs of certainty, order, communication, and knowledge transfer," legitimizing culture as a domain of inquiry and helping researchers seeking "exemplars" of "good research."[10] At the same time, however, Gagliardi notes what is lost in such a transition:

> To go from the movement to the institution means to go from the phase of the thousand options—where everything is still possible, and we have to deal with the anxiety deriving from the uncertainty of the language and of the ends, but we also can enjoy the enthusiasm and hope of new discoveries—to the phase where the options are reduced, the avenues of knowledge and the way of going along them appear with reassuring clarity but in the same time constrain the scope and the trajectory of possible developments. (Gagliardi, 1991, p. 2)

In recognition of the less desirable aspects of institutionalization, this book describes the three viewpoints as perspectives, not paradigms. There are several reasons for this. Jaggar argues that full-fledged paradigms reflect the material interests of particular groups.[11] Although it is difficult to ascertain the material interests of particular groups of researchers, the authors of studies primarily congruent with one of the three perspectives cannot be characterized as sharing particular demographic or social identities. This suggests that the three viewpoints may not be full-fledged paradigms. In a more specific use of the term "paradigm," Burrell and Morgan argue that organizational theory and research is characterized by several paradigms that have methodological and epistemological, as well as theoretical, attributes.[12] The three social scientific perspectives on cultural research are not consistently associated with particular epistemologies or methods, so this too suggests that they are not paradigms, at least in the sense that Burrell and Morgan use this term. Interestingly, Strathern suggests that pre-paradigmatic conflicts are particularly overt and intense because each viewpoint can still be overthrown relatively easily.[13] This suggestion might explain the vehemence of conflicts among the three perspectives.

In addition to refusing to treat the three perspectives as three paradigms, this book argues that the three-perspective framework itself should not be be treated as a paradigm. Instead, this text concludes by discussing the blindspots inherent in each perspective, deconstructing the three-perspective framework, and revealing the kinds of cultural issues it does not or cannot address. Why would anyone bother to read about a categorization scheme that self-destructs in this way? There may be no other intellectually honest alternative. Avoiding the claims of certainty inherent in a paradigmatic stance is congruent with the reflexivity of a cultural approach, particularly its acknowledgment of the epistemological complexities of studying subjective, socially constructed processes. Furthermore, failure to deconstruct the three perspectives would reify these categories, rather than transcend their blindspots. To make this endeavor worthwhile and to learn from it, it is essential to point out what cannot be understood as long as the three perspectives remain intact. For these reasons, the perspectives themselves, and the three-perspective framework, should not be construed as paradigms.

An Alternative Way of Writing About Theory

Some see social science as achieving intellectual progress through an on-going competition among opposing viewpoints. It is a continual struggle for supremacy, for the intellectual goal of getting closer to the truth, and for personal career enhancement. This view of the knowledge-building process legitimates and reinforces a particular style of theoretical writing. Each theoretician speaks and writes as if a particular perspective were "the truth." The theorist tries to present a highly polished, "show-stopping" argument that admits no weaknesses. This style of writing tries to present itself as finished, impenetrable, not open to attack, except in the form of normal science extensions—that is, minor, empirically based adjustments in this one-best-way to see the world.

Theoretical writing congruent with this view of social science presumes an atmosphere of a fierce debate (as in the argument earlier among the hypothetical advocates of the three social scientific perspectives). In this kind of writing, uncertainties are often not admitted; the implicit goal is to score a point, beat the competition, and destroy opposing arguments. If the theory-building process is to be demystified, and if the weaknesses of any meta-theoretical move are to be explored, an alternative way of writing about theory needs to be used.

This book is written more in the style of a conversation than a fierce debate. By using this kind of writing, one tries to create a space where different theoretical points of view can converse with minimal distortion. As in a conversation, each perspective is given its turn to speak fully, in its own words (with extensive quotations). Only after each perspective is presented without interruption, can it be criticized. This way of writing tries to preserve the integrity of each perspective, so it is not placed under pressure to assimilate to another. This approach requires respect for the integrity of each of the social scientific viewpoints—and modesty about limitations.

LIMITATIONS

This book is limited by who I am and what I have chosen to cover—the most important of these limitations being my own. This book is limited by where I stand in the social scientific argument presented earlier and by my belief that social science research cannot be value-neutral. While I try to represent each of the three perspectives even-handedly, this will be easier in some cases than in others.

For example, I appreciate the Differentiation perspective's sensitivity to inequality and the dynamics of power, as these concerns are my own. Because my political commitments and my gender make me different from many of the people I work with, I am generally uncomfortable with homogenizing assumptions about what "we all share" since such statements often leave out my views. And because these omissions are usually neither overt nor intentional, I am left deciphering silences and trying to find my place "between the lines" of a discourse. Perhaps as a result, the ambiguities described by the Fragmentation perspective are a central part of my experience. These aspects of who I am make me especially critical of the Integration perspective's emphasis on clarity and organization-wide consensus.

However, there are contradictions inherent in my position. I am a white, Anglo-Saxon Protestant. I have a relatively high income, a good education, and a good job. Perhaps because I am a beneficiary of this series of hierarchical relationships, much of my early organizational culture research, and not a few of my present ideas, have affinities with the Integration perspective. I also appreciate the Fragmentation perspective's acknowledgment of the multiple identities that people bring to and enact in their work. I see organizational life as full of unresolvable complexities, confusion, and constant flux, and I see most organizational theory (including my own) as offering clear and rational explanations of phenomena which lack these characteristics, imposing unity on difference, and offering cross-sectional views that imply a stability that seldom exists and never persists. Perhaps, because I live with all of these contradictions, I have published within, and vacillated among, all three of the theoretical viewpoints described in this book.

My belief that social science research cannot be value-neutral has implications for my writing style. Traditional social science writing enhances the authority of the author by making the author disappear, leaving only the impersonal voice of "truth" speaking, usually in the passive voice. Some scholars have argued that scientific writers should expose the limitations of the I/eye of the author, by writing in the first person and describing the interaction between what is being observed and who is doing the observing.[14] Although I have been intellectually convinced of the merit of these arguments, I-centered writing still sounds egotistical and self-indulgent to my oversocialized ears. Therefore, I have written this book in a relatively impersonal style, using a personal voice only in a few places where a discussion of my biases and limitations seemed essential.

This text is also limited by what I have chosen to include and exclude. Within the domain of organizational culture research, the book focuses on representative or particularly fine studies, rather than attempting to include everything. It primarily draws on organizational culture research published in the United States, although some published work from other countries is included. This book covers research conducted in the last fifty years (primarily in the last decade) in organizations located in Western, industrialized countries.

This is not a book written primarily for practitioners. Hopefully some will be interested, although this book does not address some important issues. For example, it does not assess the merits of the claim that there is a correlation between a firm's culture and its performance[15] and it does not offer guidelines for changing a "bad" or "weak" culture to a more desirable one. To the extent that these issues are addressed at all, it is to challenge the presuppositions that would lead one to hope for such applications of cultural research.

Although the book incorporates some references to work outside the domain of organizational culture, a comprehensive integration of the anthropological or sociological work on culture is beyond its scope. It does not explore links to noncultural organizational research or to related treatments of homogeneity, difference, and ambiguity in other disciplines, such as literary criticism, philosophy, and history. The ideas presented later could be explored differently, and perhaps more effectively, in a fuller interaction with these other traditions of inquiry. However, others could do this better than I.

OVERVIEW

The practical and intellectual utility of the three-perspective framework is clarified when it is grounded by an empirical illustration. For this reason, OZCO is described three times, from each of the three social scientific perspectives. This does not mean that the empirical basis of the three-perspective framework is a case study of one organization; as explained earlier, each of the three social scientific perspectives rests on its own substantial empirical foundation. In order to maximize the usefulness of the OZCO case material, the sequence of chapters in this book alternates between theoretical abstraction and the empirical specificity of the descriptions of OZCO.

Chapter 2 introduces the OZCO case, describing the firm, the sampling procedure, the methodology, and the style and format with which the case material is presented.

Chapter 3 offers an Integration view of OZCO, using quotations from cultural members. These employees appear to share the values and opinions of the top leadership, working together in apparent harmony and consensus. The Integration view of OZCO is summarized using a matrix framework. The definition of culture underlying this matrix is described in some detail in this chapter, as the matrix framework is utilized throughout the book to analyze the results of studies conducted from all three perspectives. Chapter 4 outlines the theoretical arguments and assumptions underlying the Integration perspective, drawing on a wide range of studies.

Chapter 5 is a return to OZCO, viewed this time from a Differentiation perspective that acknowledges subcultural inequalities and explores the dynamics of power and conflict. These data are summarized using the matrix framework. Chapter 6 restates the Differentiation perspective at a theoretical level of abstraction, exploring the results of a variety of empirical studies conducted from this viewpoint. The Differentiation perspective is extended with a discussion of the tension between claims of cultural uniqueness and an acknowledgment of environmental influences on organizational cultures.

Chapter 7 offers a Fragmentation view of OZCO, again analyzing the results using the matrix framework. Chapter 8 offers a theoretical exploration of the Fragmentation perspective, drawing on a wide range of organizational research, as well as postmodern and feminist theories.

The remainder of the book looks across the boundaries between these perspectives. Chapter 9 offers a meta-theoretical overview that encompasses all three of these viewpoints, with a focus on cultural change. Chapter 10 deconstructs the three-perspective framework, exploring the weaknesses and omissions inherent in this way of carving up the cultural domain.

This exploration of organizational cultures involves much doubling back to look at things from a different perspective. Because all paths lead back to OZCO, this case study is a point of convergence in the text. The OZCO case also serves as an antidote to what otherwise might be an overdose of theory. It offers a sustained look at a single context, embedded in a text that otherwise offers only excerpted quotations from extended cultural descriptions.[16] For all these reasons, OZCO's president, product managers, engineers, marketing staff, secretaries, assembly-line workers, and custodians are well worth listening to. The next chapter introduces OZCO and describes the methods used to collect data from its employees.

NOTES

1. See, for example, Deal and Kennedy (1982), Ouchi (1981), Pascale and Athos (1981), Peters and Waterman (1982), Riggs (1983), and Wilkins (1983).

2. See Martin and Meyerson (1988) and Wilkins (1978).

3. The three-perspective framework was first outlined in Meyerson and Martin (1987) and Martin and Meyerson (1988). Although the ideas have evolved considerably from these early papers, I remain deeply indebted to Debra Meyerson, particularly for her theoretical contributions to the Fragmentation perspective and empirical contributions to the OZCO case material. The distinction between the Integration and Differentiation perspectives was first developed in Martin and Siehl (1983) and Martin, Sitkin, and Boehm (1985).

4. The words *viewpoint, perspective,* and *culture* are used in this book because they are more succinct than saying "culture, as it is perceived from perspective x." It is important, however, to note that such shorthand is potentially misleading. A view of a culture from a particular perspective is not an objective or distanced observation of a reified object; it is subjective, participative, and only partially self-aware (e.g., Sahlins, 1976).

5. This observation about the social construction of race, and the next sections of this chapter which explain the difficulties inherent in categories and meta-theories, draw directly on a series of informal lectures given by Professors Jane Flax and Kathy Ferguson at a conference on Business Ethics, Feminism and Organizational Theory, held in Alta, Utah, in October 1989 (as an example of postmodern theoretical writing, see also Flax, 1990).

6. Reasons for this contention can be found in postmodern and feminist theories (e.g., Derrida, 1976; Flax, 1990).

7. Kuhn (1970).

8. Meyerson and Martin (1987), Martin and Meyerson (1988).

9. Gagliardi (1991).

10. Ibid., p. 2.

11. Jaggar (1983), p. 9.

12. Burrell and Morgan (1979).

13. Strathern (1987).

14. Some of these works focus explicitly on cultural research (e.g., Clifford and Marcus, 1986; Van Maanen, 1988).

15. For an assessment of the evidence regarding a culture-performance link, see Siehl and Martin (1990).

16. Short empirical case studies representing each of the three perspectives, suitable for assigning in class, are available in a volume of readings edited by Frost, Moore, Louis, Lundberg, and Martin (1991).

2

OZCO: Gathering the Data

OZCO has been the focus of several major organizational culture studies and has been mentioned frequently in a wide range of other texts.[1] These are, generally, glowing reports that any company would be proud of. The firm is described as being unusually harmonious—a haven of shared values and mutual commitment in an industry ("high" technology) that has been wracked by economic difficulties and a turbulent market.

In Chapters 3, 5, and 7, I will present three very different views of this company (an Integration, a Differentiation, and a Fragmentation perspective). The glowing portrait of OZCO, presented in the organizational culture literature cited in footnote one above, is consistent with only one of these views. Given this divergence of opinion, it is essential that I be explicit about my purpose, the sources of these data, their limitations, and the textual strategies I have used to present them.

The purpose of this case study is not to present an exposé: the "truth" about OZCO. All three of these views of OZCO represent "good faith" attempts to recount aspects of life at OZCO. Instead, my objective is to show that cultural members can and do see the OZCO culture in terms that are congruent with all three perspectives. This material is also not a systematic case study. Each of the three perspectives has been derived from an extensive body of systematic qualitative and quantitative studies that are quoted and referenced in the chapters which follow. In contrast, the OZCO material is simply a collection of different views of the OZCO culture that illustrate the ideas presented in this book by offering an extended look at a single cultural context.

SAMPLE

OZCO is one of the Fortune 500 companies. It has over 80,000 employees worldwide, although this study focuses primarily on employees who work in the company's headquarters in California. I first started collecting material about OZCO in 1978. The texts cited in footnote one above were helpful, the company produces a wide range of publicly available material (recruiting brochures, newsletters, annual reports), and coverage in the national and local media has been extensive. In 1985 and 1986, Meyerson and I began to interview a wide range of OZCO employees.

This study was unusual in that I did not ask OZCO management to sponsor or approve our study or to guide the selection of our informants. Because all interviews were conducted away from OZCO, usually in homes or public places, no official approval was necessary. I wanted the study to be, and seem, independent of and uninfluenced by the company's management. This is one of its major strengths.

The flip side of this strength, however, is that the lack of managerial assistance meant that unfortunately we could not obtain a large, stratified *random* sample of employees from all levels of the hierarchy, functional areas, and so forth. Instead, we used a *convenience* sample (a "snowball" method, based on employees' responses to two questions: "Who do you think we should talk with?" and "Who sees things the same as [or differently from] you?"). All referrals were contacted. The subjects, then, were not selected by OZCO management or by the researchers.

The sample consisted of a wide range of employees from various functional areas, hierarchical levels, and demographic groups (e.g., age, gender, ethnicity). Noting that our sample included relatively few blue collar and clerical employees, we were grateful when Alan Wilkins generously let us read the interview transcripts from his random, stratified sample of OZCO employees (see material from Ron, Joan, Terry, and Aida).[2] Below I describe the procedures used to collect our data and the textual strategies used to present them in the chapters which follow.

DATA COLLECTION

Meyerson and I conducted interviews separately and together. Usually, only a single OZCO employee was interviewed, but in the case of friends, sometimes two or three joined in a group discussion. These interviews were informal and open-ended. We encouraged people to talk about their work—any aspect of it. We tried to keep leading questions to a minimum, probing for more information ("What else?" "Go on?") if conversation lagged. As common concerns, cultural manifestations, or areas of disagreement emerged repeatedly, across employees, we began to ask specific questions and directly seek clarification, in the manner suggested by grounded theory.[3] Sometimes conversations were continued by telephone and, at the end of the data collection period, I hosted one long and informative dinner party for our most helpful informants. (Excerpts from the material collected during this dinner are presented in Chapter 10.)

Whenever possible, we tape recorded and transcribed these conversations. Otherwise, we took notes and expanded them into "field notes" shortly thereafter. Although we did our best to preserve each individual's exact words, some of our notes rely on paraphrases. Whenever we were in doubt about the wording or meaning of quotations, we checked back with our original sources.

These employees were speaking of their personal experiences at OZCO. When they were willing to generalize about the company as a whole, or some part of it, the descriptions below reflect their views. Thus the case material includes various assertions of "fact" that we have simply recorded, rather than checked against possibly more "authoritative" sources. How these employees perceive the culture is informative, whether or not others would agree with their perceptions. Whenever disagreements in perception or interpretation were noted, these discrepancies have been included.

Having gathered this mass of data, the next task was to decide how to edit and present it in a coherent text. My solution to this problem is unusual and merits explanation.

WRITING ABOUT CULTURE

This study is obviously not an ethnography (e.g., long-term participant-observation). Nevertheless, the difficulties of writing about ethnographic data are, in many ways, similar to the problems of presenting the OZCO data. In contrast to the turgid prose of most scientific writing, ethnographies are often more like beautifully written novels. The use of fictional devices in ethnographies, however, can increase the appeal and credibility of the text while drawing attention away from the limitations and uncertainties inherent in its data.

Anthropologists and humanities scholars have become increasingly interested in this tension between science and fiction.[4] Because these ideas are of such central importance to organizational culture research, they are summarized below. I focus on two aspects of cultural writing that are particularly problematic for the presentation of the OZCO case material: the structure of the narrative and the process of generalization.

Many ethnographies have a narrative structure—a "plot." This plot is a "fable of rapport" that encourages the reader to identify with the ethnographer and accept his or her authority. Geertz among others, observes that ethnographies often begin with an entry scene (i.e., "what I saw when I got off the boat and saw the chief sitting on the beach").[5] According to Van Maanen, the plethora of vivid details in such scenes, as well as the personalized presence of the narrator in the text, create the illusion that the reader was there and would have seen it the same way.[6] During the next stage in this narrative plot, the narrator-ethnographer enters the culture, suffers physical discomfort and isolation, and struggles to learn the "native's" customs and language. After a difficult initiation, the ethnographer is (apparently) accepted as "one of them." The author has become a participant in the culture being observed, an insider whose word can be accepted as authoritative. At this point, the narrator-ethnographer usually disappears into the background of the text as native informants appear to come "center stage" to enact and describe their culture.

Clifford and Marcus show how problems of generalization surface at this point in the writing process.[7] The researcher, because of space limitations, has to compress "raw" data into textual format. A series of unique events are combined into a description of a "typical" ceremony or ritual. Individual informants become interchangeable ("an informant said . . .") or merged ("The Balinese react . . ."). Feelings and thoughts are ascribed to these informants ("The Nuer believe . . ."). Their individual voices, and what they said on a particular instance, are paraphrased, transposed into generalizations, and otherwise assimilated and distorted.

In this way, specifics become generalities and parts come to stand for a whole. The fragmented, loosely connected "raw" observations and quotations of field notes are transformed into smoothly integrated abstractions, sprinkled with "rich" (concretely visualized, exotic) details. The narrative power of the plot, with entry scenes, an initiation, and an exit scene of equal eloquence combine to offer a convincing interpretation of a culture. Unfortunately, the elegance of this style of writing is a misleading way to write about culture. It seduces the reader, drawing attention away from the difficulties, such as overgeneralization, discussed briefly above.

In presenting the OZCO data, I sought a way of writing about culture that avoids narrative structure and other forms of textual seduction. Because my objective was to present multiple views of the OZCO culture, I needed a nontraditional textual structure and writing style. I decided to rely primarily on quotations from OZCO employees, keeping generalizations to a minimum and refraining from interpretations of their meanings. I made no attempt to pull this material together into a narrative or to offer a final unifying interpretation of my own, within any one or across all three perspectives.

However, any qualitative study must use some criteria for deciding which data will be quoted or discussed. In this instance, I needed to give coherence to the OZCO material and provide continuity across the three perspectives. I decided to structure the case material around the three content themes that were mentioned most frequently, and spontaneously, by OZCO employees: egalitarianism, innovation, and concern for employee physical and mental well-being. Data not germane to these three themes is not discussed in the chapters which follow.

This criterion for selecting quotations for presentation enhanced the coherence and brevity of the presentation of the OZCO material, but it is an important limitation. Other content themes *were* mentioned by fewer employees. A more complete and systematic presentation of these data would include quotations concerning a wider variety of content themes, some of which would be particular to a single perspective.

In presenting quotations regarding these content themes, I tried to preserve the individuality of my informants without providing personal or career information that would identify them. The people we interviewed spoke very openly with us and, in some cases, volunteered information that they felt could harm their careers at OZCO if their identities were revealed. We are very grateful to them. In order to protect their anonymity, we have excluded some quotations, changed their proper names (but not their genders), used general descriptions of job classifications (retaining functional responsibilities and hierarchical level), and removed any details that might identify the speaker. The organization of the text keeps individuals separate and identifiable and lets them speak for themselves, in their own words.

By using quotations, I have tried to accept the authority of these informants, without elaborating or interpreting what they have left unspoken. I have refrained from attributing thoughts, feelings, or beliefs to them. In these ways, I have tried to preserve a sense of them as independent, aware, self-reflective, politically significant actors with evidently independent minds. The OZCO case, then, is multivocal, rather than ''monophonic'' (i.e., presented from the viewpoint of a single author).[8]

Although it is impossible to write a value-neutral text that eliminates an author's biases, I have tried to reduce my input to a minimum. However, space limitations and the need to avoid redundancy make some generalizations necessary. I have tried to keep these generalizations free of my interpretations and illustrate them with quotations. In order to avoid implying that these generalizations are accurate descriptions of an ''objective'' reality, I have chosen phrasing that suggests that alternate interpretations are possible (''are seen by some as consistent with . . . ,'' ''according to some employees . . .''). Policies are described as recommendations that might not be followed (''are supposed to . . . ,'' ''should . . .''). Informal practices are described as norms that people can deviate from (''employees are encouraged to . . .''). Only events and physical artefacts are described in an unqualified fashion (''The walls were . . .'') and alternate interpretations of the meanings of these events or artefacts are included whenever available.

I have avoided language that makes universalizing assumptions, such as ''(all) OZCO employees claim. . . .'' It is inappropriate to make generalizations about all employees of the organization or all members of this sample. Statements about the relative proportions of employees (e.g., ''many'' or ''few'') sharing a particular opinion are also inappropriate. Similarly, no ''typical'' or (always) recurring events are described and no frequency modifiers (such as ''rarely'' or ''frequently'') are used. Instead, phrases like ''some employees'' and terms like ''sometimes'' are preferred. Although this language does not lend elegance or variety to the text, it carefully preserves an acknowledgment of what is not known about the prevalence and generalizability of what has been recorded.

There is one exception to this attempt to minimize generalizations. Reluctantly (because it gives an a-historical sense of never-changing accuracy), I have generally used the (eternal) present tense in this description. Because the OZCO employees spoke in the present tense, other verb constructions seemed awkward. However, since these data were collected, some things may well have changed or may now be seen, by some, in different ways.

Overall, this minimalist textual strategy weakens the authorial role. It avoids the conventions of narrative structure and eliminates many of the textual seduction strategies that foster rapport between author and reader, create false certainty, and mask overgeneralization. The result is a rather unbeautiful, loose collection of generalizations and quotations from OZCO employees, organized by three themes that emerged from employees' observations, rather than researchers' preconceptions.

However, no writing strategy can avoid the fact that an author has constructed a text. For example, I have separated the OZCO material into three chapters representing the three perspectives. I made editorial decisions that limit what is presented, for example, by organizing the case material around three content themes, excluding quotations congruent with other content themes, and omitting quotations that seemed redundant or incoherent. My biases are evident in some of these decisions. For example, the use of modifiers such as "some" or "sometimes" reflects a refusal to generalize particular reactions. This is an implicit critique of the idea, congruent with the Integration perspective, that a cultural researcher can represent cultural members using a unified, homogeneous voice of "the Other." In spite of these inescapable kinds of limitations, in presenting the OZCO material I have tried to be more of an editor than a novel writer, more a transcriber than an interpreter—so the OZCO employees can speak for themselves. In the next chapter, they do so in glowing terms that reinforce OZCO's reputation as a haven of harmony, homogeneity, and commitment to shared values.

NOTES

1. See, for example, Deal and Kennedy (1982), Hatch (1990), Hoffman (1982), Ouchi (1981), Pascale and Athos (1981), Peters and Waterman (1982), Riggs (1983), and Wilkins (1978).

2. For studies based on these data, see Wilkins (1978, 1983).

3. See, for example, Glaser and Strauss (1967).

4. See, for example, Clifford (1983), Clifford and Marcus (1986), Geertz (1988), Pratt (1986), Rosaldo (1989), Van Maanen (1988), and Visweswaran (1988).

5. Geertz (1988).

6. Van Maanen (1988).

7. Clifford and Marcus (1986).

8. See Tyler (1986), p. 132.

3

OZCO: An Integration View

This chapter presents the first of three views of OZCO, summarizes these data in the form of a matrix, and explains the ways this matrix framework can be used to represent and understand the differences among widely disparate ways of understanding cultures. In the first part of this chapter, OZCO employees talk about the ways the firm encourages egalitarianism, fosters innovation, and expresses concern about employees' physical and mental well-being. In accord with the Integration perspective, cultural manifestations are consistent with these espoused values, little dissent is evident, and little mention of ambiguity is made. In this cultural view, consistency, consensus, and clarity are evident.

FACILITATING EGALITARIANISM

One of the top priorities of the top management of OZCO is a desire to encourage an "egalitarian" approach to employee relations. For example:

> Central to OZCO's corporate culture and personnel policies is the concept of sharing with its people—sharing the responsibilities for defining and meeting goals, sharing in economic ups and downs, and sharing opportunities for personal and professional development. (annual report)

OZCO management has implemented a number of formal practices that some employees see as evidence of egalitarianism. For example, all employees are given an opportunity to be involved in a stock plan and a profit-sharing program. Everyone is required to answer his or her own telephone, whenever possible. In addition, at OZCO "perks" are not supposed to be distributed according to status. Instead, job-related need should determine who gets which space, desks, or equipment:

> If you have a reason, you get something better. Design people get better terminals. Sales people have cars, but they need them. I have a schlocky desk, but that's OK. I can still do my work. (Stuart, marketing engineer)

> The way to get a good parking space around here is to be the first one at work in the morning. (Joseph, former corporate officer)

Three other formal practices are seen by some as reinforcing egalitarianism: bottom-up consensual decision-making, lateral promotion ladders, and a commitment to avoiding mass layoffs. Each of these formal practices is discussed in some detail below.

At OZCO, consensual decision making procedures are designed to push decisions down to the lowest possible level of the hierarchy. For example, an idea for a new product or product enhancement can originate in any division or functional area. The relevant people from a variety of functional areas, all at the same level in the company hierarchy, meet to reach consensus about the idea's worth and relative importance. If the idea is deemed worthwhile, it becomes a "project" and the various pieces of the project are assigned to appropriate functional areas. In this way, ideas are generated and evaluated at relatively low levels of the corporate hierarchy. Issues can be escalated upward, repeatedly if necessary, if bottlenecks or unresolvable differences occur.

Deviations from this practice apparently are resisted. For example, new employees, unfamiliar with the OZCO way of filtering decisions up from lower levels of the divisions, are sometimes told the story of why an attempt to institute strategic planning at OZCO was considered by many to be a failure:

> Relatively recently, a "strategy retreat" was held for very senior personnel. This was the first time OZCO had considered instituting a formal, systematic strategic planning effort at the corporate level. No strategy was set during the retreat, but the process was discussed. People objected to a centralized strategy because "it was not the OZCO way." (Sally, human resources consultant)

OZCO's lateral promotion policy provides an alternative to the usual, purely vertical promotion ladder. Top performers are supposed to receive "promotions" that are horizontal (same level, different functional area) before they are moved up one level of the hierarchy. This policy is apparently not just empty rhetoric:

> Employees are encouraged to move horizontally around the organization. Lateral movements tend to homogenize divisions. Most of the [vice presidents] have worked in several divisions. The more divisions you work in, the more highly you are valued, even at the price of not developing expertise in a given area. (Bob, marketing planner)

> Nobody will think less of you, or think you are fickle if you interview around. One of the benefits of working at OZCO is the emphasis on personal development and the option of broadening yourself in different functional areas. There's not the pressure to specialize. Someone could move from marketing to finance because they want a change. This is accepted. It's not looked at as waffling or a lack of commitment. (Denise, product marketing)

Perhaps the most well known of OZCO's formal practices is its commitment to avoiding mass layoffs, whenever possible. This policy is communicated to new employees in the form of an organizational story about the "Nine-Day Fortnight":

> Back in the 1970's, when the economy slowed down, OZCO's industry was particularly hard-hit. Most companies responded by laying off workers. But, OZCO's policy has

been, and still is, to avoid mass layoffs. So, everyone at OZCO, including the president, took a ten percent reduction in pay. In return for the pay cut, employees were required to work only nine of every ten days. (adapted from Wilkins, 1983, p. 84)

Recently, the company failed to meet its profitability goals, and all OZCO employees were asked to help. OZCO management calculated that a ten percent reduction in labor costs was needed. Given the no-mass-layoffs policy, the obvious solution seemed to be an across-the-board pay cut, whereby all employees were allowed two days off per month, with pay adjusted accordingly. The impact of this policy has been apparently egalitarian:

I guess it's laid back and informal. Everyone has flex hours now. Everyone has a pay cut. (Denise, product marketing)

Everyone did it. It's like profit sharing, same concept: everyone takes the hit. Across the board at OZCO, everyone takes the good and the bad and spreads it around with only minor exceptions. (Stuart, marketing engineer)

Some informal practices are also seen as consistent with this egalitarian emphasis. For example, "Management By Walking Around" (MBWA) is encouraged. Some employees feel this practice facilitates informal interchange, improves the accessibility of high-ranking employees, and reverses the usual hierarchical priorities by having superiors come to their subordinates. In addition, employees are encouraged to communicate openly, across levels of the hierarchy, both in person and through questionnaire responses:

By using [this attitude survey] to take a critical look at our policies and practices as well as the various tenets of our management philosophy, we reinforced the processes of openness and listening that are fundamental to the OZCO way. We must continue to create opportunities for communication by listening carefully to one another's ideas, and by responding openly and constructively to one another's concerns. (internal newsletter)

Cultural forms, such as rituals, also are seen by some as reflecting a concern with egalitarianism. For example, at some point during the parties that conclude training programs and award ceremonies, the president of OZCO, Jim Hamilton, makes an effort to greet participants personally. Some employees feel his manner deliberately transcends differences in status. At one Senior Sales Seminar, top performing sales employees were socializing with corporate personnel:

Jim Hamilton walked in by himself. He just walked in and personally introduced himself: "Hi. I'm Jim Hamilton." In no way did his actions communicate any aura of superiority. He was just one of the many bodies in the room. He shook hands, talked to you, and he remembers you. In this, he shows a real appreciation. (Stuart, marketing engineer)

In most companies, corporate headquarters is a high status job assignment. Some employees feel this is not the case at OZCO, where company jargon refers to corporate space as "retirement village" because time in corporate is like taking time off because you have no profit-loss responsibility. (Sonia, corporate staff)

Physical arrangements also are seen by some as confirming egalitarian values. Employees dress casually; even the president is seen frequently in shirt sleeves. There is only one cafeteria, rather than a separate executive dining room. Perhaps most important, many OZCO employees have open offices, with relatively low partitions dividing small cubicles. Only employees with external "boundary spanning" jobs have large, enclosed offices. According to some employees, this space allocation policy facilitates open, informal communication patterns that reduce status differentials.

ENCOURAGING INNOVATION

In a fast-moving industry, the ability to innovate is a prerequisite for survival. OZCO's management stresses innovation, but with attention to the marketplace and a reluctance to take financial risks:

> OZCO's fundamental strengths: superior customer satisfaction and loyalty, technological innovation, and aggressive new product development, conservative financial policies that ensure stability, and commitment to offering products that make a genuine contribution. (annual report)

OZCO management considers new product development one of its key strengths. New products are sometimes introduced at the rate of eight per week, perhaps because the structure of OZCO is designed to give primacy to product development:

> The product division remains the basic building block of the company, with a great deal of autonomy in the design, manufacturing, and marketing of products that fit within a larger strategic framework. (Jim, president, internal newsletter)

This stress on innovation has bred a jargon all its own. Most of that jargon focuses on the work of engineers, who are encouraged to "play." They are said to leave their projects "on the bench" for other engineers to look at, play with, and develop further.

> The "next work bench" idea created lots of products. Engineers designed products for themselves—they know what they need—and they had their buddies check out their idea. (Andy, design engineer)

This commitment to innovation is not blind to marketing considerations, according to some employees. Even engineers are sometimes urged by their bosses to be sensitive to customer needs—not those needs that might be apparent after hours of technical product demonstration, but needs that customers are already aware of:

I keep telling my engineers that they now have five minutes to make a sale, not five hours like we used to. We have to focus on apparent user benefits. (Irving, vice president, product area x)

Management's emphasis on customer satisfaction has been heard, and attended to, by some engineers:

We have a lot of freedom in implementation, but we have to meet the specs. We have a lot of schedule constraints and marketplace needs. . . . I'm always thinking about the customer—not an individual, but an imaginary one. We are very objective-driven, and now the objective seems to be the customer. (Andy, design engineer)

OZCO has a reputation for producing high quality products. However, high quality often has meant very high prices. This pricing policy reflects the company's traditional deference to engineers, who have been accused of designing products first and only later worrying about cost. Recently, however, OZCO designed a product for low cost mass production, hoping its aggressive pricing would quickly establish it as a market leader. This is only one part of a marketing reorientation, designed to make a better range of OZCO products appeal to a broader range of corporate customers (not primarily engineers):

You'll notice that the last three products have names, not just numbers. The idea is to create a brand family, the way Ford names cars, and be a bigger presence at retail. (John, director of marketing, product area x)

This increased customer focus creates a need for greater coordination of new product development efforts. OZCO management has addressed this need by changing its formal structure:

In recent months, we've been taking a close look at the OZCO organization. Our goal has been to answer a fundamental question: How can we best provide our customers with complex systems and integrated solutions that require products and services from different OZCO groups? Is there a better way to organize ourselves to ensure that our focus is on the customer and understanding, supplying, and supporting needed solutions? The organizational changes just announced are designed to enhance our ability to produce and support solution selling. (Jim, president, internal newsletter)

The new structure mandates the development of products that cut across several divisions. Groups are assigned to coordinate various divisional contacts with particular client industries. For example, customer relations and marketing to the defense industry is handled at the group level. Someone is specifically designated to work as a liaison with that industry, coordinating the divisions' responses and making certain that a "system" solution is sold. This employee is supposed to figure out what is needed, including products and services, and then work with the product marketing people and engineers to identify products and services from a variety of divisions:

Marketing is industry-oriented—at the group level—not product-oriented. We do industry research. We play an integrating role as an overlap between product and industry marketing. . . . What do they need? Do they need special training? . . . A total system should work. So, it's coordinated by one group to make sure it works. (Stuart, marketing engineer)

For example, as part of this coordination effort, two manufacturing operations were merged:

During this year, we moved to consolidate portions of [two independent entities]. Some operations were merged and [these two entities], though geographically dispersed, now each report through central organizations better able to coordinate operations and future developments. (annual report)

This restructuring entailed centralization, so some of the freedoms and prerogatives of engineers had to be constrained:

Supposedly, we are now market-focused with [industry] groups geared toward specific markets. This may make OZCO a less fun place for engineers because the work is coordinated by higher forces above them which are marketing driven. Their autonomy is what made their work fun; now they are forced to coordinate more. (Dana, sales)

Other formal rules and procedures are seen, by some, as reinforcing centralization and enhancing coordination. For example, corporate staff were asked to develop a large, centralized pool of M.B.A. resumes. The divisions, rather than recruiting separately as they had done in the past, are to recruit from this central pool. Teleconferencing is also encouraged, as a means of integrating geographically dispersed employees:

Our idea is to spend money to move information rather than spending it to move people. (Kerry, information systems)

FOSTERING CONCERN FOR EMPLOYEE WELL-BEING

OZCO management expresses concern with their employees' physical and emotional, as well as material, well-being. For example, one of the firm's corporate objectives focuses on

our people: To help OZCO people share in the company's success which they make possible; to provide job security based on their performance; to insure a safe and pleasant work environment; to recognize the individual achievements; and to help them gain a sense of satisfaction and accomplishment from their work. (internal newsletter)

This holistic concern for employee well-being is regarded by some as reinforcing management's commitment to egalitarianism:

OZCO's openness and informality contribute to a non-authoritarian atmosphere. As a result, the OZCO work environment fosters individual dignity, pride in accomplishment, and the motivation to produce quality work. (employee recruitment brochure)

OZCO management's expressed concern for the personal well-being of their employees should presumably be mutual and strengthen personal ties among employees. It is not surprising, then, that OZCO employees often use the word *family* when referring to company members. One employee, explained the meaning of this word:

OZCO is like a midwestern family: good, kind, fair, community folks. (Sally, human resources consultant)

Although any family has strains, the family feeling at OZCO, according to some employees, is very real:

OZCO is like a family. . . . Even in the nicest, friendliest family you are going to find some reward and punishment mechanisms. You expect that even if it is hidden, there are high level discussions about this subtle control strategy. Even though I've had some high level organizational dealings, I haven't seen evidence of this. The parents don't seem to talk about them. This good homey feeling is pretty deep; I haven't seen that fade away. The battling is more like two brothers battling than competitive strangers. I keep thinking that there have to be things going on that I'm not seeing, but I don't think so. (Stuart, marketing engineer)

A number of the firm's formal policies are seen by some as reinforcing this family atmosphere. *Workforce rebalancing* (a jargon term for geographical and functional relocations) is apparently carried out with "kid gloves," ensuring that no move is involuntary. Spouses who relocate with an OZCO employee are supposed to be given assistance in finding jobs, schools for children, and so on. Flex hours are sometimes encouraged, in order to accommodate employees' personal lives. There are scholarship funds for employees' children. Self-improvement programs (e.g., Weight Watchers, exercise classes, athletics, etc.) are available at subsidized rates.

A holistic commitment to employee well-being is also reflected in the physical arrangements at OZCO. The open office spaces are seen by some as facilitating personal, as well as informal, work-related contacts among employees:

People get involved in each other's personal lives simply because they overhear each other on the phone. There is no privacy, so a family atmosphere is fostered. (Denise, product marketing)

The partitions dividing the open space are covered with personal photographs and mementos. Some recreational facilities and showers are available at most buildings. OZCO uses its financial resources to support a variety of formal practices and physical facilities that merge work and personal concerns.

Some informal practices are designed to express caring for employees at key points in their careers. For example, when women accept a job offer from OZCO, they are sometimes sent flowers. When a major mistake is made, employees are supposed to look at what's wrong with the process, rather than seeking an individual to blame:

> OZCO employees are supposed to ask "What was wrong with the training this person received?" (Stuart, marketing engineer)

If individual blame seems unavoidable, then the erring employee is to be given a second chance. For example, a "Second Chance" story concerns a manager who made an admittedly disastrous mistake:

> As a new manager, Peter Long's first assignment was to manage an important project. One difficulty after another was encountered, and ultimately the project was "a dismal failure." With some trepidation, Long met with the President to discuss "his future with the company." After discussing Long's poor performance in his first assignment, the President called in one of the Vice Presidents. Instead of letting the ax fall, as Long expected, the Vice President was given the responsibility of making sure that Long succeeded in an important new assignment. Long was elated at being given another chance. And, this time he succeeded. He went on to become one of OZCO's most valuable and loyal employees. (adapted from Martin, Feldman, Hatch, and Sitkin, 1983)

Jim Hamilton also uses organizational stories to illustrate OZCO's commitment to employee well-being. For example, at a public panel discussion Jim was pressed for evidence of the company's concern for working mothers. He responded with the following "Caesarean" story:

> We have a young woman who is extraordinarily important to the launching of a major new [product]. We will be talking about it next Tuesday in its first worldwide introduction. She arranged to have her [baby born by a] Caesarean [operation] yesterday in order to be prepared for this event, so you—we have insisted that she stay home and this is going to be televised in a closed circuit television, so we're having this done by TV for her, and she is staying home three months. We are finding ways of filling in to create this void for us because we think it's an important thing for her to do. (Jim, president, public panel discussion)

Jim interpreted this story in terms of OZCO's commitment to helping mothers with managerial responsibilities. He proudly cited the company's willingness to incur costs, for example, by permitting a three-month maternity leave, arranging for someone to perform the employee's job during her leave, and paying for the closed circuit television in her bedroom, so she could watch the public introduction of the product for which she had been responsible.

OZCO management reinforces this concern for employee well-being with several financial practices. For example, OZCO has a policy that prohibits the use of short-term contractors, so they will not be put out of business should OZCO's needs change. OZCO management's commitment to avoiding mass layoff by requiring company-wide pay cuts, is also interpreted, by some, as further evidence of concern for employees:

> At [the Colorado plant] they weren't selling product, long before the corporate-wide problem. They decided to cut down on pay, voluntarily initially. Then corporate decided to implement it as policy. Like a family, everyone was watching [Colorado]. The reaction was not Ann Landers-like, what can they do about that problem? Rather, the reaction was more like a family: we need to get together as a family and come up with a family decision. Jim Hamilton makes a head of the family decision. (Stuart, marketing engineer)

Concern for employee well-being is sometimes facilitated informally when financial or other considerations preclude more formal support. For example:

> As far as having childcare facilities and that sort of thing, we have as a company decided that's probably not a good thing for us to do. We think it invites into a whole series of problems that are probably better met by other institutions. We are good at making [our] products. I suspect we're not so good at delivering childcare. That doesn't mean we are not interested in the subject, and we facilitate employee groups getting together and arranging to do this themselves by helping to identify and support locations, find teachers, provide car pools, and that sort of thing, but we think we should not get in this business ourselves. (Jim, president, public panel discussion)

According to these employees, then, OZCO's commitment to egalitarianism, innovation, and employee well-being is real. This commitment surfaces in a wide variety of cultural manifestations, including externally espoused values, formal practices, informal practices, jargon, rituals, stories, and physical arrangements. Because the matrix framework is used throughout this book to summarize and contrast widely disparate approaches to the study of culture, it is defined and discussed in some detail below.

A MATRIX FRAMEWORK FOR UNDERSTANDING CULTURES

This book, like any overview of cultural literature, has to grapple with the fact that researchers have failed to come to an agreement about what culture is and what it isn't. These definitional differences aren't merely academic quibbles. Because researchers use the same term to mean very different things, it is very difficult for any reader to decipher what is being said, to understand why one researcher's conclusions are so different from another's, and to draw conclusions about the practical implications of this body of work.

A theoretical framework is, therefore, needed. It should be able to represent, with minimal distortion, quite different approaches to studying culture. At the same time, it should be capable of clarifying why these differences occur and how they relate to each other. The matrix framework described below can accomplish these objectives. Rather than offering yet another abstract definition of culture, the matrix framework focuses on the cultural manifestations researchers actually study, when they claim to be studying culture. *When the manifestations of a culture are arrayed in the form of a matrix, the pattern of interpretation underlying that matrix reveals how a given study is defining culture.*

Defining Manifestations of a Culture

Three kinds of cultural manifestations are frequently studied: forms, practices, and content themes. Cultural forms are aspects of organizational life that, before cultural research became popular, were often dismissed as trivial. It has become increasingly clear that these forms can provide important clues as to what employees are thinking, believing, and doing. The most commonly studied cultural forms include: rituals,[1] stories,[2] jargon, humor, and physical arrangements (i.e., architecture, interior design, and dress codes).

While cultural forms have traditionally been dismissed as trivial, practices have long been the primary focus of organizational research. Formal practices are generally written down and therefore are more easily controlled by management. Several types of formal practices have been of particular interest to cultural researchers: organizational structure, task and job descriptions, technology, rules and procedures, and financial controls. In contrast, informal practices evolve through interaction and are seldom written down. Informal practices include, for example, unwritten norms, communication patterns, and standard operating procedures.

Content themes are common threads of concern that are seen as manifest in a subset of forms and practices. These themes can be deliberately espoused to an external audience (e.g., when a corporate objective of fostering innovation is publicized). Content themes can also be internal, either espoused deliberately (such as, when a president declares that "conflict should be openly confronted") or they may emerge as tacit, deeply held assumptions (e.g., the unstated presupposition that financial planners must take a long-term perspective).

Assembling the Pieces of a Cultural Puzzle in Matrix Form

When content themes are combined with forms and practices, we have the pieces of a cultural puzzle. The next step is to put them together. The manifestations of a given culture can be arranged in the form of a matrix. For example, Table 3-1 summarizes the manifestations of the OZCO culture described in this chapter. The column headings of such a matrix are, moving from left to right, formal practices, informal practices, and forms, such as rituals, stories, jargon, humor, and physical arrangements. Different content themes provide the rows of the matrix. A cell entry in this matrix is a practice or form that is relevant to a content theme. For example, in the matrix in Table 3-1, the first content theme, egalitarianism, was manifested in several formal practices, an informal practice, and a variety of cultural forms; the second theme, innovation, was manifested in formal and informal practices, as well as jargon, and so on.

This book began with an informal definition of culture. The matrix framework can be used to restate that definition in more formal terms. *The manifestations of cultures in organizations include formal and informal practices, cultural forms (such as rituals, stories, jargon, humor, and physical arrangements), and content themes. Interpretations of these cultural manifestations vary. The pattern or configuration of interpretations (underlying a matrix of cultural manifestations)*

Table 3-1   OZCO: An Integration view

Content themes		Practices	
External	*Internal*	*Formal*	*Informal*
Egalitarian sharing		Participation in stock plan and profit sharing	"Management by walking around" as status equalizer
		Answer own telephone	
		"Perk" distribution based on need not status	
		Consensual decision making	
		Lateral promotions	
		No mass layoffs; across-the-board pay cuts	
Innovation		New products aimed at marketplace	Products developed at rate of eight per week
		New structure to integrate industry and product marketing	Engineers design products for other engineers
		Centralized recruiting	
		Teleconferencing	
Holistic concern for employee well-being	Relocation voluntary; assistance for spouse	Facilitates self-help day-care arrangements	
	Scholarship funds	New employees sent flowers	
	Flex hours		
	Self-improvement programs	Blame training rather than individual	
	No short-term contractors		

constitutes culture. If culture is defined as the pattern of interpretations underlying a matrix, it is important to consider how the cells in that matrix relate to each other. These intercell relationships reflect how a given study is defining culture in a more accurate and specific way than most formal definitions of culture.

What the Matrix Framework Can Do

This matrix approach to analyzing culture can encompass a variety of ways of thinking about cultures in organizations, including the three social scientific perspectives that are the focus of this book. For example, a practice or form can

Forms			
Stories	*Ritual*	*Jargon*	*Physical arrangements*
Strategic planning is not the "OZCO way"	President's behavior at award ceremonies	"Retirement village"	Casual dress
			One cafeteria
"Nine-day fortnight" story			Open offices
			No reserved parking
		"Play"	
		"On the bench"	
"Second chance" story		"Family"	Open office facilitates personal contact
"Caesarean" story		Workforce rebalancing	Decoration of office with personal mementos
			Recreation facilities

be consistent with a theme, as when egalitarian values are congruent with the design of equally desirable office spaces. They can be inconsistent, as when egalitarian values are coupled with highly unequal pay distributions. Or, a relationship between manifestations may be unclassifiable as either clearly inconsistent or consistent.

Furthermore, a matrix can represent individual, group, or organizational levels of analysis. For example, a single matrix can summarize an Integration study that focuses on values and interpretations that all members of an organization apparently share. A Differentiation study might require several matrices, each one representing a different subculture, or it might be summarized using a single, organization-wide matrix riddled with inconsistencies. A Fragmentation study might utilize one matrix for each issue of concern, so issue-specific differences and similarities among individuals might be explored. Alternatively, a Fragmentation study might be represented with a single organization-wide matrix where relationships among themes, practices, and forms were not clearly inconsistent or consistent. All these kinds of matrices can be seen as cultural maps, showing where boundaries of consensus and lack of consensus are drawn.

What goes into a matrix can be all that seems clear—all that cultural members agree about. It could include what they clearly disagree about, or what seems ambiguous. Thus the matrix framework can encompass studies that see culture as an oasis of clarity in an otherwise ambiguous world, view organizational cultures as riddled with subcultural conflict, or portray the essence of contemporary cultures as ambiguous.

For example, Table 3-1 reflects an Integration perspective on the OZCO culture, as indicated by consistency among manifestations, organization-wide consensus, and the absence of ambiguity. More specifically, action consistency (between themes and practices) and symbolic consistency (between themes and forms) appear horizontally, across the rows of the matrix. Content consistency (across the various themes) appears vertically, in the left-hand column of the matrix. Organization-wide consensus implies that a single matrix is sufficient to represent OZCO's culture. None of the cell entries is given an ambiguous interpretation. The pattern of interpretation underlying this matrix clearly portrays OZCO as an oasis of consistency, consensus, and clarity.

The matrix framework can also be used to summarize both cross-sectional and longitudinal approaches to the study of culture. A matrix is a snapshot; it offers a view of a culture at one point in time. Matrices of the same culture at different times can be compared in order to represent, in a systematic way, how that culture has changed.

In addition, the matrix framework can represent a variety of other types of cultural research: studies which focus on the easily observable and those which insist on in-depth analysis; studies which view culture from an outsider's point of view and those which attempt to see it from an insider's perspective; materialist (including practices) and ideational (excluding practices) approaches to the study of culture; studies which seek to understand one or just a few cultural contexts and those which are enamored of abstracting across contexts; as well as studies which specialize in just a few manifestations and those which prefer a more generalist approach. It would be time consuming (and of interest to relatively few) to describe how the matrix framework can represent all these points of view. However, the specialist versus generalist debate is of sufficient importance that it merits some discussion.

THE SPECIALIST VERSUS GENERALIST DEBATE

Specialists study only one or two types of cultural manifestations. Specialization is easily observable when the matrix framework is used to summarize the results of a study, since most columns are empty or underutilized, while one or two others are full. For example, Schall defines culture in terms of communication activities, Kilmann emphasizes behavioral norms (informal practices), I have studied organizational stories, and Beyer and Trice have focused on rituals.[3] Perhaps the most common specialist approach is to define culture in ideational terms, excluding formal and informal practices, such as structure, technology, pay, job definitions, and so on.[4]

In contrast, generalist research examines a wide range of cultural manifestations. Smircich offers a persuasive defense of this approach, drawing a distinction between (more specialist) studies that treat culture as a variable and those (more generalist) studies that approach culture as a root metaphor for conceptualizing organizational life:

> Some theorists advance the view that organizations be understood AS cultures. They leave behind the view that a culture is something an organization HAS, in favor of the view that culture is something an organization IS. (Smircich, 1983b, p. 347)

When culture is used as a root metaphor for organizational life, organizations are analyzed and understood in expressive, ideational, and symbolic—as well as material and economic—terms.[5] Given how different the generalist and specialist approaches are, it is not surprising that each has its advocates and its critics.

Advantages and Disadvantages of the Specialist Approach

Specialist studies can be informative about whatever cultural manifestation has been studied (although generalizing about an entire cultural context from data concerning only one or two types of manifestations is probably not justified). A specialist approach to the study of culture has a clear advantage: it is an attempt to carve up intellectual territory so that the study of culture does not overlap with other areas of inquiry. This is the deliberate creation of an intellectual "ghetto." It makes it easier to demonstrate that cultural research can make a unique contribution to organizational theory.

However, the advantages of a specialist approach to understanding culture are obtained at the cost of excluding much of critical importance. Such a restricted approach precludes cultural researchers from examining the variables—such as formal and informal practices—that have long been the core concerns of organizational research. Specialist, ideational definitions of culture are particularly problematic because the exclusion of materialist considerations makes it difficult to "conceptualize the processes of cultural transmission and change and to relate them to economic and political realities" (Keesing, 1981, p. 73).

These shortcomings are fatal flaws when cultural research has an organizational focus. Most organizations are set up for economic and/or political objectives. Employees understandably place great weight on utilitarian considerations, such as pay, tasks that must be performed, or political struggles that must be won in order to ensure personal and organizational financial survival. When cultural research excludes practices from the study of culture, it excludes much of what constitutes organizational life.

The exclusion of practices from culture is particularly objectionable to those, like myself, who are concerned with conflicts of interest within an organizational hierarchy. From this point of view, cultures do not exist only in the realm of ideas and values; they constitute a specific material condition of existence that some consider oppressive and exploitative. It is misleading to portray cultures in organizations as arcane, ungrounded worlds of ideas and values, disconnected from the practicalities of earning a paycheck for doing work, a portion of which is, in any job, distasteful, stressful, and for some, physically taxing. It is therefore essential that the study of culture include (but not be restricted to) structural and economic factors, such as formal or informal practices. For these reasons, if a researcher's goal is to gain a deep understanding of an entire cultural context, or of culture in more general terms, then it is essential to abandon a specialist approach and examine a wider range of manifestations.

Advantages and Disadvantages of the Generalist Approach

Cultural research that adopts a generalist approach, however, is faced with different kinds of criticisms. Generalist approaches treat culture as a "kitchen sink," a receptacle for unexplained complexities, error variance, and other mysteries of failed empiricism. Critics ask, "What isn't culture? And if culture includes everything, then how can the results of cultural studies be distinguished from other domains of research? Isn't it likely that the results of cultural research will be 'old wine in new skins,' rather than a new contribution to knowledge? How can culture make any discernibly unique, original contribution to organizational theory?" Each of these issues is addressed below.

If culture is usefully regarded as a metaphor for organizational life (and I think it is), then everything of importance to cultural members should be examined. Although useful insights have been garnered from specialist research, a generalist approach can yield understandings that so far have "fallen between the cracks" of organizational research that examines causal relationships among small sets of variables. Furthermore, a generalist approach that includes study of all kinds of cultural manifestations, including formal and informal practices, takes culture research out of an intellectual ghetto, facilitating exploration of linkages with other domains of organizational theory. For example, quantitative cultural studies of espoused values and self-reports of group behavior bear a marked resemblance to studies of organizational climate and sometimes even use similar or identical measures.[6] As another example, Schall's study of culture as communication activities has much in common with research in the field of communication and with organizational studies of the disjunctions between formal and informal communication networks. If such intellectual overlaps were explored more fully by cultural researchers, the relationship between culture and other areas of organizational theory could be strengthened.

A generalist approach undoubtedly carries dangers of being "old wine in new bottles." Indeed, given that organizational culture research examines some of the same contexts as other kinds of organizational studies, some congruence of results would be expected. However, it is up to cultural researchers to demonstrate that this approach adds insights not otherwise available in organizational research. For example, one of the purposes of this book is to show that cultural research, unlike other traditions of organizational inquiry, offers an unprecedented understanding of interplay of homogeneity, conflict, and ambiguity in organizations.

WHAT THE MATRIX FRAMEWORK CANNOT DO

Although the matrix framework and the three social scientific perspectives have some insights to offer, they are just one among many ways to "carve up" this domain of inquiry. For example, other overviews have classified organizational culture studies by their orientations toward functionalism, methods, or epistemology.[7] There are good reasons for emphasizing these issues. In the early 1980s some scholars hoped the study of organizational culture (based on an interpretive approach and qualitative methodologies) would provide an alternative to the structural-functionalist assumptions, managerial bias, and quantitative methods that dominated organizational research.

That hope has not been fulfilled. Reviews of the last decade of organizational culture research have concluded that most studies—even interpretive ones—approach culture in utilitarian functionalist terms as a new management tool.[8] In addition, these studies have used a broad and innovative range of qualitative and quantitative methods. This domain of inquiry, then, has not become an exclusive haven for interpretive, qualitative research.

Rather than examining what methods are used to study culture or what functions it might serve for managers, this book carves up this domain of inquiry by focusing on why vehement disagreements among the three social scientific perspectives have characterized this field. The result, I hope, is a different kind of understanding of what cultural approaches can contribute to organizational theory and research.

HAVENS OF HOMOGENEITY AND HARMONY

In this chapter OZCO employees describe their company from an Integration perspective, as a haven of homogeneity and harmony. This is not an unusual kind of cultural portrait. Indeed, if people were to make the mistake of reading only Integration studies of culture they might conclude that a vast number of organizations have succeeded in creating cultures where inconsistencies, shared dissent, and ambiguity are exceedingly rare, if not unheard of. The next chapter analyzes the commonalities among Integration studies of liberal arts colleges, small family-owned businesses, the Los Angeles Olympic Organizing Committee, large electronics corporations, like OZCO, and funeral homes. In all of these organizational cultures, homogeneity and harmony apparently prevail.

NOTES

1. Rituals generally have several defining characteristics. They are carefully planned and executed, often with formal rehearsals. Rituals are enacted in a social context, with clearly demarcated beginnings and endings and well-defined roles for organizational members. They usually incorporate other cultural forms, such as company jargon or stories. Trice and Beyer (1984) offer a fourfold typology of interpretations of ritual meanings (technical and expressive, latent and manifest) and distinguish rituals (enacted repeatedly) from ceremonies (enacted once).

2. Organizational stories are not personal anecdotes, known only to one person. They usually focus on an event sequence (not a lengthy excerpt from an employee's biography or a company's history). The central characters are organizational employees and the event sequence is, apparently, true. For reviews of some of this literature, see Martin (1982) or Martin, Feldman, Hatch, and Sitkin (1983).

3. Kilmann (1985), Martin (1982), Schall (1983), Trice and Beyer (1984).

4. See, for example, Pennings and Gresov (1986), pp. 322-323, Porras (1987), and Tushman and Romanelli (1985).

5. Smircich (1983b), p. 348.

6. Examples of such studies include Denison (1990), Enz (1988), and Kilmann (1985). The overlap and disjunctions between climate and culture research are discussed in Schneider (1990).

7. For example, Calas and Smircich (1987), Ouchi and Wilkins (1985), Smircich (1983b), Sypher, Applegate, and Sypher (1985).

8. See Barley, Meyer, and Gash (1988), Calas and Smircich (1987), Stablein and Nord (1985), and Sypher, Applegate, and Sypher (1985).

4

The Integration Perspective: Harmony and Homogeneity

Studies written from the Integration perspective describe a cultural unity that has no place for doubt, uncertainty, or collective dissent. Many, *but not all,* Integration studies portray leaders as culture creators and culture transformers—high-ranking managers who have the capacity to envision and enact a culture that inspires intense loyalty, strong commitment, increased productivity, sometimes even greater profitability. Many managers would like to create a culture, reflective of their own values, that would generate both loyalty and productivity. No wonder, then, that the Integration perspective has become so popular among researchers who write primarily to a managerial audience. It is misleading, however, to imply that only managerially oriented researchers produce studies written from an Integration point of view. As outlined below, this perspective has a wide range of adherents, particularly in the United States.

Studies congruent with the Integration perspective have three characteristics. First, a set of content themes (usually values or basic assumptions) are described as being shared by all members of a culture, in an organization-wide consensus. Second, these content themes are said to be enacted, consistently, in a wide variety of cultural manifestations. Third, cultural members are described as knowing what they are to do and why it is worthwhile to do it. In this realm of clarity, there is no place for ambiguity. These three defining characteristics of the integrationist viewpoint (*organization-wide consensus, consistency, and clarity*) are explored in more detail below.

Before proceeding, it is important to define what is meant by an "Integration study" of culture and to specify the reasons why particular studies are and are not cited in the pages that follow. *An Integration study is a specific piece of research that is primarily, but usually not exclusively, conducted in accord with the premises of the Integration perspective defined above. The Integration perspective, like the other social scientific perspectives, is characteristic of a particular written product, not an individual researcher.*[1]

This chapter (and the chapters describing the Differentiation and Fragmentation perspectives) contain quotations and references to studies that are primarily congruent with a single perspective. Excerpts from some of these studies are included in order to illustrate the fact that each of the three social scientific perspectives is based on an extensive body of empirical literature. Explanatory material that I have added to these quotations is marked with brackets.

All or even most studies congruent with a given perspective could not be included in these references. There are simply too many. For example, the Integration perspective has become the dominant view of organizational researchers and practitioners in the United States. One review of a limited sample of journals counted almost 200 recent articles, most of which were conducted from this perspective.[2] Limitations in manuscript length and reader patience also make it impossible to discuss all of a cited text (or all of the writings of a given researcher). Therefore, those who are unfamiliar with particular researchers and texts quoted or referenced in this book are encouraged to read some of this work in its entirety, so that the context from which a quote is taken can be seen and the fairness and accuracy of descriptions can be assessed.

ORGANIZATION-WIDE CONSENSUS

The core of the Integration perspective is the lure of organization-wide consensus. Clark's description of "organizational sagas" (a precursor of organizational culture) states this point cogently:

> An organizational saga is a powerful means of unity in the formal workplace. It makes links across internal divisions and organizational boundaries as internal and external groups share their common beliefs. With deep emotional commitment believers define themselves by their organizational affiliation and in their bond to other believers they share an intense sense of the unique. (Clark, 1972, p. 183)

In Integration views of culture, people at all levels of an organizational hierarchy are said to agree about potentially divisive issues. For example:[3]

> Just as individuals process information, so also do groups and units of people. In doing so they develop collective belief systems about social arrangements. . . . They include beliefs about, among other things, organizational purpose, criteria of performance, the location of authority, legitimate bases of power, decision-making orientations, style of leadership, compliance, evaluation, and motivation. (Quinn and McGrath, 1985, p. 325)

Integration studies often describe organization-wide consensus in (harmonious) familial terms, which merge the (supposedly separate) public and private domains, so that organizations are seen as families and families of employees are described as part of the organization. For example, some OZCO employees, such as Denise and Stuart, quoted in Chapter 3, spoke of OZCO using a family metaphor. Other examples of familial language come from Schein's study of organizational founders and Ouchi and Jaegar's examination of "Theory Z" cultures:

The people who were comfortable in this environment and enjoyed the excitement of building a successful organization found themselves increasingly feeling like members of a family and were emotionally treated as such. Strong bonds of mutual support grew up at an interpersonal level, and Murphy [the founder] functioned symbolically as a brilliant, demanding, but supportive father figure. (Schein, 1991a, p. 23)

The slowness of evaluation and the stability of membership promote a holistic concern for people, particularly from superior to subordinate. This holism includes the employee and his or her family in an active manner. Family members regularly interact with other organization members and their families and feel an identification with the organization. (Ouchi and Jaegar, 1978, p. 688)

Perhaps because of the Integration perspective's emphasis on interpersonal, sometimes even familial closeness, organization-wide consensus is often described in highly emotional terms. For example, a study of the Los Angeles Olympic Organizing Committee concludes with a description of a party held for employees:

A vice president who had been on the road for several days with the torch relay . . . told about the runner going over a winding road in the hills of West Virginia and encountering a man standing alone on the top of a hill with a trumpet playing "America the Beautiful" as the torch passed. There was not a dry eye in the house. The speaker himself broke down, overcome by emotion, and could not continue for several minutes. The staff filed out to the strains of ceremonial music, clutching their commemorative mugs and pins reading "Team 84" that were handed to them at the exit. (McDonald, 1991, p. 37)

This emotional language leaves no room for dissent. For example, in the quotation above, no "eye in the house" failed to cry, responded with skepticism, or felt embarrassed about the chauvinism, fervor, or abundance of tears.

Consensus is another name for conformity. Some Integration research has frankly responded to the harsh criticism that this perspective prescribes, as well as describes, a corporate form of fascism or cult religion:

Those white-shirted, polite, competent, hard-working [IBM] employees of twenty years ago were often regarded as corporate "fanatics," or even corporate "fascists," because they appeared not to display in superficial ways their "American individuality." White shirts were mistaken for laundered minds. The shirts are now colored, but it appears that their wearers are still politely service-oriented, highly competent, and hard working (everything may change but the beliefs). And in our culture, any evidence of a reduction in obvious "individuality," which naturally accompanies increases in organizational commitment, will produce criticism from those who overvalue individuality. (Pascale and Athos, 1981, p. 186)

Even if pressures toward consensus sometimes make it necessary to over-ride the desires of individuals, some Integration studies find this justified because unity provides an antidote to the conflicts of interest that can divide and paralyze an organization. Integration studies sometimes acknowledge conflict or deviance, interpreting them as reasons for seeking a transcendent, more powerful unity—one that gains the consent, even the enthusiastic commitment, of the governed.

CONSISTENCY

Many Integration studies acknowledge that organization-wide consensus is not easy to achieve. It must, researchers argue, be reinforced by a myriad of interconnected cultural manifestations, each of which is consistent with the others. For example:

> Each ideal type [of culture] represents a set of interconnected parts, each dependent on at least one other part. (Ouchi and Jaegar, 1978, p. 685)

An Integration study usually includes three kinds of consistency: action, symbolic, and content. Examples of each are discussed in the following sections.

Action Consistency

Action consistency occurs when content themes are consistent with an organization's formal and informal practices. For example, in the Integration view of OZCO's culture, some employees described management's espoused value of egalitarianism as consistent with a wide variety of formal and informal practices, including company participation in the United Way charity, the company's stock plan, profit-sharing, answering one's own telephone, "Management By Walking Around," need-based distribution of "perks," "bottom-up" consensual decision-making, and lateral promotions. In more abstract terms, action consistency occurs when

> the structural elements and organizational processes making up the design type are strongly underpinned by provinces of meaning and interpretive schemes that bind them together in an institutionally derived normative order. (Hinings and Greenwood, 1987, p. 2, quoted in Greenwood and Hinings, 1988, p. 295)

For example, Barley's study of funeral work examined practices consistent with a content theme emphasizing the denial of death:

> The funeral director seeks to create the appearance of normality or naturalness whenever the living are in the presence of the dead. This intention underlies strategies that organize the execution of many different activities; for example, preparation of the body, removal of the deceased from a home. (Barley, 1991, p. 44)

Symbolic Consistency

A second type of consistency is symbolic. It occurs when the symbolic meanings of cultural forms, such as physical arrangements, stories, rituals, and jargon, are described as congruent with content themes. For example, the Integration view of OZCO's culture offered egalitarian interpretations of Jim Hamilton's behavior at company rituals, "retirement village" jargon, and the story about the failure of corporate strategic planning. Physical arrangements, such as casual dress norms, a single cafeteria for all employees, and open office spaces also were described as reinforcing egalitarian themes.

Symbolic consistency is also evident in Pettigrew's study of public school headmasters.[4] According to this study, headmasters tried to introduce new values in their schools by reinforcing desired changes with cultural forms. For example, they created rituals or told organizational stories that expressed appreciation for the types of behaviors they were seeking to encourage. Similarly, at IBM rules were said to apply equally—to all employees. This espoused value was once put to a severe test, according to an Integration interpretation of the "Rule Breaking" story:

> A twenty-two-year old bride weighing ninety pounds, whose husband had been sent overseas and who, in consequence, had been given a job until his return. . . . The young woman, Lucille Berger, was obliged to make certain that people entering security areas wore the correct clearance identification. Surrounded by his usual entourage of white-shirted men, Watson [the president] approached the doorway to an area where she was on guard, wearing an orange badge acceptable elsewhere in the plant, but not a green badge, which alone permitted entrance at her door. "I was trembling in my uniform, which was far too big," she recalled. "It hid my shakes but not my voice. "I'm sorry," I said to him. I knew who he was alright. "You cannot enter. Your admittance is not recognized." That's what we were supposed to say. The men accompanying Watson were stricken; the moment held unpredictable possibilities. "Don't you know who he is?" someone hissed. Watson raised his hand for silence, while one of the party strode off and returned with the appropriate badge. (Rodgers, 1969, pp. 153–154, quoted in Martin, Feldman, Hatch, and Sitkin, 1983, p. 440)

Martin, Feldman, Hatch, and Sitkin found that versions of this and six other "common" organizational stories were told in a wide range of large and small, public and private organizations.[5] When we analyzed the scripts (the common elements) in various versions of these seven common stories, we assumed that these stories had only one interpretation—one that was consistent with the espoused values of top management. Such an assumption is a hallmark of an Integration study.

Other Integration studies focus on the ways leaders and enthusiastic employees can foster the development of symbolic consistency through attention to dress norms and the physical arrangements of the work space. For example:

> The architecture and office layout of Action reflected Murphy's assumptions about creativity and decision making. He insisted on open office landscaping; preferred cubicles for engineers instead of offices with doors; encouraged individualism in dress and behavior; and minimized the use of status symbols, such as private offices, special dining rooms for executives, and personal parking spaces. Instead, there were many conference rooms and attached kitchens to encourage people to interact comfortably. (Schein, 1991a, pp. 21–22)

The colorful look of the [Olympic] Games is called "festive federalism." A conscious effort was made to select a color scheme for use in buildings, uniforms, pageantry, and all printed material that will not reflect political themes. The predominant magentas, aquas, vermilions, purples and periwinkle blues of the palette are not found in any country's flag. . . . Although most employees were expecting red, white, and blue as the colors, the festive federal look of colorful bars, stars, and confetti has caught on and is evident even in crudely made employee notices for parties. Indeed, one large staff party not officially related to the L.A.O.O.C. called itself "Venuization Sensation" (for the process of sending employees permanently out to the competition venues for the duration of the Games) and required all people attending to wear a minimum of three festive federal colors. (McDonald, 1991, pp. 31–32)

Content Consistency

A third kind of consistency occurs when content themes are consistent with each other. For example, in the Integration view of OZCO, the theme of encouraging innovation is consistent with the theme of valuing egalitarianism in the distribution of perks and rewards to those who deserve or need them, rather than to those who have the highest status. And this egalitarianism seems consistent with a humanitarian concern for the emotional and physical well-being of all employees—again independent of their status.

Similarly, Ouchi describes "Theory Z" cultures as having three mutually consistent content themes: a holistic concern for the physical and psychological well-being of the employee and his or her family; a long-, rather than short-term perspective on decisions about products and people; and a desire for "shared values," rather than "red tape" as ways of controlling deviant behavior.[6] Obviously, such broad-based, personal concern about employees would not be appropriate, and the development of "shared values" would not be possible, if only a short-term perspective were being taken. Thus, in an Integration view of a culture, content themes reinforce each other, creating an internally consistent ideology.

Dealing with Inconsistency

Action, symbolic, and content consistencies are not always easy to see. Every once in a while, an Integration study will mention an inconsistency, but usually the study will go on to describe a deeper consistency that resolves the apparent conflict. For example:

Without understanding these [underlying basic] assumptions, one cannot decipher most of the behavior observed, particularly the seeming incongruity between intense individualism and intense commitment to group work and consensus. Similarly, one cannot understand why there is simultaneously intense conflict with authority figures and intense loyalty to the organization without also understanding the assumption "We are one family who will take care of each other." (Schein, 1985, p. 11)

In another example, Barley's study of funeral directors suggests ways of tapping the consistencies that are said to underlie apparent inconsistencies in the ways people think about their work:

> At first glance, preparing a body, choosing a decor for a funeral home, and removing deceased persons from their homes appear to have little in common besides being routine activities of funeral work. Yet, a semiotic analysis suggests that, in at least one funeral home, these three activities are inextricably linked to a common interpretive scheme. Each of the activities is based on a denotative code whose structure is identical. The codes of posed features, furnishings, and removals all create a metonymical array of metaphorical signs that intimate that perceived opposites are similar. The redundancy of structure in the coding rules at the denotative level is reinforced by synonymous, hence redundant, connotative codes. Taken together, the three codes converge to form an interrelated semiotic system. (Barley, 1983, pp. 409–410)

CLARITY AND THE EXCLUSION OF AMBIGUITY

Cultures, according to the Integration perspective, exist to alleviate anxiety, to control the uncontrollable, to bring predictability to the uncertain, and to clarify the ambiguous. For example, Barley defines culture as the product of sense-making activity that brings clarity into employees' working lives:

> Organizations are speech communities sharing socially constructed systems of meaning that allow members to make sense of their immediate, and perhaps not so immediate, environment. (Barley, 1983, p. 393)

Such sense-making is necessary, from an Integration viewpoint, in order to control behavior which disrupts harmony and predictability. For example, in Barley's study of funeral directors:

> For the purpose of this discussion, however, we need only consider those complications that are understood to arise out of mourners' expressive behaviors and are deemed "uncontrollable" in that they are not open to the funeral director's direct intervention. From the funeral director's point of view, acutely expressive behavior can interrupt the pacing of funeral events, upset the "dignity" of the scene, and thereby hamper his work. Expressive behaviors are unresponsive to planning, scripting, or routinization, and their probability cannot be predicted with accuracy. Nevertheless, funeral directors do attempt to divert such disruptions by influencing participants' perceptions in ways that they think might render the emotional tone of the funeral scenes more manageable. (Barley, 1991, p. 43)

Sense-making, as a kind of clarity creation, is an essential aspect of the basic assumptions that lie at the heart of Schein's approach to studying culture. These assumptions are derived from values that emerge from clear, "correct" solutions to problems which previously had seemed to be ambiguous:

The value gradually starts a process of cognitive transformation into a belief and, ultimately, an assumption. If this transformation process occurs—and it will occur only if the proposed solution continues to work, thus implying that it is in some larger sense "correct" and must reflect an accurate picture of reality—group members will tend to forget that originally they were not sure and that the values were therefore debated and confronted. (Schein, 1985, p. 16)

In a similar fashion, Clark defines an "organizational saga" or story as providing clarity, creating meaning out of meaninglessness, and sometimes even replacing uncertainty with the conviction of a religious convert.[7]

Metaphors for the Integration Perspective

Three metaphors capture essential elements of the Integration perspective: a hologram, a clearing in a jungle, and a monolith. Because of its emphasis on consistency, an Integration study is like a hologram:

A hologram is a device [that creates an image] by focusing two beams of laser light on a sheet of film. . . . The film can be broken up into many pieces; yet, no matter how small the pieces are, each is still encoded with the information necessary to reproduce a three-dimensional portrayal of the object. (Dennings, 1986, p. 8)

In a hologram, any fragment encapsulates the essence of the whole; in an Integration portrait of a culture, interpretations of any single manifestation are consistent with the interpretations of all the other manifestations mentioned. Therefore, interpretation of any one manifestation recapitulates the whole in embryonic form.[8]

Because the Integration perspective restricts attention to those cultural manifestations that seem to be consistent and to generate organization-wide consensus, culture becomes that which is clear:

An area of meaning carved out of a vast mass of meaninglessness, a small clearing of lucidity in a formless, dark, always ominous jungle. (Berger, 1967, p. 23, quoted in Wuthnow, Hunter, Bergesen, and Kurzweil, 1984, p. 26)

The Integration perspective defines culture as that which is clear, relegating all else to a jungle that is seen as lacking both form and meaning.

The matrix framework can be used to summarize the essential elements of the Integration perspective. Organization-wide consensus implies that a single matrix is sufficient to represent an organization's culture. Content consistency appears vertically in the left hand column, as consistency of the various content themes that are espoused externally or enacted internally. Action consistency appears horizontally as consistency between these content themes and the organization's formal and informal practices. Symbolic consistency appears horizontally as consistency between the content themes and the cultural forms, such as stories, rituals, jargon, and physical arrangements. The picture of culture that emerges from such an Integration view is a unbroken monolith. Every cell entry is somehow consistent with every other cell entry.

DEFINING CULTURE FROM AN INTEGRATION PERSPECTIVE

It is essential in any domain of research to define the topic being studied, so that it is clear to readers what is and what is not being discussed. Given the commonalities described above, it seems reasonable to expect that Integration studies would define culture in a similar way. They do—and they don't. Table 4-1 contains a sampling of definitions of culture taken from research written predominantly from an Integration point of view.

These definitions generally concur that culture should be defined as that which is shared, but the definitions disagree about what exactly is being shared. For example, in Table 4-1, Davis's definition (1) mentions shared beliefs and values, while Siehl and Martin's definition (2) includes shared patterns of meaning, values, beliefs, and expectations, Sathe's definition (3) emphasizes shared understandings, Schein's definition (4) stresses basic assumptions, and Schall's definition (5) focuses exclusively on communication rules. In spite of these differences in focus, Schein makes it clear what these Integration definitions have in common:

> What this "model" does say, however, is that only what is shared is, by definition, cultural. It does not make sense, therefore, to think about high or low consensus cultures, or cultures of ambiguity or conflict. If there is no consensus or if there is conflict or if things are ambiguous, then, by definition, that group does not have a culture with regard to those things. (Schein, 1991b, pp. 247–248)

Integration definitions of culture vary in the extent to which they are specialized and the extent to which they value depth. The specialist versus generalist debate was introduced in Chapter 3. Among the Integration definitions in Table 4-1, perhaps the clearest representative of a generalist approach is Sergiovanni and Corbally's (definition 6), a laundry list of all the manifestations included in the matrix framework. A clear example of a specialist approach is Schall's (definition 5) of culture as communication rules, which restricts attention to a single column of the matrix (informal practices). This definitional difference of opinion can be misleading, as many of the more specialized definitions of culture, such as Siehl and Martin's definition and Sathe's are taken from cultural studies that encompass a wide range of cultural manifestions.

Integration definitions and research also vary in the extent to which they value depth. For example, some Integration studies define culture in terms of content themes that are externally espoused, to such audiences as researchers or the public, rather than enacted internally, through behavioral interaction with other cultural members. Externally espoused content themes are relatively superficial, often platitudinous statements (usually espoused values or self-reports of behavioral norms). These kinds of espoused content themes could be (and sometimes are) included in annual reports or organizational "mission statements." For example, some Integration studies have focused on such externally espoused themes as a desire to enhance innovation, claims of egalitarianism, the value of teamwork and cooperation, and so on.[9] In a quantitative study of espoused

Table 4-1 Defining culture from an Integration perspective

1. The pattern of shared beliefs and values that give the members of an institution meaning, and provide them with the rules for behavior in their organization. (Davis, 1984, p. 1)

2. Organizational culture can be thought of as the glue that holds an organization together through a sharing of patterns of meaning. The culture focuses on the values, beliefs, and expectations that members come to share. (Siehl and Martin, 1984, p. 227)

3. Culture is the set of important understandings (often unstated) that members of a community share in common. (Sathe, 1985, p. 6)

4. I distinguish among these elements by treating basic assumptions as the essence—what culture really is—and by treating values and behaviors as observed manifestations of the cultural essence. (Schein, 1985, p. 14)

5. An organization might then be studied as a culture by discovering and synthesizing its rules of social interaction and interpretation, as revealed in the behavior they shape. Social interaction and interpretation are communication activities, so it follows that the culture could be described by articulating communication rules. (Schall, 1983, p. 559)

6. A standard definition of culture would include the system of values, symbols, and shared meanings of a group including the embodiment of these values, symbols, and meanings into material objects amd ritualized practices. . . . The "stuff" of culture includes customs and traditions, historical accounts be they mythical or actual, tacit understandings, habits, norms and expectations, common meanings associated with fixed objects and established rites, shared assumptions, and intersubjective meanings. (Sergiovanni and Corbally, 1984, p. viii)

7. To analyze *why* members behave the way they do, we often look for the *values* that govern behavior, which is the second level. . . . But as the values are hard to observe directly, it is often necessary to infer them by interviewing key members of the organization or to content analyze artifacts such as documents and charters. However, in identifying such values, we usually note that they represent accurately only the manifest or *espoused* values of a culture. That is they focus on what people *say* is the reason for their behavior, what they ideally would like those reasons to be, and what are often their rationalizations for their behavior. Yet, the underlying reasons for their behavior remain concealed or unconscious. To really *understand* a culture and to ascertain more completely the group's values and overt behavior, it is imperative to delve into the *underlying assumptions*, which are typically unconscious but which actually determine how group members perceive, think, and feel. (Schein, 1984, p. 3)

8. Organizational theorists often claim that culture is best understood as a set of assumptions or an interpretive framework that undergirds daily life in an organization or occupation. However, despite such theoretical pronouncements, few organizational researchers have actually bothered to study the deep structure of a work setting. Instead, most have focused on symbolic phenomena that lie on the surface of everyday life: stories, myths, logos, heros, and assorted other verbal or physical artifacts. For this reason, cultural research typically belabors the obvious while failing to reveal the core of the interpretive system that lends a culture its coherence. (Barley, 1991, p. 39)

content themes, Kilmann "measured culture" by asking respondents to answer a questionnaire with items, for example, that asked respondents to report whether cultural members do or do not "encourage creativity" or "try to please the organization."[10] Such relatively superficial content themes may be espoused by cultural members because of a desire to present oneself or one's organization in a socially desirable manner, either as an intentional, impression management strategy or as a less conscious distortion of perception or memory.

In contrast, Schein (definition 7) and Barley (definition 8) argue that a focus on these kinds of content themes or on other kinds of cultural manifestations (such as formal and informal practices, stories, or rituals) is undesirable because these are all relatively superficial cultural manifestations. Instead, Schein and Barley argue that cultural studies should focus on deeper content themes, labeled *basic assumptions,* because such themes are less subject to rationalization and self-conscious manipulation. For example, Schein suggests the following basic assumptions may serve as content themes for a cultural analysis: humanity's relationship to nature (dominant, submissive, harmonizing, etc.); the nature of reality and truth (what is real and what is not); the nature of human nature (good, evil, or neutral); the nature of human activity (active, passive, self-developmental, etc.); and the nature of human relationships (cooperative, competitive, etc.).[11] One (somewhat tautological) rationale for this focus on deeply held assumptions, offered in Integration studies, is that culture should be defined in terms of those manifestations that are most likely to elicit organization-wide consensus. For example:

Basic assumptions, in the sense in which I want to define that concept, have become so taken for granted that one finds little variation within a cultural unit. (Schein, 1985, p. 18)

This debate about depth versus superficiality can be illuminated by examining the results of three Integration studies of the same organizational culture, referred to here by a pseudonym—GEM Co. These three studies all work within an Integration definition of culture as that which is shared, but they all come to quite different conclusions about the nature of GEM Co.'s culture because they place different emphasis on the importance of depth. Martin, Anterasian, and Siehl, in the most superficial of the three studies, content-analyzed the externally espoused values in the annual reports of 100 very large corporations.[12] In comparison to the other companies, GEM Co. expressed less concern about the well-being of its employees, emphasizing instead bottom-line issues such as profitability and products—appropriate concerns for an annual report.

A second study by Siehl and Martin focused on internally enacted content themes at GEM Co.[13] Four content themes emerged from a study of cultural forms, such as stories, rituals, and jargon (symbolic consistency): "people are our most important asset," "the company's products and people are unique," "the family of an employee is part of the company," and "never take a short-term perspective." At least three of these themes express a humanitarian concern for employee well-being.

In a third, independently conducted research project, Dyer studied GEM Co. using Schein's emphasis on internally enacted, fundamental assumptions.[14] The themes which emerged from the observation of formal and informal practices (action consistency) and cultural forms (symbolic consistency) included: "long-term perspective on employees' careers," "egalitarianism," "truth through confrontation," and "protect women." A deeper look at the cultural manifestations expressive of these apparently humanitarian content themes revealed evidence of physical and verbal abuse, as well as overt sexism. In this case, the depth of this study's insights stem from an examination of supposedly superficial manifestations.

Depth, then, is an issue about which Integration studies differ. The three studies of GEM Co. suggest that content themes externally espoused in public contexts (or in questionnaires asking for self-reports of values or norms) will be relatively superficial, in the sense that they are probably more influenced by self-presentation and social desirability concerns than the internally enacted content themes that emerge from observation of cultural members at work. Dyer's results suggest that studying supposedly superficial manifestations, as well as basic assumptions, can yield in-depth understanding.

There is a final way in which definitions of culture in Integration studies differ. Many, but not all, Integration definitions stipulate that culture must be unique to a given organizational context.[15] For example, Selznick argues that it is vitally important for an organization to define its distinctive competence, that is, its ability to do a kind of work that other organizations cannot do. This distinctive competence then becomes the focal point of the institution's culture. Similarly, Clark contends that an organization's saga gives believers "an intense sense of the unique" and a "collective understanding of unique accomplishment."[16] Schein also defines the task of the organizational culture researcher as a search for the unique:

> Rather, our problem is to distinguish—within a broader host culture—the unique features of a particular social unity in which we are interested. (Schein, 1985, p. 8)

Schein argues that different organizations may focus on assumptions that are similar, but that in any one organization, the pattern of mutually reinforcing assumptions will be unique. Ott concludes that one of the

> very few areas of general consensus about organizational culture [is that] each organizational culture is relatively unique. (Ott, 1989, p. 52)

This is an overstatement, as will be shown in subsequent chapters of this book, but many Integration studies share this emphasis on uniqueness.

Integration studies, then, tend to define culture as that which is shared and, usually, that which is unique to particular contexts. These definitions vary in the extent to which they are specialized and in the extent to which they value depth. Some of these Integration definitions focus on deeper content themes, such as basic assumptions, while others have a more superficial focus. One of the reasons these definitions are important is that they can be misleading; there is often a discrepancy between how an Integration study defines culture and what it actually studies. The next sections of this chapter examine how Integration studies cope with evidence of the dissent, conflict, and ambiguity that is excluded by these definitions of culture.

WHEN INDIVIDUALS DEVIATE

Although one of the defining characteristics of the Integration perspective is organization-wide consensus, perfect unanimity is unlikely to occur. At the very least, it is reasonable to presume that occasionally an individual will deviate. Some Integration studies simply do not mention this possibility, while other Integration studies recognize it—with evident ambivalence, as they both deny the possibility of dissent and admit that differences of opinion may occur. For example, some of the studies quoted earlier in this chapter claim unanimity ("there was not a dry eye in the house," "family members feel," and "from the funeral director's point of view") and also admit the possibility of deviance ("the people who were comfortable in this environment," "at least in one funeral home," and "on the whole, the group").

A few Integration studies explicitly recognize the difficulties experienced by individual cultural deviants. For example, one book examining the implications of Integration research for individual career development concludes:

> If fundamental and irreconcilable misfits between the individual and the organization are apparent, it may be best for the individual to leave. Biting the bullet may be less costly than an eventual withdrawal, for both parties. (Sathe, 1985, p. 140)

Similarly, O'Reilly, Chatman, and Caldwell indirectly recognize deviancy by advocating a fit between individual job applicants and the "cultures" (as measured by externally espoused values and self-reports of behavior) of large accounting firms.[17]

More rarely, Integration research will recognize a discrepancy between an individual and an organization's culture and try to suspend judgment about the desirability of this state of affairs. For example, one study explores five different reactions to individual cultural deviance (isolation, closure, accommodation, dominance, and transcendence):

> Isolation is a passive reaction to contradiction that seeks to maintain one of the competing positions by closing off other aspects of the dynamic, tension-causing relationship. Closure may come through denial, formalization, buffering, or some other mechanism but tends to result in separation. Accommodation is a passive approach to contradiction that suggests a problem-solving strategy resulting in compromise, and perhaps the subordination of one or more of the competing positions. Dominance is a dynamic strategy for maintaining continuity and suggests confrontation and conquest of the opposing positions. Transcendence . . . is the capacity to engage paradox in a Janusian fashion, to transcend one's own schismogenic tendencies, to see the unities in oppositions, and to move above and reframe the contradictions. (Quinn and McGrath, 1985, p. 331)

Although this study tries to avoid negative judgments of individual deviance, isolation and closure are described in terms that have negative connotations ("passive," "closing off," "denial," "separation"). Accommodation and dominance, described in more positive terms, both require partial or complete domination of one point of view by another. Transcendence describes a higher unity, a more abstract frame, that encompasses oppositions. All of these alternatives (or at least the first four) implicitly portray deviance as an undesirable state or advocate its absorption into a kind of unity.

It might seem benign to advise individuals to avoid organizational cultures where they might be deviants. Ouchi analyzes the difficulties inherent in this position:

> Type Z companies have a tendency to be sexist and racist . . . That is, the top management is wholesome, disciplined, hard-working, and honest, but unremittingly white, male, and middle class. (Ouchi, 1981, p. 91)

Many Integration studies implicitly or explicitly assume that the organizations they examine place unusual emphasis on organization-wide consensus. This is an objectivist position: some cultures are said to be "objectively" more unified than others. This conclusion is put into question by the subjective issues discussed in Chapter 1. Putting aside that point of disagreement until Chapter 9, if the organizations examined in Integration studies do place an atypical emphasis on organization-wide consensus, then these organizations may be particularly likely to exclude women and racial or ethnic minorities from the top levels of the hierarchy. Although statistics regarding the race, gender, and ethnicity of employees are not generally available, Martin and Casscells persuaded the Equal Employment Opportunity Commission to make available summary statistics for a group of organizations lauded in Integration studies (including, for example, Hewlett-Packard, Cummins Engine Company, IBM, Levi Strauss, Proctor and Gamble) and for a group of randomly selected companies in similar industries. As a group, the companies described in studies congruent with the Integration perspective were significantly more likely to exhibit occupational segregation by race and gender, with women and some minorities under-represented in managerial or technical-professional positions.[18]

One explanation for these findings is that evaluation criteria in the companies lauded in Integration research often emphasize humanitarian content themes and place great value on subjectively assessed interpersonal skills, such as "fits in," "works well with team members," and "has respect of subordinates."[19] The unavoidable subjectivity inherent in assessing these skills permits prejudice to be exercised in subtle, often unintentional ways. Perhaps this is why women and minorities earn more and are promoted more often in less "humanistic" cultures where interpersonal skills are considered less important and where performance appraisal criteria are more "objective" (i.e., number of products sold).[20]

These results regarding women and minorities are congruent with sociological research on what has been termed "homosocial reproduction." When upper- and middle-class white men predominate in the top levels of an organization (as they usually do in Western industrial societies), they tend to hire and promote similar others who share their values.[21] Ferguson, for example, concludes that

> the more similarity there is in outwardly identifiable characteristics, such as race, sex, dress, language, and style, the more likely is an aspirant to be seen as the "right kind of

person'' and given access to positions of discretion and power. Thus, the patterns of racial, sexual, and class stratification of the larger society are reproduced in the organization. (Ferguson, 1984, p. 106)

This research suggests that if the organizations described in Integration studies are more likely to exhibit organization-wide consensus, it may be because they exclude from positions of power those whose values and demographic identities are different.

There is another response to deviance, congruent with the Integration perspective, which is seldom mentioned or explored empirically in these studies, although it might well be. The presence of a few, relatively unpowerful deviants can serve to perpetuate and strengthen a hegemony:

> To validate it by being a mistake. . . . To be wrong, so the other can be right; to be bad, so the other can be good; to be unnatural, so the other can be natural: to be Different. (Farley, 1985, p. 270)

All of these alternative responses to deviance—including advising deviants to leave the organization, isolation within it, accommodation, dominance, and inclusion (as an example of what not to do)—strengthen the unity that is the focus of an Integration view of culture.

INTEGRATED CULTURES: THE KEY TO ORGANIZATIONAL EFFECTIVENESS?

Some, *but not all,* Integration studies move from description to prescription, arguing that unity is attractive because of the benefits it brings to individual employees and to the organizations where they work. Not all integration studies claim a link between culture and organizational effectiveness, but those that do generally focus on cognitive clarification, commitment, or productivity.[22]

Some Integration studies argue that consistency, organization-wide consensus, and clarity have cognitive benefits: cultural members know what they are expected to do.[23] For example, in Barley's study of the funeral directors' activities, the content themes (i.e., making death look lifelike) offer a unifying interpretation for tasks that might otherwise seem unrelated or meaningless. Integration studies describe cognitive clarification as serving several individual-level functions: alleviating the anxieties associated with ignorance and confusion; helping individuals retrospectively make sense of their own activities; and making them more aware of role expectations and the organization's history.[24]

Underlying these discussions of cognitive clarification is a traditional concept of the self. According to this view, individuals can rely on their own experiences to develop accurate cognitive models of how the world works:

> The dominant assumption in our society [is] that experience gives access to truth. It is assumed that we come to know the world through experience. There is little question of experience being open to contradictory interpretations guaranteed by social interests

rather than by objective truth. From early childhood we learn to see ourselves as unified, rational beings, able to perceive the truth of reality. We learn that as rational individuals we should be non-contradictory and in control of the meaning of our lives. (Weedon, 1987, p. 80)

This view of the self is congruent with an emphasis on consciousness, autonomy, free will, and self-control. In this view, the self is assumed to be unitary, rather than split into levels of consciousness or multiple, partial identities defined by one's role in a family, organization, or society. Individuals are seen as wanting clarity and consistency in order to avoid the anxiety and unpredictability inherent in an acknowledgment of ambiguity.

Some Integration studies argue that cultures characterized by consistency, consensus, and clarity generate an increased sense of loyalty, commitment, and enthusiasm.[25] For example, McDonald's description of the Olympic Organizing Committee clearly communicates a sense of excitement and an intense commitment to the tasks of this temporary organization. Similarly, experimental studies have shown that organizational stories generate more commitment than other forms of communicating information, such as statistics or statements of espoused values.[26] Other Integration studies argue that cultural uniqueness (the claim that an organization's culture is somehow distinctive) gives cultural members an extra reason to remain loyal to the organization.

Some Integration research argues that organizational commitment is particularly important in contemporary industrial societies where traditional involvements in the community, religion, and extended kinship networks have been eroded by factors such as geographic mobility. A unified organizational culture, according to these studies, can provide substitute outlets for employees' need to belong. Conforming to this viewpoint, some Integration research stipulates that the supposed benefits of unified cultures are limited to a particular type of "humanistic" culture, like OZCO, that emphasizes factors such as familial warmth and holistic concern for the physical and mental well-being of employees. Ouchi, for example, offers this explanation for his findings that members of a "Theory Z" culture had fewer mental and physical health problems and fewer divorces than members of a less unified culture.[27]

In an extension of these claims, some Integration studies contend that cognitive clarification and increased commitment should contribute to increased productivity; employees should have a clearer idea of what they are expected to do and more reasons for wanting to do it well. This claim is implicit in the work of Barley and McDonald and explicit in many other Integration studies.[28]

The most controversial claim, made in relatively few Integration studies, is that a culture characterized by organization-wide consensus, consistency, and clarity will produce improved financial performance. Empirical support for this claim is understandably scarce, since it is difficult to find measures of financial performance that are comparable and reliable within and across industries. And it is even more difficult to find measures of culture that are sufficiently deep, sensitive to contextual idiosyncrasies, and comparable within or across industries.[29] Careful reviews of this literature to date, conducted by those who remain optimistic about such claims and those who think such claims are misguided, generally agree that no evidence meeting these methodological criteria has yet been presented.[30]

Although some remain convinced that adequate evidence can be or even has been found, Siehl and Martin contend that such evidence will not be forthcoming.[31] Putting aside for the moment questions about whether functional "effects" of culture are appropriate to consider and whether the key variables (culture and performance) can be adequately measured, financial performance is determined by so many other variables (including product mix, economic conditions, market segmentation, etc.), that the variance unambiguously attributable to culture is unlikely to be large.

Much of the current revival of interest in organizational culture may have been due to claims concerning the financial benefits of unitary cultures. In the hope that such cultures can provide a new key to profitability, many corporations have invested considerable time and money. Some scholars, managers, and consultants have even put their reputations and livelihoods on the line. The possibility that unitary cultures may not result in increased financial performance (or may not even exist) is upsetting to many. They may ask, "If culture cannot increase profitability, what good is it?"

Some Integration studies respond to such questions by stressing the advantages of having clear expectations and high levels of commitment, sometimes as a means of increasing productivity, sometimes as a goal of separate worth, and sometimes as a means of increasing control over employees. Markets control behavior through direct rewards; hierarchies control employees through rules and procedures. Ouchi suggests it may be less expensive and more efficient to use internalized value consensus, rather than direct rewards or rules and procedures, as a means of control in organizations.[32] Effectiveness arguments such as this reinforce the hope that convincing evidence of a link to financial performance will eventually be found. Schein, however, adds an important caveat: cultural attributes that lead to effectiveness in one environment may lead to failure in another.[33]

To summarize, some but not all Integration studies make claims that cultures characterized by consistency, organization-wide consensus, and clarity will lead to greater organizational effectiveness, as indicated by greater cognitive clarity, commitment, control, productivity, and profitability.

INTEGRATION VIEWS OF CULTURAL CHANGE

Given the supposed benefits of consistency, organization-wide consensus, and clarity, it is not surprising that Integration studies conceptualize cultural change in terms of establishing, maintaining, or returning to a stable unified state.[34] Below, each of these aspects of the cultural change process is discussed from an Integration point of view.

Most Integration studies of the initial establishment of a culture focus on a leader who is described as taking an active role in the culture creation process.

For example, Clark describes the cultural change process at three liberal arts colleges. In each case, a leader is given credit for masterminding the establishment of a distinctive organizational culture. According to Clark, Reed College was established by an unconventional leader:

> William T. Foster, a thirty-year-old, high-minded reformer, from the sophisticated East of Harvard and Bowdoin went to the untutored Northwest, to an unbuilt campus in suburban Portland in 1910, precisely because he did not want to be limited by established institutions, all of which were, to his mind, corrupt in practice. (Clark, 1972, p. 180)

Dr. Foster's vision created great excitement which, forty years later, still generated commitment from

> a faculty proud of what had been done, attached deeply to what the college had become, and determined to maintain what was for them the distinctive Reed style. (Clark, 1972, p. 182)

Schein also offers a leader-centered vision of the cultural change process, describing how a founder, Mr. Jones, used personal example and close supervision to instill his values in employees:

> He would show up at his stores unexpectedly, inspect even minor details, and then "teach" the staff what they should be doing by personal example, by stories of how other stores were solving the problems identified, by articulating rules, and by exhortation. He often lost his temper and berated subordinates who did not follow the rules or principles he laid down. Jones expected his store managers to be highly visible, to be very much on top of their own jobs, and to supervise subordinates closely in the same way he did. In later years these assumptions became a major theme in in his concept of "visible management," the assumption that a "good" manager always had to be around to set a good example and to teach subordinates the right way to do things. (Schein, 1991a, p. 16)

Schein is careful to note that this culture creation process is not automatic. Sometimes founders do not wish to become involved in the day-to-day management of an organization and sometimes they try—and fail.

Once a culture is established, most Integration studies argue that it must be actively, continually maintained, monitored, and renewed. Some activist studies go beyond a leader-centered focus to discuss what lower-level employees can do to facilitate this process of cultural renewal. For example, writing from an Integration perspective, Kanter describes how subordinates contributed to the institutionalization of participative management at Honeywell.[35] Pressure for the change was initiated at the "grass roots" level at the middle and lower echelons of the organization. Top managers endorsed the change goal and individual "prime movers" mobilized employees and implemented systems to be sure the change was introduced effectively. Both informally and formally, lower-level employees helped maintain the cultural change momentum.

Other activist studies generally take a leader-centered view of cultural maintenance and renewal.[36] A leader is the source of a cultural vision that generates an organization-wide consensus, enabling the firm to maintain itself successfully, survive difficult crises, and reorient itself to changed environmental circumstances (see, e.g., Pettigrew's private school headmasters, Tichy and DeVanna's transformational leaders, Siehl's culture-creating group manager, and Selznick's inspirational leaders).[37] Nadler summarizes this point of view in what he terms the "magic leader principle":

> All the successful reorientations we have observed are characterized by an individual leader who is able to serve as a focal point for the change and whose presence, activity, and touch have some special feel or magic. Large-scale organizational change appears to require active, dynamic, and visible leadership to help articulate the change and to capture and mobilize the hearts and minds of the people in the organization (Bennis and Nanus, 1985; Tichy and DeVanna, 1986). (Nadler, 1988, p. 77)

This leader-centered, activist version of the Integration perspective is appealing to managers, as evidenced by the success of several popular books on this subject.[38] It is attractive, in part, because this viewpoint promises high-ranking executives that their efforts can make a difference:

> [These studies] offer a seductive promise to entrepreneurs: namely that a founder can create a culture, cast in the founder's own image and reflecting the founder's own values, priorities, and vision of the future. Thus a founder's personal perspective can be transformed into a shared legacy that will survive death or departure from the institution—a personal form of organizational immortality. (Martin, Sitkin, and Boehm, 1985, p. 99)

Activist Integration studies often seem to assume that normative control of the cultural change process is possible and desirable. Some of these studies focus on the transformation of current employees' values and attitudes. Others argue that since people's values are hard to change, executives might find it more effective and efficient to hire employees with the desired values. In either case, activist Integration studies are advocating a form of "value-engineering." Other researchers argue that culture cannot and should not be controlled by management. For example:

> Culture operates as a form of normative control beyond the volition of the individual. . . . While cultures might control people, it was almost unthinkable that people could control culture. (Barley, Meyer, and Gash, 1988, p. 44)

The possibility and desirability of managerial control of culture, then, is an issue, about which Integration studies disagree.

In accord with a skeptical view of the viability (and in some cases, the desirability) of managerial control of the cultural change process, some Integration studies take a more passive stance toward cultural change, particularly with regard to a leader's role. These studies contend that once internal cultural consistency and consensus is established, a culture will maintain itself in this form with little extra maintenance effort.[39] This can create cultural inertia as a system becomes tightly coupled, elaborated, and rigid, like a scientific paradigm in an advanced stage of development.[40] For example:

> In the short term, congruence of organizational elements seems to be related to effectiveness and performance. A system with high congruence, however, can also be one that is resistant to change. It develops ways of buffering itself from outside influences and may be unable to respond to new and unique situations. (Nadler, 1988, p. 68)

Integration studies that emphasize cultural inertia tend to be pessimistic about the possibility (and sometimes even the desirability) of management control of the cultural change process. These studies place relatively greater emphasis on finding a fit between an existing culture and various business strategy options.[41]

Whether an Integration study takes an activist or passive approach, the process of change is usually described in dramatic terms: a unity is established, becomes resistant to change, and then collapses. This collapse is system-wide, and is sometimes referred to as a "second-order" change process.[42] A new organization-wide unity then may be substituted for the old one. In a review of studies of cultural change, Greenwood and Hinings describe the Integration perspective's view of change in some detail. The unity becomes established and resistant to major change:

> Changes will take the form of structural adjustment to the guiding assumptions of the design archetype. Changes inconsistent with the prevailing meanings will not exist or will be suppressed. (Greenwood and Hinings, 1988, p. 304)

When change comes, it is a system-wide collapse, followed by the substitution of a new unity:

> Structures become de-coupled from the old legitimating interpretive scheme, and connected—re-coupled—to a new one. The organization has emerged in a different design archetype. (Greenwood and Hinings, 1988, p. 307)

If a new unity is not attained, this is seen as a failure in the Integration view of the change process. For example:

> This is a track where there is a failure to obtain coherence, involving sustained movement from a coherent archetype without attaining a reorientation. Incomplete de-coupling occurs without completed re-coupling. These tracks are examples of failed or resisted attempts at reorientation. (Greenwood and Hinings, 1988, p. 308)

To summarize, an Integration account of the cultural change process emphasizes the establishment, maintenance, collapse, and re-establishment of cultural unities. When cultural change occurs, it is described as entailing an organization-wide cultural transformation, whereby an old unity is replaced—hopefully—by a new one. Conflict and ambiguity appear, even in Integration studies. These gaps or breaks in consistency, organization-wide consensus, and clarity are interpreted as evidence of the deterioration of culture before a new unity is established. In this way, Integration studies acknowledge the existence of conflict and ambiguity, while continuing to define culture as the absence of these elements.

The Integration perspective has been the subject of considerable controversy. Some of the criticisms have been methodological, others more substantive. Both kinds of critiques are represented in the concluding sections of this chapter.

METHODOLOGICAL CRITIQUES

Most Integration studies assume an objectivist position and most methodological critiques have also been written from an objectivist stance, implicitly assuming that substantive differences between the three perspectives could be resolved, and truth could be found, if better data collection and analysis procedures were used. However, it should be noted that an alternative kind of critique, more subjectivist in orientation, would focus on different issues, such as: What problems does the language of the text circumvent, ignore, or mask? How have the voices of cultural members been distorted or excluded? Working within the objectivist tradition of the Integration perspective itself, this section discusses a few methodological difficulties that are particularly troublesome for Integration research: the sampling dilemma, the potential for bias due to characteristics of researchers, and the tensions between operationalizing culture and studying a tautology. More extensive discussions of methodological and epistemological difficulties in culture research are available elsewhere.[43]

Integration research has utilized a wide range of methods: quantitative analysis of questionnaire data; quantitative content analysis of texts and conversations; structured and open-ended interviews; short- and long-term participant and non-participant observation; semiotic analysis, and so on. Many of these methods are qualitative and so represent a methodological anomaly within the largely quantitative (at least in the United States) field of organizational studies. Cultural research (and, given its popularity, the Integration perspective in particular) has been reasonably successful in legitimating qualitative methods, renewing interest in subjective phenomena, and encouraging researchers to question their assumptions about objectivity.[44]

Qualitative Integration studies have been criticized, using a standard usually reserved for quantitative research, for inadequate sampling procedures. Most qualitative Integration studies focus on a single (or a small number of) organization(s), usually selected for convenience reasons (sometimes involving a paid consulting relationship). In accord with an unfortunate norm in qualitative research, the number of informants and their characteristics (e.g., hierarchical status, gender, functional responsibilities, etc.) are often not reported. Systematic random, stratified samples with appropriate comparison groups are rare.[45] In most Integration studies, the number of informants is relatively small and the sample is usually disproportionately or exclusively clustered at the upper and middle levels of a hierarchy.

There are good reasons for these sampling deficiencies. Top management approval for a study is usually necessary, and these officials have good reason to restrict researcher access to troubled organizations and discontented employees. Furthermore, trust and openness improve the quality of qualitative data, and rapport cannot be established with large numbers of randomly selected informants. Good qualitative research is exceptionally time-consuming and labor intensive, making large samples of subjects—not to mention organizations—difficult, although not impossible.

In contrast, quantitative Integration research generally includes relatively large numbers of organizations and individual respondents. Most of these studies also report more systematic selection procedures at both the organizational and individual levels of analysis. These systematic sampling procedures are made possible because purely quantitative studies tend to utilize rather superficial, specialized measures of culture (usually focusing on externally espoused content themes).

All culture researchers have to face the same trade-off: the deeper and more detailed their understanding of an organization's culture, the smaller and less systematic their samples. However, most of the qualitative (and some of the quantitative) Integration studies have resolved this dilemma in a manner that reinforced their theoretical perspective. They have generally focused on high morale organizations and relatively high-ranking (or committed) employees. (Similarly, most of the OZCO employees who volunteered observations congruent with an Integration view were high- or middle-level managers or technical/ professional personnel.) These are the people most likely to endorse an Integration view of a culture:

> Advantaged groups, whose interests are served by prevailing structures, will wish organizational arrangements to express coherence, or a common orientation, in order to minimize the latent disruption of discordant structures. Purposes of political control and preservation of privilege are advanced by giving attention to the coherence of organizational design. (Greenwood and Hinings, 1988, p. 297)

For example, Barley seldom mentions the funeral director's employees, who presumably wash the dead bodies, clean up the embalming room, and set out chairs and flowers for the funeral service. Do they too see their activities in terms of a lifelike presentation of death? And did an overemphasis on the highly committed design department cause McDonald's description of the Olympic Organizing Committee's culture to be overly enthusiastic?

A second source of potential bias is possible, particularly in those qualitative studies where researchers had face-to-face contact with individual employees. In these Integration studies, the research team was generally composed of well-educated, well-dressed professionals, entirely or predominantly white, middle class, and male. These attributes are similar to those of management, particularly in the kinds of private-sector organizations selected for most Integration research. To what extent would employees who did not agree with prevailing views of management be willing to express these reservations to researchers who, usually, had been approved by and looked like management?

A third difficulty stems from the fact that Integration research sometimes teeters on the edge of tautology as it excludes from consideration all data that does not reflect its particular definition of culture. Some Integration studies define culture as that which is shared on an organization-wide basis; only that which seems to be shared is then included as part of the culture. For example, funeral directors' activities that did not meet Barley's criteria for consistency were eliminated from his analysis. This is not evidence of methodological sloppiness; it was inherent in Barley's careful mode of analysis. Similarly, in Martin, Anterasian, and Siehl's content analysis of the content themes in annual reports, only those themes that generated considerable cross-organizational consensus were included in the content analysis scheme.[46] Other Integration studies restrict attention to particular manifestations, such as basic assumptions or formal practices, that are seen as most likely to generate consensus.

As can be seen in these examples, choices of sampling procedures, the composition of research teams, and operationalizations of culture can increase the chances that Integration research will find what it is looking for: organization-wide consensus, consistency, and clarity. These methodological "solutions" enhance the managerial bias of Integration research by circumventing evidence of dissenting views.

At this point readers who work from an objectivist position might argue that concerns about the validity of the Integration perspective could be reduced to empirically resolvable questions: Are these Integrationist descriptions of cultures accurate or not? In other words, do some cultures "objectively" generate more consensus, consistency, or clarity? Certainly, it would be helpful to gather data from larger and more systematic samples (when possible), utilize demographically mixed research teams, and study a wider range of cultural manifestations. Problems with the Integration perspective, however, are not so easily resolvable.

SUBSTANTIVE CRITIQUES: A PREVIEW
OF THE OTHER PERSPECTIVES

Methodological improvements are of limited use in this research domain. Many trenchant criticisms of the Integration view cannot be reduced to empirically resolvable questions if the Integration perspective is asking the wrong questions for the wrong reasons. For example, some critics of this perspective observe the platitudinous quality of externally espoused values and the blandness of many basic assumptions and conclude that such commonalities are not what is most important. For example:

> We have to ask what all the members of a whole society do, or what they all do together, that requires them to share these general understandings. There are such things, but I think they tend to be rather banal and not at the level usually meant in discussions of general cultural themes. (Becker, 1982, p. 516)

> The ideas which people share in common are relatively general, relatively innocent, relatively powerless, and relatively non-controversial. Such ideas also don't explain very much. (Weick, 1979b, p. 9)

Other critics are more severe, arguing that such common ideas are neither power-less nor innocent. Instead, the apparent neutrality and inclusiveness of these cultural manifestations reveals the bias of those who are dominant:

> Perhaps "reality" can have "a" structure only from the falsely universalizing perspec-tive of the dominant group. (Flax, 1987, pp. 633–634)

> Corporate culture [researchers] have done an excellent job of staying within "positive/functionalist" assumptions while using the rhetoric of "myth," "rituals," and "quali-tative methods." Rather than opposing the "dominant discourses" they have extended them, one more time, for the same instrumental purposes of prediction and control (Barley, Gash, and Meyer, 1988). . . . To the extent that "culture" has been appro-priated, incorporated, into the functionalist, positivist, technical interest—made part of the "traditional organizational literature"—the organizational culture literature may be dominant but dead. (Calas and Smircich, 1987, pp. 18, 39)

From this critical perspective, the methodological shortcomings described above are not merely careless; they are dangerous. Integration studies reify a view of culture as homogeneity and harmony, usually asserting this view as "objective truth." Because unanimous agreement is unlikely, organization-wide consensus is bound to entail the imposition of someone's authority on someone else. Inte-gration studies are criticized for legitimating intellectual and organizational prac-tices that ignore, downplay, or exclude the ideas, opinions, and interests of those who individually or collectively deviate from a supposedly dominant viewpoint. This dominance is reinforced when Integration studies focus on concepts (such as basic assumptions and transcendence) that avoid difference by moving to higher levels of abstraction. Some statistical techniques used in quantitative Integration studies (reports of averages without between-group analysis of variance, the use of Q-sorts, etc.) serve similar functions. From this viewpoint, Integration studies contribute to a vicious hegemonic cycle whereby this research serves the interests of members of dominant groups, while ignoring those who see things differently.

To summarize, Integration studies appear objective and politically unbiased from the perspective of those who accept and benefit from established relations of authority. Those who wish to dissent from established relations of authority find their concerns silenced by the Integration perspective. In the next chapter, the employees of OZCO speak from a different point of view, one that focuses on differences of opinion and sees conflicts among interest groups as an essential element of an organization's culture.

NOTES

1. The importance of this focus on a particular study, rather than on all the writings of a researcher, is illustrated by Schein's research inside and outside the cultural domain. This chapter argues that Schein's studies of founders and his description of cultural change fit primarily within an Integration perspective. However, his noncultural studies take quite a different point of view. For example, his early work (1961) examined how prisoners of

war resist brainwashing and his studies of socialization (e.g., Schein, 1978) focused on the tension between the individual and the organization, underscoring the need for a lack of conformity under some conditions. It is therefore very important to speak of a particular Integration study, rather than an Integration researcher.

2. Barley, Meyer, and Gash (1988) and Calas and Smircich (1987) discuss the increasing dominance of the Integration view, particularly in the United States.

3. The Integration perspective has some similarities to research which views organizations as interpretive systems. One important difference is that the latter tends to be quite careful in its specification of the sources and limitations of an "organization's" interpretation (e.g., see Daft and Weick, 1984, p. 285).

4. Pettigrew (1979). Other Integration studies illustrating symbolic consistency can be found in Gagliardi (1991), Pfeffer (1981), and Pondy, Frost, Morgan, and Dandridge (1983).

5. Martin, Feldman, Hatch, and Sitkin (1983).

6. Ouchi (1981).

7. Clark (1972), p. 179.

8. This metaphor was first suggested by Pondy (1983).

9. Goodhead (1985), Kilmann (1985), Siehl and Martin (1990).

10. Kilmann (1985). Rousseau (1989) has also studied culture using questionnaire measures of espoused values and self-reports of behavior or behavioral norms.

11. Schein (1985).

12. Martin, Anterasian, and Siehl (1988).

13. Siehl and Martin (1990).

14. Dyer (1982).

15. This discussion of uniqueness is adapted from Martin, Feldman, Hatch, and Sitkin (1983).

16. See Selznick (1957), p. 139, and Clark (1972), p. 183.

17. O'Reilly, Chatman, and Caldwell (1991).

18. Martin and Casscells (1985). Statistics were requested for all companies mentioned in Deal and Kennedy (1982), Ouchi (1981), Pascale and Athos (1981), and Peters and Waterman (1982). The EEOC would release only data for groups of companies; particular companies may differ from these group averages.

19. See, for example, Ouchi (1981) and Pascale and Athos (1981).

20. Studies supporting this contention include Hess and Ferree (1987), Kanter (1977), and Pettigrew and Martin (1987).

21. Kanter, (1977), Moore (1962).

22. Reviews of this literature, written primarily from an Integration perspective, include Ouchi and Wilkins (1985) and Ott (1989). For a more critical assessment of this literature, I would suggest Alvesson and Melin (1987), Barley, Meyer, and Gash (1988), Stablein and Nord (1985), Sypher, Applegate, and Sypher (1985), and Turner (1986).

23. References to this kind of Integration research, with particular focus on the cognitive impacts of organizational stories, include Martin (1982), Martin, Feldman, Hatch, and Sitkin (1983), Sims and Gioia (1986), and Sproull (1981).

24. Schein (1984) offers a cogent explanation of the anxiety-relieving functions of integrated cultures, and Weick (1979a) discusses enactment in similar terms, with particular reference to retrospective sense making.

25. Examples of this kind of research include Clark (1972), Lincoln and Kallberg (1985), Martin and Powers (1983), O'Reilly (1989), Ouchi (1981), and Pettigrew (1979).

26. Martin and Powers (1983).

27. Ouchi (1981).

28. Some unusual and richly detailed studies include Cole (1971), Dellheim (1987), and Rohlene (1974).

29. Financial performance studies using problematic, superficial measures of culture (i.e., values and behavioral norms espoused to an external audience in annual reports or self-report questionnaires) include Denison (1990) and Martin, Anterasian, and Siehl (1988). These issues are discussed in more depth in Siehl and Martin (1990).

30. For a careful, optimistic review of this literature, see Saffold (1988). For a less optimistic assessment, see Siehl and Martin (1990). Both reviews include detailed discussions of methodological difficulties inherent in this kind of research.

31. Siehl and Martin (1990).

32. Ouchi (1980).

33. Schein (1985).

34. Other accounts with a similar orientation toward an organization-wide gestalt, but without a primary emphasis on cultural issues, include Miller (1980), Quinn and Cameron (1983), Torbert (1976), and Tushman and Romanelli (1985).

35. Kanter (1984).

36. Examples include Kilmann (1985), Ouchi (1981), and Pascale and Athos (1981).

37. For example, see Bennis (1984), Pettigrew, (1979), Selznick (1957), Siehl (1984), and Tichy and DeVanna (1986).

38. For example, Deal and Kennedy (1982), Ouchi (1981), Pascale and Athos (1981), Peters and Waterman (1982).

39. Examples of researchers who stress the deeper, more difficult-to-change aspects of culture include Berger and Luckmann (1967), Sathe (1985), and Selznick (1957).

40. Kuhn (1970).

41. For example, Deal and Kennedy (1982), Sathe (1985).

42. Bartunek (1984) and others refer to such radical, discontinuous shifts as second-order changes. Other studies of this kind of change, often with little explicit focus on culture, include Argyris and Schon (1978), Hedberg (1981), Miller and Friesen (1980), Sheldon (1980), Sproull (1981), and Tushman and Romanelli (1985).

43. See, for example, Clifford and Marcus (1986), Meyerson (1991b), and Van Maanen (1988).

44. Reviews supporting this contention include Calas and Smircich (1987) and Ouchi and Wilkins (1985).

45. Exceptions to this include Ouchi (1981) and Siehl (1984).

46. Martin, Anterasian, and Siehl (1988).

5

OZCO: A Differentiation View

This chapter presents the second of the three views of OZCO. In this account employees challenge OZCO's commitment to the values of egalitarianism, innovation, and concern for employee well-being, espoused in the first, Integration view of this firm. In accord with the Differentiation perspective, this account exposes inconsistencies and views organization-wide consensus as a myth. Difference and conflict replace homogeneity and harmony.

CHALLENGING CLAIMS OF EGALITARIANISM

There are those who question the reality of OZCO's commitment to egalitarianism. The rhetoric, they claim, masks a hierarchy that is, in the words of one employee,

> more adhered to than anywhere that I have ever seen. (Sally, human resources consultant)

In addition, some functional areas are apparently "more equal" than others. Some employees say that engineering, in particular, receives preferential treatment:

> I wouldn't recommend [that a person come to work for OZCO] unless he had a technical background. . . . So I'd tell a person that. People come to me all the time and say, "Hey, I heard it's a good company. What could they do for me?" You know, until you have a technical background—let's be truthful, you know. (Maria, personnel clerk)

According to some employees, these inequalities are made visible in OZCO's physical arrangements. Although employees eat at the same cafeteria, status and functional differences are reflected in self-chosen seating patterns. Engineering and marketing staff, it is said, "never" eat together. And, although cross-status interaction is sometimes observed, some say it is limited:

> I wouldn't hesitate to sit down with my immediate boss, his boss, or his boss's boss. But I wouldn't sit with anyone higher than that. And, of course, I wouldn't eat with engineers. (Dan, product marketing)

Some employees reinterpret OZCO jargon, denying that it reflects egalitarianism across levels of the hierarchy or functional areas. Although corporate headquarters may be referred to as "retirement village," it is located "upstairs," along with Engineering and Quality Control. Engineers work in "the Labs," a word sometimes referred to with deference. The labs, like most of the rest of the company, have open office spaces. However, the walls of the engineers' partitions are higher, supposedly to provide "room for thought." In contrast, people in marketing "have to go off-site to think."

Rather than being an egalitarian panacea, open office spaces can create tension. Some employees find the lack of privacy uncomfortable:

> There was one guy I worked with that made me very uncomfortable. I had to go to great lengths to avoid him. I even tried earplugs, so that I wouldn't have to hear his very personal, agonizing phone conversations. (Denise, product marketing)

Hoffman and Hatch studied the effects of the apparently egalitarian physical arrangements at OZCO.[1] These researchers note that open office spaces make employees' behavior visible. Conversations can be, and are, easily overheard. Supervisors can literally oversee (by gazing over partitions) the work of their subordinates. From this perspective, the OZCO policy of "Management By Walking Around" (MBWA) becomes a way of keeping an eye on employees.

Hoffman even suggests that casual dress norms and informalities, such as the use of first names, have an inegalitarian effect because they give the impression that superiors know their subordinates personally. Those employees who prefer more interpersonal distance feel uncomfortable, particularly when superiors express concern with their private lives. Thus, these informalities can exacerbate the tensions between hierarchical levels. Rather than being a source of egalitarian harmony, according to Hoffman and Hatch, these cultural manifestations sometimes create resentment, and, occasionally, overt conflict.

Although formal practices may be designed to foster egalitarianism, the informal ways these policies are implemented are, according to some employees, definitely not egalitarian. For example, "perks" are supposed to be distributed according to job-related needs, but some employees observe that who gets what depends on a manager's "pull":

> If my manager has extra money, after everything is taken care of, then we get some perks. (Stuart, marketing engineer)

In addition, although bottom-up consensual decision-making might seem to be an unequivocally egalitarian practice, most important decisions at OZCO require agreement across divisional boundaries. To reach that kind of consensus, some employees feel they have to resort to hierarchical sources of authority:

> For example, I was trying to get some guys in [another product area] to learn about my product before its introduction, so they would be ready to pump it. They had better things to do, so I had to go to their boss to get their help. The problem is you use up social capital when you do this. (Tom, marketing engineer)

Status differences among functional areas are also sometimes seen as influencing the decision-making process. For example:

> There are lots of internal competition and status differentials. Product management is more prestigious than sales and purchasing, and purchasing likes to spite the other divisions. In group level meetings there is a lot of finger pointing, rather than coherence into a united force. (Denise, product marketing)

Although OZCO's lateral promotion policies are supposedly egalitarian, in that they are backed by evaluation procedures that should not reward functional specialization, some employees see inconsistency. As part of the evaluation process, employees are ranked in comparison to others in different functional groups at the same hierarchical level. Some employees say this ranking process encourages specialization because, in order to be relatively better, one needs expertise. Furthermore, opportunities for lateral movement are not equal; according to these employees, the lateral promotion policy is apparently implemented with a sensitivity to power differentials:

> Opportunity to move around and ultimately advance depends on relative power and status of division and division manager. (Dana, sales)

Furthermore, some employees believe that chances for promotion, which depend on training, and thus the opportunity to go to school, vary by department:

> Anybody that goes to school and shows that much enthusiasm towards their job and that type of thing, I think, moves themselves into line for a promotion and things like that. It has worked for me. . . . But, like I said, then again, I know of departments that would never allow you to go to school. You know, they cannot afford to have their people missing half a day or missing a week or a quarter of a day—that type of thing. And they don't need that. Some divisions just don't need somebody that is that well trained. They just need somebody for Part A and Part B, you know. It is really important to know what the divisions are like. (Ron, operations staff)

According to some employees, even the company's commitment to avoiding mass layoffs is not egalitarian in practice. For example, some higher status employees claim to suffer more than an equal share of the burden imposed by OZCO's across-the-board pay cut. In exchange for less pay, employees are generally allowed to take two days a month off:

> Voluntary Time Off sounds good, but if you have lots of work, then time off is a joke. It is really a pay cut when you have lots of work. If you don't, then the time off is really not voluntary. I guess it's my choice, but I have too much work to take time. In the last six months, I've only taken two days off. (Stuart, marketing engineer)

In addition, some functional areas were apparently exempted from the pay cut. For example, one group did not "take a hit" because it was deemed strategically critical to the company's long-term success. In short, according to these employees, a closer look at OZCO's commitment to egalitarianism reveals that some employees are "more equal" than others.

IMPEDIMENTS TO INNOVATION

In order to promote the development of innovative, complex products that provide integrated solutions to customer needs, OZCO recently reorganized. The traditional dominance of engineers, over the product development process, was constrained by a new emphasis on unity and coordination. OZCO's divisional structure was supplemented by "groups," "sectors," and "customer/industry managers," designed to coordinate divisions' responses to customer needs. A number of formal and informal practices were instituted, in order to facilitate integration and centralization, thereby encouraging innovation and better product marketing.

When this emphasis on innovation is reinterpreted from a Differentiation perspective, the focus changes. The reorganization is seen as an attempt to reduce the dominance of one group (engineering), increase the authority of another group (marketing), and maximize coordination across groups by requiring more centralized, cross-functional control. According to some employees, this attempt to make product development more market-driven and more integrated was not successful because the company retains a highly differentiated structure. First, the corporation is dispersed geographically. Plants are located in over twenty U.S. cities. Research and manufacturing facilities, as well as sales and support offices, are established all over the world. In addition, sometimes several divisions set up to service one product. Although these divisions recognize a need to work together, they are autonomous. They have their own methods of product appraisal and their own methods of evaluation.

According to some employees, OZCO's accounting and incentive systems also promote divisional differentiation. Divisions are rewarded, independently, for new product development. In addition, divisions are separate profit centers, each with their own incentive system. The new industry-oriented marketing coordination groups, on the other hand, are considered a corporate overhead expense. As a result of this structural differentiation, it is perhaps not surprising that some employees question the success of the marketing integration efforts of the industry-oriented groups. These employees claim that coordination by superentities, such as groups and sectors, is done only in response to a problem, when a "lack of links" is apparent, or when obvious turf battles are taking place.

Other informal practices, it is claimed, further undermine efforts to coordinate across divisions. For example, corporate staff have made an attempt to centralize the recruiting process by creating a resume pool. Some employees claim that divisions continue, illegally, to do their own recruiting "on the side." Informal patterns of interaction also sometimes strengthen divisional boundaries. Employees get together informally once or twice a month to discuss what's happening within the division. Cross-divisional gatherings of this sort are apparently rare.

Some employees say that the product development process also exhibits a lack of integration and coordination. Although various divisions may work under the same product umbrella, they have sometimes have their own spin-off products and services. Divisions don't communicate adequately, some employees claim, to these other interdependent divisions, or to corporate staff, about a new product. Sometimes divisional employees even take pride in getting products to the marketplace before corporate employees have figured out whether or not they even want it.

Although this autonomy is understandable, given OZCO's decentralized formal structure, some employees say the development of unique and marketable new products is apparently impeded. Although many new products are developed, the products produced by different divisions are sometimes seen as redundant. Some employees in other divisions, on which the product may ultimately depend, feel they cannot do their part to affect the design of the product and make it successful. Most important, marketing considerations are sometimes ignored:

> Still, labs are developing products. There is lots more of this than they would like to acknowledge. They like doing their own thing and don't like taking directions from a marketing group. There is not much up front marketing planning. It was an incredible thing for OZCO to have [a new product] come out so coordinated, . . . as a package. At OZCO that is a big deal. (Dana, sales)

Part of the perceived problem seems to come from the way the marketing effort is structured. As some employees see it, marketing is treated as an integrating function, involving interdependent divisions. In a marketing decision, all the relevant divisions are supposed to be involved. In contrast, engineering decisions are sometimes treated as independent. These problems with OZCO's marketing effort have not gone unnoticed or unacknowledged:

> I don't think OZCO is bad at marketing. It's just that we needed to accelerate the marketing to complement the engineering. (Jim, president, internal newsletter)

In spite of the push to make product development market-driven, products still get developed in the lab by engineers, for engineers:

> They crank out products without looking if there is a need or niche. The engineers don't talk to the sales people who are out in the field. That's why we are successful in the engineering marketplace—our products speak to their need. And, that's why we're dying in the business marketplace. For most businesses, we really don't address the marketplace questions because of the way we develop products. (Denise, product marketing)

According to some employees, engineers get the credit, and the blame, for whatever new products are developed. For example, OZCO entered a new high-growth area with a product that had some clear technical advantages over its competitors. The engineers had apparently done this part of the job well, but, flouting the dominance of one of their competitors, they decided to adopt product characteristics that differed from the industry's norm:

> It was a conscious decision on our part. The [characteristics make the product] better, so we used it. (Irving, vice president, product area x)

This was an engineering-driven decision and some employees felt it "doomed" sales of the product by retail outlets. Because of the unique product characteristics, technical and marketing support was minimal. Furthermore, retail profit margins were severely limited because of a shortage of high-margin compatible products to sell. These employees felt strongly that this product's history clearly revealed OZCO's conflicting priorities, showing why the company has found it difficult to develop innovative, marketable products.

LACK OF CONCERN FOR EMPLOYEE WELL-BEING

Some employees listen with considerable skepticism to OZCO rhetoric about concern for employees' personal well-being:

> They really don't care about you as a person. Now I realize we're all here to do a job and it is very hard, I know, to draw that line as to when personal feelings or things shouldn't be heard and the job should come first. . . . But, some people do have more problems—even personal problems. I've seen some people being very cold towards people's personal problems. And I just feel we should have a little more sympathy for people 'cause I always think to myself, "That could be me someday." And I would like to think that if that ever happened to me, I would want somebody to treat me fairly and have some understanding. And I don't see it happening here now. (Aida, personnel clerk)

Perhaps the most pointed criticism is that apparently humanitarian policies, such as personal development opportunities, flex hours, and the informalities that make OZCO a nice place to work, are simply compensation in lieu of decent pay:

> They pay, especially now, really shitty. (Denise, product marketing)

> Well, their pay scales are low. You see lots of problems. I can compare, being that I worked in another industry where they had more financially—pay scales, but they weren't consistent. OZCO is consistent—and offers or clouds you with all these other things. But the finance, you know, doesn't compensate the job. (Maria, personnel clerk)

The use of family terminology is also met with cynicism by some employees:

> Along with this very nice, humanitarian theme goes the midwestern mommy and daddy: daddy makes the decisions and takes care of the family and mommy does the supplementary stuff. (Sally, human resources consultant)

Some employees believe that the traditional gender ideology of OZCO's management has fostered inequities in pay and promotions for women. Noting OZCO's publicized preference for promoting insiders, rather than hiring outsiders, one OZCO employee questioned why a senior woman, who earned considerably less than he, had not been given a promotion to the position he had been hired (from the outside) to fill:

I found out what she made and then what I made. Then I thought, well, something has got to be wrong and then I found out she had had a fight for the job that I had and they did not take her because of her attendance. I was making more than her . . . and, you know—wondering why she didn't get my job because I had come from the outside and she had been with OZCO, you know, because they take their employees first before they go to outsiders. (Jack, operations staff)

According to some employees, pay and promotion inequities experienced by women at OZCO are exacerbated because the company's concern for employees' personal well-being takes a form that supports traditional-housewife, rather than working-mother roles for women. For example, at a public panel discussion the president of OZCO was asked if the company was concerned about "the deterioration of the family" and if it was "doing things like providing, for example, day care centers for working mothers" employed at OZCO. Jim Hamilton did not respond by observing that high-quality day care was an important part of the company's concern for the well-being of the families of its employees. Instead, he observed:

Well, I think we are, of course, concerned about family values. I think they are on the decline, and I think that is a problem. . . . There aren't a lot of other institutional ways to re-implant that kind of values set in young people as they grow up. As far as the corporation acting as a proxy to the family, I think it's not a great one. Again, I think we can provide a whole range of benefits and that kind of thing, but when you're thinking about it from a family values point of view, that really isn't a substitute for what really happens in the strong family relationship. (Jim, president, public panel discussion)

Later in the discussion, after being pressed to give more specific evidence of OZCO's commitment to the well-being of working mothers, Jim told the Caesarean story recounted in Chapter 3. While Jim offered this story as evidence of the company's concern for the personal well-being of women employees, some of the audience felt that the story expressed an unconscionable disregard for the mother's pain after the Caesarean operation and for the possible health benefits of a more natural timing for the baby's birth. From this perspective, the company's provision of a closed circuit television in the mother's bedroom, in order to continue her involvement with the introduction of a new product, was an inexcusable intrusion into her privacy. Although Jim's version of the story includes no record of the new mother's opinion on these matters, the story can be reread from this critical viewpoint:

We have a young woman who is extraordinarily important to the launching of a major new [product]. We will be talking about it next Tuesday in its first worldwide introduction. She arranged to have her [baby born by a] Caesarean [operation] yesterday in order to be prepared for this event, so you—we have insisted that she stay home and this is going to be televised in a closed circuit television, so we're having this done by TV for her, and she is staying home three months. We are finding ways of filling in to create this void for us because we think it's an important thing for her to do. (Jim, president, public panel discussion)

Negative reactions to the Caesarean story include hisses, as well as more articulate criticisms:

> Not only was it an outrageous statement, it was stupid. It didn't occur to him to ask, "Where are our values here?". . . Didn't it occur to him that this kid deserves his own timing? (Janet, attendee, public panel discussion)

> Sounds like an Intel comment. It smells macho like Intel. It really doesn't sound like OZCO, although there are not really any senior women managers. [The woman who had the Caesarean] is one of the highest ranked women here. My division is pretty isolated from that junk. There are more women than men [in my division], even though I know women aren't at the top yet. (Dana, sales)

According to some employees, Jim Hamilton's (mis)interpretation of this story (as expressing concern for working women) is one sign of a widespread lack of sensitivity to gender issues at OZCO. Perhaps this is why, these employees suggest, there are so few women in senior management positions at OZCO. Some employees characterize the company's management as an "old boys' network"; the top management team, for example, is composed of only men. Although there are some women in the middle management ranks, they are generally clustered in gender-segregated jobs and work groups. These "pink-velvet ghettos," according to some employees, tend to have lower status, lower pay, and fewer well-developed career ladders.

Some employees say other forms of discrimination, for example, against blacks, Hispanics, Filipinos, and Vietnamese, are also serious problems at OZCO. Because of the small numbers involved and because of clustering (for example, at lower levels and in particular jobs), some employees say that it is hard to get management to acknowledge the seriousness and pervasiveness of discriminatory problems. These employees are worried that OZCO's concern for employee well-being does not include minorities and/or women as fully as their white male co-workers.

HOTBEDS OF CONTRADICTION AND CONFLICT

According to this Differentiation view, OZCO is characterized by contradiction and conflict. Employees challenge the sincerity of management's commitment to egalitarianism, innovation, and employee well-being. Instead, these employees see pervasive inequality and inequity, the perpetuation of impediments to innovation, and an insensitivity to the well being of OZCO employees, particularly those who hold lower status jobs and have demographically different identities.

Table 5-1 presents this Differentiation view of OZCO in the form of a matrix. Cell entries are frequently inconsistent, as when espoused values are contradicted by informal practices and cultural forms, such as stories, jargon, and physical arrangements. These inconsistencies are clear; there is little ambiguity included in this matrix. Perhaps most important, this Differentiation matrix is the polar opposite of the Integration view of OZCO's culture, presented in Table 3-1.

This chapter's description of OZCO can be presented in a single matrix because it focuses on the ways middle management and lower-level employees challenge the Integration view of OZCO's "dominant" culture. Other kinds of Differentiation studies must be represented with several matrices, one to represent each subculture. Although the OZCO data are not sufficiently detailed to delineate relevant subcultures, there is evidence that marketing, engineering, and perhaps other status-specific or function-specific subcultures may exist. (Apparently, women and/or minorities, in spite of widespread disaffection, have not evolved coherent subcultures, with the possible exception of some "pink-velvet ghettos.") For example, Figure 5-1 includes a Differentiation view of OZCO with five major subcultures: top management, engineering, marketing, production, and lower-level employees. If subcultural differences were explored further, it is likely that some subculture-specific content themes (related for example to function-specific tasks and responsibilities) would be relevant. The three themes used to link the three portraits of OZCO could be supplemented in this way.

In this chapter, OZCO employees question the validity of claims that the company has managed to create a culture where egalitarianism, innovation, and concern for employee well being are truly valued. If this Differentiation view is to be believed, the Integration portrait of OZCO is either misleading corporate propaganda or a wistful description of what might be desired—not a realistic description of how the company really functions. Which of these two perspectives is correct? Chapter 4 summarized the case for the Integration viewpoint: a

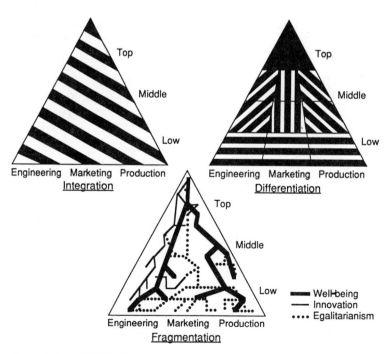

Figure 5-1.   OZCO: Three perspectives.

Table 5-1 OZCO: A Differentiation view

Content themes		Practices	
External	*Internal*	*Formal*	*Informal*
	Egalitarianism is questioned		Engineers get privileges
			"Management by walking around" as means of control
			"Perk" distribution based on managers' pull and surplus budget
			Authority and status may override consensual decision making
			Ranking encourages specialization
			Opportunities for lateral promotion depend on power of manager
			Voluntary time off has differential impact
	Impediments to innovation	Autonomous divisions with independent systems of •product appraisal •evaluation •incentives •accounting	Divisions each do recruiting on the side
			Divisional informal gatherings
			Divisions develop spin off products independently
		Group level integration only in response to problems	Marketing not integrated
			Engineers develop products without marketing considerations
	Lack of holistic concern for employee well-being		Lack of personal concern
			Humanitarian policies in lieu of fair pay
			"Family" implies patriarch and "Daddy" gets paid more
			No female general managers, few minorities and women clustered in "pink velvet ghettos"

		Forms	
Stories	*Ritual*	*Jargon*	*Physical arrangements*
		"Upstairs" "The Labs"	Seating in cafeteria by status and function
			Higher partitions for engineering than marketing
			Open offices cause discomfort
			Casual dress etc., causes intrusion into personal lives
"Caesarean" story questions sensitivity to employee's family			

wide range of studies claimed to show that under the right kind of vision-creating leadership, organizations can develop cultures based on shared values, harmony, and homogeneity. The Differentiation research to be discussed in the next chapter challenges this conclusion. According to these studies, the Integration perspective is a myth, created and perpetuated for the benefit of top management, to cover up the contradictions and intergroup conflict that inevitably characterize organizational cultures.

NOTE

1. Hatch (1990), Hoffman (1982).

6

The Differentiation Perspective: Separation and Conflict

According to the Differentiation perspective, the apparently seamless unities of the Integration perspective mask a series of overlapping, nested organizational subcultures. These subcultures co-exist, sometimes in harmony, sometimes in conflict, and sometimes in indifference to each other. The Differentiation perspective unveils the workings of power in organizations, acknowledges conflicts of interest between groups, and attends to differences of opinion. This chapter introduces the Differentiation perspective and extends it to incorporate insights about environmental influences on the development of cultures in organizations.

Differentiation views of organizational culture have three defining characteristics. First, interpretations of content themes, practices, and forms are often inconsistent. Second, the Differentiation perspective is suspicious of claims of organization-wide consensus. To the extent that consensus exists, it is seen as located primarily within subcultural boundaries. Third, within subcultural boundaries, clarity reigns, while ambiguity is relegated to the periphery. These defining elements of the Differentiation perspective (*inconsistency, subcultural consensus, and the relegation of ambiguity to the periphery of subcultures*) are explored in more detail below, using quotations from studies that illustrate this viewpoint.

INTRODUCTION TO DIFFERENCE

Integration studies focus on that which is similar, often moving to higher levels of abstraction that sidestep difference by encompassing it. Because abstractions have a higher logical status, they are sometimes seen as having a firmer claim to importance or even a moral priority. Thus, claims of difference are often seen as "lower level, fragmenting, particularistic sorts of concerns," while similarities are considered "higher level, integrative, and universalistic sorts of concerns."[1] This process of valuing that which unifies, and devaluing that which differentiates, can be observed at all levels of organizations. Managerial advocates of unity may urge a recalcitrant labor force to accept a firmwide wage freeze "because we are all in this together." A white-dominated union making up a list of grievances to be brought to the bargaining table may refuse to give black workers' claims of racist discrimination a top priority because "it may create internal dissent at a time when the union must stick together." A group of women employees, drawn from all levels of a hierarchy, may dismiss the problems of Chicana assembly-line workers as secondary, "Let's achieve the goals all the women in this company share before we focus on the needs of any specific group of women."

Note that each of these examples of valuing that which unifies is based on a dichotomy: management versus labor, whites versus blacks, non-Chicana versus Chicana women. Western thought has been founded on dichotomous thinking, for example, rational/emotional, active/passive, presence/absence.

> Meaning is produced precisely through binary oppositions. Thus, in the opposition masculine/feminine, each term only achieves significance through its structural relationship to the other: "masculine" would be meaningless without its direct opposite "feminine" and vice versa. (Moi, 1985, p. 105)

Differentiation studies work within this tradition, using oppositional thinking to define subcultural differences. Some take oppositional thinking one step farther, arguing that binary oppositions are inevitably hierarchical; one of the two terms is generally treated as having more power, status, or value:

> Western culture has proven to be incapable of thinking not-the-same-as without assigning one of the terms a positive value, and the other, a negative. (Jardine, 1988, p. xxv)

For example, in each of the dichotomies above, the second of the two terms (labor, blacks, Chicanas; emotional, passive, absence) is often seen as having less power or value than the first.[2]

A critique of the hierarchical nature of dichotomous thinking is congruent with the Differentiation perspective. Just as the Integration perspective is most congruent with a managerial point of view, so the Differentiation perspective is most congruent with the views of groups that lack the power and status of top management. For example, some theorists explain top management's preference for the Integration perspective and less powerful groups' preference for a Differentiation viewpoint by stressing conflicts of interests between classes:

> Because their class position insulates them from the suffering of the oppressed, many members of the ruling class are likely to be convinced by their own ideology; either they fail to perceive the suffering of the oppressed or they believe that it is freely chosen, deserved, or inevitable. They experience the current organization of society as basically satisfactory and so they accept the interpretation of reality that justifies that system of organization. They encounter little in their daily lives that conflicts with that interpretation. Oppressed groups, by contrast, suffer directly from the system that oppresses them. . . . The pervasiveness, intensity, and relentlessness of their suffering constantly push oppressed groups toward a realization that something is wrong with the prevailing social order. Their pain provides them with a motivation for finding out what is wrong, for criticizing accepted interpretations of reality and for developing new and less distorted ways of understanding the world. These new systems of conceptualization

will reflect the interests and values of the oppressed groups and so constitute a representation of reality from an alternative to the dominant standpoint. (Jaggar, 1983, p. 370)

To summarize, Differentiation studies do not usually deny the existence of the similarities, consistencies, and unities that are the focus of Integration studies. However, Differentiation research goes one step farther, exploring the viewpoints of subcultures that see things differently. This is crucially important because similarity and dissimilarity are asymmetrical, in that there are far more ways to be dissimilar than to be similar.[3] Some Differentiation studies stop at this point, simply describing a subculture. Other Differentiation studies stress opposition to management, placing power, and the potential for conflict, at the center of attention. Every person is seen as having complicity in relations of dominance. Everyone is always either in power—enabling, prohibiting—or subordinated. In these latter Differentiation studies, subcultural relations are seen as inevitably hierarchical; no place is neutral. The next sections of this chapter discuss examples of inconsistency, subcultural consensus, and the channeling of ambiguity in Differentiation research.

INCONSISTENCY

Differentiation views of cultures are textured by the acknowledgment of inconsistency, which is a form of oppositional thinking. The simplest case of inconsistency occurs when one manifestation is interpreted in two different ways. For example, in Smircich and Morgan's study of an insurance company, the president and the staff are described as having inconsistent interpretations of a recent project:

> For the president, [the project] sought to define the situation in a way that created a high priority, future-oriented program. . . . [He stressed] the relative success of [the project] in getting rid of the backlog of work. For the staff, [the project] . . . was just another sign of the inadequate way the fragmented organization was being run. They saw it as the act of a manager who was afraid to confront the real issues, who insisted on seeing the organization as a team, whereas the reality was that of a poorly managed group characterized by narrow self-interest, and noncooperation at anything but a surface level. (Smircich and Morgan, 1982, p. 267)

Whereas Integration studies stress consistency, Differentiation studies offer inconsistent interpretations of cultural manifestations. Differentiation research has drawn attention to three kinds of inconsistency: action, symbolic, and ideological. Examples of each are given below.

Action Inconsistency

Action inconsistency occurs when an espoused content theme is seen as inconsistent with actual practices.[4] For example, in Chapter 5 OZCO employees described the company's espoused egalitarian values as inconsistent with a variety of formal and informal practices, including the distribution of "perks" according to a manager's "pull" and surplus budget, rather than an employee's task-based need; the interpretation of MBWA as a means of maintaining control over subordinate behavior, rather than making management more accessible to lower level employees; "consensual" decision-making as being controlled, in an inegalitarian manner, by upper levels of the hierarchy and certain functional areas, and so on.

These are examples of inconsistency that derive from conflicts of interest between employees who have more power (e.g., the president of the insurance company or OZCO managers with "pull") and those who have less. Inconsistencies can also stem from an external conflict of interest between the dominant coalition within an organization and the organization's external environment, as represented by the law or public opinion. Siehl reports examples of this kind of action inconsistency at an oil refinery located in a "red neck" area of Texas.[5] The refinery's top management team spoke frequently and at length about the importance of combating the evils of racism and sexism. However, no management disapproval was expressed when one of the few women to hold a blue-collar position at the refinery put on her hard hat—only to find her co-workers had left a raw egg inside. This was only one of many sexist and racist "jokes" observed at the refinery. Apparently, the oil refinery's management spoke approvingly of the need to combat racism and sexism, but did not follow up this rhetoric with consistent action because they were not really committed to change; they just wanted to protect this white male enclave from outside "interference" by external advocates of affirmative action, such as the Equal Employment Opportunity Commission, lawyers, and law enforcement agencies.

Studies of loose coupling also often draw attention to action inconsistency. For example, Meyer and Rowan's study of school systems describes inconsistencies between externally espoused rhetoric and actual priorities in the classroom.[6] When addressing external audiences, such as school boards and government funding sources, school administrators stressed the importance of "the numbers": test scores, inventories of school books, and the number of classrooms and desks. In contrast, when addressing teachers, administrators made little mention of these quantitative variables, focusing instead on the process of education. Meyer and Rowan concluded that public talk about "the numbers" was empty rhetoric that buffered the teachers from outside interference, so that the work itself, the unquantifiable art of teaching, could continue undisturbed.

Brunsson carries this loose coupling argument one step farther, with a particular focus on inconsistent environmental demands:

> For example, companies are required, by powerful counterparts, not only to make high profits, but also to provide many jobs, good employment conditions and little pollution. (Brunsson, 1986, p. 166)

In order to conform to these conflicting environmental demands, organizations often need to develop internal inconsistencies:

The use of three kinds of output—talk, decisions and products—provides an important possibility. Organizations may reflect inconsistent norms by systematically creating inconsistencies between talk, decisions, and products. They can talk in consistence with one group of norms, decide according to another, and produce according to a third. (Brunsson, 1986, p. 171)

Symbolic Inconsistency

Symbolic inconsistency, between espoused content themes and cultural forms, is also evident in many Differentiation views of culture. For example, in the Differentiation portrait of OZCO, egalitarian rhetoric is inconsistent with a variety of forms, including jargon ("upstairs" and "The Labs"); status-stratified seating arrangements in the cafeteria; and higher wall partitions for engineers rather than marketing personnel.

Symbolic inconsistencies can also point to deviations from official organizational policy. For example, the oil refinery described earlier had a safety record that was quite respectable, compared with the records of other nearby refineries. However, the most popular organizational story at the refinery concerned "The Labor Day Explosion," when disregard for safety rules caused an employee's death. Two inconsistent interpretations of this story were offered. Some employees said the story was "the exception that proved the rule," reinforcing management's emphasis on the company's "excellent" safety record. Other employees said that the "Labor Day Explosion" proved that the refinery, in spite of many people's best efforts, was a dangerous place to work.

Differentiation research often describes organizational stories as having two conflicting interpretations. For example, the "Rule Breaking" story described in Chapter 4 might be interpreted differently, depending for example, on the status of the interpreter. A manager might say, "Everyone here should obey the rules, even the president." A lower-status employee might conclude, "She was lucky she didn't get fired. What a risk she took!" or "She was lucky she stood up to him; otherwise she would have been fired."

A different kind of symbolic inconsistency can be seen by examining the jargon employees use. For example, a study of two large consulting firms revealed that, in spite of rhetoric about the importance of cooperation and teamwork, employees' jargon was rife with metaphors of violent conflict:

The interviews were filled with images of cards and players, wars, teams, battles, armies, pugilistics, and wounds. Game (with a particular emphasis on sports) and military (with a vicarious interest in espionage) scenarios repeatedly emerged along with a discerning sense of their use. (Riley, 1983, p. 427)

Analysis of inconsistencies in the interpretation of cultural forms, such as stories, rituals, and jargon, often reveals an "underbelly" of conflict that is not acknowledged in managerial rhetoric that stresses teamwork, harmony, egalitarianism, or cooperation.[7]

Ideological Inconsistency

A third form of inconsistency occurs when content themes conflict with each other. For example, in the Differentiation view of OZCO, the priority given innovation often conflicted with the espoused value of egalitarianism, as not all groups contributed equally to fostering innovation. This ideological inconsistency may account, in part, for the advantages apparently given to engineers in "The Labs."

Another example of ideological inconsistency comes from Martin, Anterasian, and Siehl's study of externally espoused values in annual reports of 100 randomly selected, large companies.[8] Cluster analysis revealed that a subset of these firms placed significantly more emphasis on the value of taking financial risks, for example, through divestitures, mergers, and acquisitions. Such risks can threaten employee job security. This subset of firms was also significantly more likely to espouse humanitarian content themes, such as caring for employee well-being. Possibly, the humanitarian rhetoric served as a smoke screen, deflecting attention from the less humane implications of valuing financial risk-taking. This explanation describes inconsistency in intentional terms. Alternatively, the management of these companies may have sincerely advocated both risk-taking and humanitarian values, but may have been forced by uncontrollable economic factors to threaten employees' job security. Inconsistencies may be intentional and they may occur unintentionally because managers must operate in constrained situations.

The Differentiation perspective's emphasis on inconsistency has methodological implications. While Integration studies seek similarities underlying apparent disparities (as in Barley's analysis of funeral director's work), Differentiation studies seek to understand the inconsistencies underlying apparently unifying abstractions. For example, Gregory analyzes employee-generated taxonomies of relatively abstract categories by seeking dissimilarities:

> I might ask the follow-up structural question, "What kinds of companies are there?", after discovering "company" as a concept during a more open-ended question. The one or more "kinds of companies" elicited, together with the cover term, "companies," form a contrast set. A contrast set is part of a lexical/semantic field and gets its name from the principle that categories (in this case concepts for various "kinds of companies") stand in limited contrast to one another (Spradley, 1979: 158); they have some similarity, hence their inclusion, and some dissimilarity, hence the need for separate terms. (Gregory, 1983, pp. 367–368)

Any two entities are likely to be similar in some ways and dissimilar in others, like a cup that is half full and half empty. Differentiation studies focus on inconsistencies that Integration research tends to ignore.

CONSENSUS WITHIN SUBCULTURAL BOUNDARIES

Differentiation studies vary in the number of subcultures they examine and the extent to which they describe conflict among subcultures. The simplest type of

Differentiation study is a portrait of a single subculture. In these studies other subcultures are mentioned only in passing. This kind of Differentiation work is quite similar to Integration research, except that inconsistencies are mentioned and consensus is subcultural, rather than organization wide.

A second type of Differentiation study, represented by the portrait of OZCO in Chapter 5, is conducted at the organizational level of analysis. All aspects of the culture are described as riddled with inconsistencies. There is a "dominant" view of the company's culture that is articulated by top management and some employees; that "dominant" view is challenged by a wide variety of lower level employees. In this kind of study, the Differentiation perspective emerges in opposition to an Integration view of the culture as unitary. Subcultural differences among lower level employees are alluded to (at OZCO, e.g., between engineering and marketing), but these are not fully developed into portraits of conflicting subcultures.

A third kind of Differentiation research focuses on at least two well-developed subcultures. These subcultures have a clearly defined, often conflicting relationship with each other. In addition, many but not all of these Differentiation studies include an oppositional stance to top management's viewpoint. For example, Young describes a shop floor with a dominant culture, an enhancing subculture (work-wear machinists), and a counterculture (bag machinists).[9]

These three kinds of Differentiation studies can be contrasted using the matrix framework. A single-subculture study would be represented by a single matrix. The second type of Differentiation study would require one matrix to represent a unified view of the "dominant" culture (as in the Table 3-1 summary of the Integration view of OZCO) and a second matrix to represent the challenge to that "dominant" view (as in the Table 5-1 summary of the Differentiation view of OZCO). The third type of Differentiation study would require one matrix to represent each subculture. (For example, Young's study of the shop floor could be summarized using three matrices.) Within and across all these matrices, all three types of Differentiation studies would include evidence of inconsistency. Because ambiguities would not be seen as part of any of these subcultural domains, ambiguities would not be included in any of these matrices.

The third kind of Differentiation research usually focuses on particular types of subcultures.[10] Louis uses oppositional thinking to define each of these types of subcultures by its orientation to top management: enhancing subcultures, countercultures, and orthogonal subcultures. Examples of each are discussed here.

In an enhancing subculture, top management's views are reproduced in an exaggerated form, as in (to pick an extreme case) a hand-picked team of fanatics, sycophants, or true believers. (Enhancing subcultures are usually the only kind of subculture mentioned in Integration research. For example, McDonald's Integration view of the Olympic Organizing Committee, described in Chapter 4, included an enhancing subculture—the design group of which the author was a member.)[11]

Countercultures are pockets of resistance to the views espoused by top managers. For example, according to Martin and Siehl, the dominant culture at General Motors (GM) emphasized traditional values of deference to authority, fitting in, and being loyal. In his division of GM, Vice President John DeLorean created a counterculture. He told organizational stories and created rituals that questioned the need for deference to authority. He used physical arrangements and dress to signal, in a highly visible way, carefully calibrated limits to acceptable deviance. For example, the dominant culture had clear expectations about how executives should dress:

> GM's dress norms in the 1960's required a dark suit, a light shirt, and a muted tie. This was a slightly more liberal version of the famous IBM dress code that required a dark suit, a sparkling white shirt, and a narrow blue or black tie. . . . [In contrast] DeLorean's dark suits had a continental cut. His shirts were off-white with wide collars. His ties were suitably muted, but wider than the GM norm. His deviations were fashionable, for the late 1960's, but they represented only a slight variation on the executive dress norms of the dominant culture. (Martin and Siehl, 1983, pp. 57, 61)

DeLorean also used formal practices to reinforce these alternative values. For example, he instituted a pay bonus for those who resisted demands for unquestioning loyalty, particularly when this resistance resulted in improved divisional sales. GM's dominant culture permitted DeLorean's deviance to persist for quite a while, in part because the counterculture members accepted the dominant culture's commitments, for example, selling as many cars as possible, maximizing profit, and maintaining control over subordinates.

A deeper alienation from management can be seen in a description of the conflict between supervisors and a counterculture of submarine operators at Disneyland:

> Supervisors in Tomorrowland are, for example, famous for their penchant of hiding in the bushes above the submarine caves, timing the arrivals and departures of the supposedly fully loaded boats making their 8 1/2 minute cruise under the polar icecaps. That they might also catch a submarine captain furtively enjoying a cigarette (or worse) while inside the conning tower (his upper body out of view of the crowd on the vessel) might just make a supervisor's day—and unmake the employee's. In short, supervisors, if not foremen, are regarded by ride operators as sneaks and tricksters, out to get them and representative of the dark side of park life. (Van Maanen, 1991, p. 61)

Because the Differentiation perspective is particularly sensitive to differences in power and conflicts of interest between groups, few Differentiation studies contain subcultures that are purely orthogonal, that is, neither positive nor negative in orientation toward management or each other. (This is an indication of the prevalence of oppositional thinking within the Differentiation perspective.) When orthogonal subcultures are described, they usually are occupational groupings.[12]

> Of most interest is the contrast between hardware and software engineers. The former are described by the latter as narrow, concrete, speak "technologese" rather than English, undereducated, hard drinking, interested only in the blood and guts of the machine. The latter are seen by the former as undisciplined, loose, airy-fairy types, dreamers, talkers not doers. (Van Maanen and Kunda, 1989, pp. 73–74)

Whereas these two types of engineers had roughly equal status, other Differentiation studies focus on occupational groupings with an unequal status relationship. For example, Barley observed how the introduction of CT scanners into hospitals upset the usual relationships between (high status) radiologists and (lowly) technicians. Because the technicians now knew more about how to operate and interpret the results produced by the CT scanners, roles were reversed. Clandestine teaching by technicians further tarnished the authority of the radiologists, so

> the technologists began to regard the inexperienced radiologists with disdain. To account for the new interaction patterns, the technologists formulated the view that the radiologists knew less than they rightfully should and that their ignorance created unnecessary work and kept the CT operation from running smoothly. (Barley, 1986, p. 93)

Some types of subcultures do not fit cleanly within this typology of enhancing subcultures, countercultures, and orthogonal subcultures. For example, some group identities (such as race, age, ethnicity, and gender) can coalesce into what might be termed demographic subcultures. These demographic subcultures, because of racial and gender segregation, sometimes partially coincide with occupational subcultures. When this happens, these subcultures often receive derogatory labels (usually by those who are not members), such as "pink-velvet ghetto" for a job classification occupied predominantly by women professionals.

Usually Differentiation studies allude to these demographic issues in passing, focusing primarily on an occupational category. For example, Rosen discusses gender-related dress codes for three occupational categories at an advertising agency: business types, creative people, and clerical workers:

> There is an explicit dress code for those performing business functions, but none for those performing creative functions. The dress code, in fact addressed only to business males, states that suits (of appropriate color, tailoring, and fabric—not polyester, for example) must be worn at work. Female business clothing norms have yet to be formally codified, although women are expected to dress according to variations on the theme of formality [such as wearing dresses]. The difference in dress norms between roles in the agency corresponds to its power hierarchy. The clerical workers and most creative people are not in the main contest for wealth and power and are not as socially constricted in their behavior. By contrast, the behavior of the business people is highly circumscribed. . . . Through these closures the borders of the powerful are in part maintained. (Rosen, 1991, pp.79–80)

This example is complex, in that it refers to hierarchical factors (the contest for wealth and power), occupational differences (business, creative, clerical), and demographic identities that coincide with occupational groupings (the business types were mostly men and the clerical workers were mostly women).

In Van Maanen's rank ordering of the occupational subcultures at Disneyland, as in Rosen's study of the advertising agency, occupational differences contain hierarchical echoes of class and gender differences:

A loose approximation of the rank ordering among these groups can be constructed as follows: (l) the upper-class prestigious Disneyland Ambassadors and Tour Guides (bilingual young women in charge of ushering—some say rushing—little bands of tourists through the park); (2) ride operators performing [coveted] ''skilled work'' such as live narration or tricky transportation tasks like those who symbolically control customer access to the park and drive the costly entry vehicles such as the antique trains, horse-drawn carriages, and Monorail; (3) all other ride operators; (4) the proletarian Sweepers (keepers of the concrete grounds); and (5) the sub-prole or peasant status Food and Concession workers (whose park sobriquets reflect their lowly social worth—''pancake ladies,'' ''peanut pushers,'' ''coke blokes,'' ''suds divers,'' and the seemingly irreplaceable ''soda jerks''). (Van Maanen, 1991, pp. 61–62)

Although occupational and class differences are spelled out in some detail here, gender is not mentioned except in two cases where the gender was female: ''bilingual young women'' and ''pancake ladies.''

A more detailed and explicit treatment of gender and racial differences is evident in Bartunek and Moch's study of subcultural differences at a large bakery. The machinists were a subculture of white men who were strongly opposed to the packing department employees, most of whom were women. Bartunek and Moch recount how the machinists used jokes to express their disdain for these women.

One story, told on several occasions in our presence, compared machinists' tool boxes with women's purses. One machinist would tell another that he owned his own work tools. He then would ask how much the other machinist thought these tools were worth. After several low estimates, the first machinist would proclaim that his work tools were worth several thousand dollars. The machinists would then change roles, the second asking the first how much his tools were worth. After the second machinist proclaimed the true value of his tools, the first machinist would ask the second, ''And what do the silly bitches carry in their purses?'' Together the two participants would call out ''Kotex!'' Those listening, usually under the windows in the cafeteria, would smile and nod approval. (Bartunek and Moch, 1991, p. 112)

At this bakery, a committee was formed to suggest improvements in the working environment. To their disgust, the machinists were asked to construct a non-smoking area in the cafeteria. They used this as an opportunity to enact their resistance to black bakery employees:

One of these proposals was for a no-smoking area in the cafeteria. The machinists installed the area in the space traditionally used by Black employees, smokers and non-smokers alike. (Bartunek and Moch, 1991, p. 113)

In most Differentiation studies, demographic groupings are mentioned ''in passing,'' rather than analyzed in depth. In some studies, such as Kanter's examination of women sales managers and Fernandez' description of black managers,[13] those who are demographically different, within an occupation, are few in number and may not form a distinctive subculture. In other Differentiation studies, members of demographic groups do form distinct subcultures, perhaps because their numbers are sufficiently high.[14] Although Differentiation research is more sensitive to demographic issues than is Integration research, in-depth organizational studies of gender or race subcultures are still relatively rare.

CHANNELING AMBIGUITY OUTSIDE SUBCULTURAL BOUNDARIES

The third defining characteristic of the Differentiation perspective is its orientation toward ambiguity. Here some definitions are necessary. Inconsistency is used in this book to refer to a clearly oppositional (dichotomous) difference; this kind of inconsistency is not ambiguous. In contrast, ambiguity arises when a lack of clarity, high complexity, or paradox make multiple (not single or dichotomous) interpretations plausible.[15]

Differentiation research generally excludes ambiguity from an arena of subcultural clarity. A subculture, then, is seen as creating a "coherent meaning system"[16] or providing clear solutions to problems shared by a group.[17] Subcultures are also said to bring clarity into a domain that would otherwise be overwhelmed by the unknown and uncertain. Thus a subculture, like a myth,

> renders an unintelligible complexity into a complexity that is more intelligible. In doing so, it provides the illusion of understandability, knowledge, and the capacity to predict as replacements for ignorance, uncertainty, and the sense of being at the whim of a capricious nature. (Lucas, 1987, p. 152)

A few Differentiation studies acknowledge ambiguity more fully, as a form of chaos, but then proceed to exclude ambiguity from that which is defined as culture. For example, Rosen describes subcultural conflicts as the core of his view of culture. He then dismisses claims of harmony and unity as capitalist "promises" and argues that the only other option is chaos:

> Culture is understood as built on the edge of chaos. . . . The rituals of Spiro and Associates, and in general the rituals of bureaucracy, are promises of order and continuity. . . . They promise the continuity of employment and ego definition in capitalist society. This "ritual veils the ultimate disorder, the nonorder, which is the unconceptualized, unformed chaos underlying culture" (Moore and Myerhoff, 1977, p. 17). (Rosen, 1985, pp. 47–48)

From the Differentiation perspective, as from the Integration viewpoint, ambiguity is the "chaos underlying culture"—it is not part of culture.

To summarize, Differentiation research describes each subculture as an island of localized lucidity. Attention is restricted to cultural manifestations that either are, or are not, inconsistent with each other. The potential complexities of the cultural domain are thereby reduced to dichotomies. Even when conflicts are present, things are clear enough so that cultural members know they disagree on particular issues or interpretations. In this way, subcultural differentiation "fences in" differences in perspective, leaving uncontrolled, untransformed am-

biguity "outside" or "underneath" these realms of clarity, in the interstices between subcultures. A metaphor may be a helpful way to also summarize this view: subcultures are islands of clarity; ambiguity is channeled into the currents that swirl around the edges of these islands. Table 1-1 summarizes these elements of the Differentiation perspective and contrasts them with the characteristics of the other two cultural viewpoints.

DIFFERENTIATION AT THE ORGANIZATIONAL LEVEL OF ANALYSIS

Because the Differentiation perspective focuses attention on subcultures, one might conclude that this viewpoint simply moves down a level of analysis, presenting a mini-Integration view of culture within subcultural boundaries. This mini-Integration critique is not warranted because Differentiation studies include inconsistencies, while Integration research focuses only on consistencies. With this caveat, however, this critique does accurately characterize the first kind of Differentiation research described earlier: the single-subculture study. It also characterizes some aspects of the second kind of Differentiation research, which contrasts a supposedly "dominant" view of the culture (congruent with an Integration viewpoint) with a countercultural view that challenges important elements of the "dominant" view.

The shortcomings of the mini-Integration critique and the magnitude of the difference between the Integration and Differentiation perspectives become most evident in Differentiation studies that distinguish between two or more subcultures. In this third type of Differentiation study, meanings do not evolve in isolated subcultural havens. Instead, in accord with the oppositional patterns of thinking described in the introduction to this chapter, subcultural differences evolve in reaction to surrounding influences. The ways members of a subculture interpret their experiences make sense only when each subculture is considered in a wider organizational context, in relation to other subcultures. When this third kind of Differentiation study turns to the organizational level of analysis, it must focus on the configuration of relationships among subcultures. The map to this terrain must be able to encompass a variety of different orientations toward management including enhancing subcultures, countercultures, orthogonal subcultures, and various demographic groupings which may or may not reflect subcultural differences. This is not the monolithic view an Integration account would offer.

A DIFFERENTIATED VIEW OF THE SELF

The Differentiation perspective also differs from an Integration view at the individual level of analysis. The complexity of relationships among subcultures can have implications for how individual self-identity is conceptualized. Subcultures can overlap. They can be nested within each other and they can be subdivided.

For example, within an engineering division, there may be different product groups, with members in several geographical locations. Blue-collar job classifications or gender groupings may be present within each of these classifications. Some of these differences may develop into subcultures.

Because of this subcultural complexity, individuals can belong to more than one subculture at once. Therefore, the Differentiation perspective is based on a self-concept that stands in stark contrast to the unitary, autonomous view of the self underlying the Integration perspective. When a person belongs to more than one subculture, that individual can feel "pulled into" several potentially conflicting groups, none of which captures all aspects of the person's identity. For example, Bell describes the bi- or tricultural pulls experienced by some upwardly mobile black women, who may work in an organization dominated by white men, feel limited affinities with white women, and no longer fit comfortably in the black communities where they were raised.[18] According to this view, multiple subcultural identities create self-concepts that are stable and compartmentalized rather than unitary, contextually responsive rather than autonomous.

When the self is conceptualized as compartmentalized and situationally responsive, it becomes particularly important to distinguish behavioral conformity from ideological commitment. From a Differentiation perspective, the "consensus" or "consent" of the relatively powerless is suspect. Feldman, for example, found three common responses to the conformity pressures at the American Telephone & Telegraph Company: acceptance based on conscious suppression of personal interests, secret rejection, and acceptance based on unconscious distortion.[19] Differentiation studies have focused primarily on the last two of these alternative responses, both of which are discussed below.

Secret rejection can be difficult for an observer to detect. It entails a splitting of the self, so that outward conformity is combined with internal resistance.

> There are, for instance, times in all employee careers when they put themselves on "automatic pilot," "go robot," "can't feel a thing," "lapse into a dream," "go into a trance," or otherwise "check out" while still on duty. . . . Much of this numbness is, of course, beyond the knowledge of supervisors and guests because most employees have little trouble appearing as if they are present even when they are not. It is, in a sense, a passive form of resistance that suggests there still is a sacred preserve of individuality left among employees in the park. (Van Maanen, 1991, p. 75)

Hochschild studies a similar form of internal resistance in occupations that require "emotional work." She observes that flight attendants, for example, are required to maintain an emotional facade (by smiling or tolerating obnoxious behavior) that may be at odds with their internal feelings. Maintaining this emotional dissonance is a constant strain.[20] When people's jobs constrain what emotions they can express, limit where they can move, or underutilize their intellectual capacities, private thoughts and feelings often seem to be the only "sphere of freedom." For example:

> Black women's experiences suggest that Black women may overtly conform to the societal roles laid out for them, yet covertly oppose these roles in numerous spheres, an

opposition shaped by the consciousness of being on the bottom. . . . That these activities have been obscured from traditional social scientists should come as no surprise. Oppressed peoples may maintain hidden consciousness and may not reveal their true selves for reasons of self-protection. (Collins, 1986, p. 23)

Other Differentiation studies focus on what Feldman labels acceptance based on unconscious distortion. This distortion occurs because it can be difficult for members of less powerful groups to see their subordination as unjust; a dominant culture can silence dissent, making it difficult for the less powerful to articulate, enact, or even see an alternative way of life. This is a description of "false consciousness." Jermier offers two descriptions of a blue-collar worker at a manufacturing plant.[21] In the first description, the protagonist accepts management's assurances about the safety of his work and occupies his mind with consumerist fantasies. The only breaches in this false consciousness are vague and fleeting glimpses of an alternative reality—a partially articulated unease that is quickly dismissed. In the second half of this portrait, the same individual is overtly alienated, disbelieving management's claims of safety, angry about his exploitation, and well aware of the costs of joining the consumerist "rat race." Although Jermier's study is unusual in its portrayal of two starkly different psychic realities, Differentiation research generally assumes a self-concept that is compartmentalized by conflicting subcultural demands. In summary, the Differentiation view differs from an Integration perspective at the individual, subcultural, and organizational levels of analysis.

DEFINING CULTURE FROM A DIFFERENTIATION PERSPECTIVE

Differentiation studies define culture in terms that are surprisingly similar, in some ways, to the definitions used in Integration research: culture is defined as that which is shared. Table 6-1 presents a range of these Differentiation definitions.[22] In contrast to Integration definitions, however, Differentiation definitions specify that it is a group, rather than an entire organization, that is doing the sharing. See, for example, Trice and Morand's definition (1), Louis's definitions (3) and (10), Gregory's definition (5), Smircich's definition (11), and Van Maanen and Barley's definition (12).

Some (but not all) Differentiation studies define culture as unique or distinctive to a particular group (see, e.g., Louis's definition [10], Smircich's definition [11], Van Maanen and Barley's definition [12], and Gregory's definition [13]).[23] This theme of cultural uniqueness was also present in many Integration definitions of culture. Because this issue of distinctness transcends the boundaries between the Integration and Differentiation approaches to the study of culture, and because there is reason to believe that this claim of cultural uniqueness may not be well founded, this issue is discussed separately in the concluding sections of this chapter.

The most important aspect of these definitions is that they vary in the extent to which they admit the possibility that subcultures may co-exist with some form of

Table 6-1 Defining culture from a Differentiation perspective

1. Organizational subcultures may be defined as distinct clusters of understandings, behaviors, and cultural forms that identify groups of people in the organization. They differ noticeably from the common organizational culture in which they are embedded, either intensifying its understandings and practices or deviating from them. (Trice and Morand, in press, p. 1)

2. Culture's utility as a heuristic concept may be lost when the organizational level of analysis is employed. Work organizations are indeed marked by social practices that can be said to be "cultural," but these practices may not span the organization as a whole. (Van Maanen and Barley, 1985, p. 32)

3. Organizations are referred to as "culture-bearing milieus". . . . The [top of the] organization, vertical and horizontal slices, and other formal unit designations [such as department] all represent typical sites in and through which cultures may develop. . . . As such, they serve as breeding grounds, if you will, for the emergence of local shared meanings. (Louis, 1985, pp. 75–79)

4. [Studies] of culture most often portray organizational systems. . . . as working together in a shared cohesive totality. The theoretical position expressed in this paper develops an alternative stance—a perspective of organizational cultures that expects organizations to have subcultures and allows for rival images and competing systems of meanings. (Riley, 1983, pp. 414–415)

5. More researchers have emphasized the homogeneity of culture and its cohesive function than its divisive potential. This paper suggests, however, that many organizations are most accurately viewed as multicultural. Subgroups with different occupational, divisional, ethnic, or other cultures approach organizational interactions with their own meanings and senses of priorities. (Gregory, 1983, p. 359)

6. From this perspective, internal conflict becomes a frequent feature of organizational cultures. Subcultures can obviously clash over issues, programs, and missions. Also, they can exist side by side for long stretches of time without conflict, and clearly can be compatible. . . . In turn, the concept of power comes into focus since it would logically be generated and differentially distributed in and among subcultures. It follows that a political view of organizational behavior becomes relevant. (Trice and Morand, in press, p. 8)

7. From the perspective we have elaborated, the study of cultural organization is therefore closely bound to the study of organizational conflict. (Van Maanen and Barley, 1985, p. 48)

8. In a political-cultural approach to organizational analysis, conflict rather than being ruled out a priori, is the ground from which interest groups collectively construct the figure of organizational culture. (Lucas, 1987, p. 153)

9. Cultural arrangements, of which organizations are an essential segment, are seen as manifestations of a process of ideational development located within a context of definite material conditions. It is a context of dominance (males over females/owners over workers) but also of conflict and contradiction in which class and gender, autonomous but overdetermined, are vital dynamics. Ideas and cultural arrangements confront actors as a series of rules of behavior; rules that, in their contradictions, may variously be enacted, followed or resisted. (Mills, 1988, p. 366)

10. A set of understandings or meanings shared by a group of people. The meanings are largely tacit among members, are clearly relevant to a particular group, and are *distinctive* to the group. (Louis, 1985, p. 74)

11. In a particular situation the set of meanings that evolves gives a group its own ethos, or *distinctive* character, which is expressed in patterns of belief (ideology), activity (norms and rituals), language and other symbolic forms through which organization members both create and sustain their view of the world and image of themselves in the world. The development of a world view with its shared understanding of group identity, purpose and direction are products of the *unique* history, personal interactions and environmental circumstances of the group. (Smircich, 1983a, p. 56, emphasis added)

Table 6-1   (cont.)

12. Only when members of a group assign similar meanings to facets of their situation can collectives devise, through interaction, *unique* responses to problems that later take on trappings of rule, ritual, and value. (Van Maanen and Barley, 1985, p. 34, emphasis added)

13. A culture is conceptualized as a system of meanings that accompany the myriad of behaviors and practices recognized as a *distinct* way of life. (Gregory, 1983, p. 364, emphasis added)

organization-wide consensus. At one extreme, Trice and Morand's definition (1) assumes the existence of an overarching, "common" organization-wide culture, in which subcultures are embedded. Louis's definition (3), like many other Differentiation definitions, focuses on groups as the site where subcultural development may begin, but does not explicitly exclude the possibility of organization-wide consensus. Van Maanen and Barley's definition (2) argues that organization-wide unity *may* not occur. At another extreme, some Differentiation definitions set out to articulate an alternative to the Integration perspective by describing subcultures as oriented toward each other, rather than emerging in opposition to some "dominant" culture articulated by top management (see, e.g., Riley's definition [4] and Gregory's definition [5]).[24]

The definitions also vary in the extent to which they emphasize power differences and conflicts of interest between groups. Some Differentiation studies define organizational cultures as hierarchically ordered clusters of subcultures, putting conflict and power in the forefront of their analysis (see, e.g., Riley's definition [4], Gregory's definition [5], and Lucas's definition [8]), while others do not mention conflict or allow for the possibility that both organization-wide consensus and subcultural conflict might co-exist (see, e.g., Trice and Morand's definition [6] and Van Maanen and Barley's definition [7]).

To summarize, like Integration studies, Differentiation research defines culture as that which is shared. Unlike Integration research, however, Differentiation studies define the boundary of a culture at the group level of analysis, focusing on consensus within subcultures. Some Differentiation definitions deliberately set out to provide an alternative to the Integration approach, denying the possibility of organization-wide consensus, while other studies allow that subcultures might co-exist with some kind of organization-wide sharing. Differentiation definitions vary in the extent to which they define culture in terms of uniqueness and the extent to which they emphasize conflict.

As was the case with the Integration definitions of culture discussed in Chapter 4, these Differentiation definitions can be misleading. Although in some cases these Differentiation definitions sound much like an Integration definition of culture, the tone of a Differentiation study is quite different, even when evidence of organization-wide consensus is being discussed. This difference is discussed next.

THE POSSIBILITY OF ORGANIZATION-WIDE CONSENSUS

Some Differentiation research describes an organization-wide culture that co-exists with various subcultures. However, that organization-wide culture is interpreted quite differently than it would be in an Integration study. For example, in a study of the machinists on the shop floor, Young sees statements that apparently assert organization-wide commonality as a place where subcultural differences are subtly articulated:

> In this company, the existence of solidary values was explicitly marked by widely held views concerning the firm, assertions of its unique qualities, and regular statements of collective identity by shop floor groups. These were also the features of company culture proclaimed by its managers. Yet a closer appraisal suggests that precisely these statements of collectivity also constitute the vehicles whereby different interests among shop floor workers asserted superiority and celebrated sectional boundaries. Unity and division existed in tandem. (Young, 1991, p. 91)

Brunsson also offers a vision of the co-existence of organization-wide unity and subcultural development. He begins with the premise that there is sometimes a conflict between the acceptance of inconsistency and the need for action:

> So the problem for these organizations is how to produce both consistency and inconsistency, how to be both integrated a..d dissolved. (Brunsson, 1986, p. 174)

Brunsson argues that an organization can respond by decoupling over issues, using some issues as a magnet for conflict (usually those where action is not essential) and other issues as an arena for action. Organizations can also decouple into subunit structures, some of which can produce conflictive talk and inconsistent decisions, others which can produce coordinated action. Finally, organizations can decouple over environments, responding to some segments of the environment with evident inconsistency and internal conflict, and reacting to other segments with clear and unified actions. Brunsson incorporates into his description some evidence of organization-wide unity, although his emphasis on subunit differentiation and inconsistency is more characteristic of a Differentiation perspective. The three kinds of decoupling (regarding issues, subunits, and environments) are described as occurring simultaneously, suggesting an unusually complex configuration of difference.

It is important to distinguish Differentiation research from Integration studies that acknowledge the existence of an occasional inconsistency or the rare (usually enhancing) subculture. The cultural descriptions of Young and Brunsson, for example, are riddled with inconsistencies. Subcultural differentiation is their primary focus; unifying cultural elements are only a secondary consideration. Differentiation research does not see elements of organization-wide unity as mediating or transcending the potential for chronic, deep conflicts of interest between groups. Thus Differentiation studies do not argue that organizational productivity is enhanced by an appropriate balance of integrating and differentiating forces, as Blau, Chandler, and Lawrence and Lorsch have done.[25]

Other Differentiation studies describe managerial attempts to create organization-wide consensus with evident skepticism and stress employee resistance. For example, Kunda examines employees' reactions to deliberate attempts to create shared values through participation in rituals. To the extent that employees internalize the espoused values of management, Kunda interprets this as false consciousness:

> When institutionally prescribed roles include definitions of appropriate emotions, they require "deep acting": the performer must try and "feel" rather than feign role-prescribed emotions. Consequently, participation in ritual enactments of the member role at Tech—no matter how tentative—may lead to what [Hochschild] calls emotional dissonance: members are included to experience the emotions they display as authentic. Over time, cognitive and emotional dissonance may serve to blur the boundary between the performer's perception of an acted role and the experience of an "authentic self." (Kunda, 1991b, p. 23)

According to Kunda, Tech employees resist the dominant culture in moments of transition, before or after a ritual, when more informal interaction is permitted. In these moments, for example,

> members of the audience assume a "wise" or "cynical" stance that focuses on creatively exposing hidden meanings, debunking explicit intents, parodying conventions, and conveying an instrumental interpretation of events and an awareness of their theatrical nature. (Kunda, 1991b, p. 25)

Similarly, Rosen's study of an advertising agency includes a description of management's attempt to generate organization-wide consensus around a set of shared values.[26] Rosen analyzes these cultural control efforts, claiming that managers co-opt employees in ways that employees are not aware of. He then proceeds to show the hierarchical and functional differences of opinion that persist, in spite of management's attempts to create an organization-wide unity that denies conflicts of interest between groups. Other Differentiation studies concur, portraying managerial cultural manipulation as a relatively impotent form of control. For example, Sunesson studied the culture of social workers, concluding that that they are largely successful in liberating themselves from their bureaucratic managers.[27]

In summary, these examples indicate that Differentiation research varies in its treatment of organization-wide consensus. Some Differentiation studies describe attempts to create organization-wide consensus as successful efforts that nurture various forms of false consciousness and limited resistance; other Differentiation studies see such cultural control attempts as unlikely to succeed. Even the Differentiation studies that see organization-wide consensus on some issues as a possibility, however, supplement this unity with descriptions of inconsistency and subcultural difference that would be alien to an Integration account.[28]

WHEN INDIVIDUALS DEVIATE

In Differentiation accounts, deviants are often heros or heroines who try to resist managerial inducements to conform. The danger of course is that deviants can be fired. In the following example, the author of one participant-observation study dared to deviate and was abruptly terminated:

I was fired from Disneyland for what I still consider a Mickey Mouse offense. The specific violation—one of many possible—involved hair growing over my ears, an offense I had been warned about more than once before the final cut was made. . . . Dismissal began by being pulled off the ride after my work shift had begun by an area supervisor in full view of my cohorts. A forced march to the administration building followed where my employee card was turned over and a short statement read to me by a personnel officer as to the formal cause of termination. Security officers then walked me to the employee locker room where my work uniforms and equipment were collected and my personal belongings returned to me while an inspection of my locker was made. The next stop was the time shed where my employee's time card was removed from its slot, marked "terminated" across the top in red ink, and replaced in its customary position (presumably for Disneylanders to see when clocking on or off the job over the next few days). As now an ex-ride operator, I was escorted to the parking lot where two security officers scraped off the employee parking sticker attached to my car. (Van Maanen, 1991, p. 76)

Before such radical steps are taken, less extreme, but still powerful compliance pressures are used to bring individual deviants into line. In many of these Differentiation studies, deviance is associated with some kind of demographic difference. For example, women are often pressured to conform to informal norms developed for and by men:

Crompton and Jones' (1984) study of a British company found that . . . the organizational culture stressed a need to "fit in" with the social as well as the technical "requirements" of the company: failure resulted in a sense of not being accepted or perceived as a "full participant" and hence not being considered for advancement. Given that the "social" consisted primarily of a company sports and social club geared to "male sports" ("football for the young men, bowls for the older men") female employees were disadvantaged. In this "predominantly male" organizational culture women were not able to fit in, did not feel themselves to be full organization members, and hence did not join the available union nor gave full commitment to the company. (Mills, 1988, pp. 364–365)

These are examples of individual deviance. Even the women deviants at the British company described above apparently did not coalesce into a subculture, perhaps because of insufficient numbers.[29] When deviance becomes collective, it is easily encompassed within the Differentiation perspective as either a counterculture or an orthogonal subculture.

DIFFERENTIATED VIEWS OF EFFECTIVENESS

As detailed in Chapter 4, many Integration studies claim that a particular type of cultural unity will be associated with some kind of improved organizational effectiveness. For example, a culture might provide cognitive clarification, engender commitment, increase productivity, and even improve financial performance. Some Differentiation studies do not question the basic premises of these claims; they simply observe that, because of the prevalence of inconsistency and the dearth of organization-wide consensus, such benefits are unlikely to be forth-coming or are gained at the cost of some disempowered group. In the following case, Morgan and Smircich observe that high levels of commitment were clearly absent in the top management team of the insurance company:

> Although the president sought to shape a reality of cooperation and urgency in the face of adverse conditions, it is apparent from the talk of executive staff that he did not succeed in generating these feelings among these staff members. Indeed, the reality for them was basically one of disharmony, disaffection, and noninvolvement. (Smircich and Morgan, 1982, p. 266)

Other Differentiation studies take a dim view of "value engineering" to im-prove effectiveness and question the ethics of those who would intrude into people's "hearts and souls" for the sake of selling more hamburgers:

> The companies studied are the cream of America's corporate crop, and range from IBM to MacDonalds Hamburgers. The dedication and quasi-religious commitment which the new manager seeks to instil into his employees sometimes sits a little oddly with the nature of the company goal: it may be inspiring to hear of sales staff risking their life in a snow storm to ensure that the company goal of regular delivery of supplies is main-tained, but when the reader learns that the product is a high-salt, high calorie junk food, doubts about whether some of this shining dedication is perhaps misplaced begin to arise. (Turner, 1986, p. 108)

> Viewed as a control device, corporate culture asks us to put our heart and soul into our work. There is, however, surely a limit to which we are willing to sell our hearts and souls for the production and sale of soap, aspirin, entertainment, research, or com-puters. . . . The [culture] movement is frightening to the extent that people are ex-pected to fall in line with a culture organized for the commercial purposes of others and over which they have little influence. (Van Maanen and Kunda, 1989, p. 92)

Rather than questioning whether culture does improve effectiveness, these Dif-ferentiation studies suggest that such "benefits" are all too easily achieved in a manner that benefits some groups at the expense of others.

Some Differentiation studies offer a deeper objection, arguing that culture determines what is considered to be effective.[30] For example, managers may place top priority on financial performance, but engineers may place greater emphasis on producing innovative products.[31] Even if employees do share mana-gerial definitions of effectiveness, Differentiation studies may interpret this as evidence of false consciousness. When organizational practices benefit some employees more than others, some of the disadvantaged, like the advantaged, may justify this inequality as an economic necessity.[32] In the following case, Rosen described how Walter, the president of the Spiro agency, announced a salary freeze that was not a salary freeze:

> At 9:00 a.m. that morning Walter [the president] announced that the agency experienced record billings. One hour later a message of austerity mixed with benevolence is communicated. All salaries are to be frozen, but this freeze "isn't a salary freeze." . . . From Walter . . . "to the lowest person here" all will suffer, imply-ing a normatively equitable condition. (Rosen, 1991, pp. 87–88)

Rosen analyzes the ways that Walter's speech offers an ideological explanation (that all will suffer equitably) which obscures the ways that shareholders and managers will suffer less:

> Management's increased equity value and dividend return is not included in this equation, as this is presumably an immaculate marginal return on capital divorced from salary considerations. . . . Walter's discussion obscures the securing of profit by capital. . . . By proposing stock dividends, credits to retained earnings, bonuses, and pay raises as different in kind from one another, capital proposes the various allocations of funds as independent, when each is a related distribution of income. (Rosen, 1985, p. 44)

In this way, some aspect of organizational effectiveness (in this case decreased salary costs) is reinterpreted as evidence of exploitation; employees' acceptance of managerial justifications for their practices are interpreted, in these studies, as evidence of false consciousness. In Differentiation research, the effectiveness question becomes: "Who benefits from this kind of effectiveness?"

In addition, some Differentiation studies offer their own brand of effectiveness—quite different from those found in Integration accounts. Three studies show the range of these effectiveness claims. Jamison expounds the benefits of belonging to a counterculture:

> [Movement or counter-cultural organizations] provide members (and organizers) with the capacity to share beliefs and engage in behaviors that are distinct from the dominant bureaucratic pattern; such participation in the creation of ongoing organizational culture is perhaps as important as any promised goal. (Jamison, 1985, p. 486)

Brunsson explains how action and symbolic inconsistencies help local governments respond effectively to the contradictory demands of a segmented environment composed of various constituencies with conflicting viewpoints.[33] Van Maanen describes the (on and off-the-job) drinking behavior of officers in London's Metropolitan Police Department.[34] He argues that the supposed conviviality and informality of these occasions, as well as the potential excuse of inebriation, permit officers to voice grievances and work through conflicts that might otherwise cause disruption at work. These Differentiation studies, not surprisingly, portray differences as functional and conflicts as potentially constructive. For example:

> We should use difference as a dialogue, . . . developing a dialectic, a tension between opposites that illuminates the differences and similarities between things in apparent opposition. . . . We need to use these differences in constructive ways rather than in ways to justify our destroying each other. (Tate, 1983, pp. 101–102, quoted in Christian, 1985, p. 198)

To summarize, Differentiation accounts vary in the extent to which they make claims that particular cultural configurations lead to improved organizational effectiveness. Some Differentiation studies claim that, because of inconsistencies and a lack of organization-wide consensus, supposed benefits do not occur.

Other Differentiation studies question the wisdom and ethics of value engineering for profit. Finally, some Differentiation studies see conflict expression as constructive—a different approach to deciding what effectiveness might be.

DIFFERENTIATION VIEWS OF CULTURAL CHANGE

Most Differentiation studies offer an analysis of a particular subcultural configuration at a single point in time. When Differentiation studies *do* discuss change, they generally focus on subcultures rather than an individual leader. Leadership, when it is made visible, is exercised by groups whose members—usually—remain nameless. The individual in these accounts is submerged in his or her group identity. At the organizational level of analysis, after the change, the configuration of subcultures has shifted, creating a new (im)balance of power. Three quite different examples of this kind of research are summarized below. Unlike most other Differentiation accounts of change, these three studies focus on change triggered by an unexpected environmental "jolt."

Meyer explains how an abrupt change in the environment (a doctors' strike) created realignments of subcultures within hospitals.[35] The hospitals responded quite differently to this environmental jolt. Some anticipated it and planned, so that its impact was minimally disruptive. Others, caught unaware, were forced to make more radical shifts in order to survive. Meyer's description of each hospital's reaction to the strike includes the maneuvers of various groups, including hospital administrators, nurses, doctors, and other staff.

In a second Differentiation study of cultural change, Abolafia and Kilduff, describe how four subcultures (buyers, sellers, bankers, and government agencies) reacted to the 1980 crisis in the silver futures market in a manner which served their interests and altered what happened.[36] These subcultures tried, variously, to profit from speculative opportunities, ensure the solvency of insiders, and protect the "integrity" of the market. In this account, the subcultural actors did not respond passively to a jolt from the environment; they succeeded in turning events to their own advantage. This proactive stance toward environmental sources of change is congruent, for example, with Weick's research on environmental enactment and with aspects of Pfeffer and Salancik's work on the management of environmental influences.[37]

In a third study, Bartunek describes how an environmental jolt (the recommendations of the Second Vatican Council) caused changes in the interpretive schemes and structures of a religious order of nuns.[38] Although the change was initiated by the order's environment, the form it took was mediated by the order members' actions and interpretations. This study, then, combines the external causality of Meyer's environmental jolts with Abolafia and Kilduff's proactive emphasis on environmental enactment. Bartunek describes the reactions of various subcultures within and outside of the order, such as the international church leadership, "provincial" and "inter-provincial" governing bodies within the United States, groups of order members located in different regions of the United States, and national "ministries" (mission-specific national associations of order members, cross-cutting other organizational divisions). In this complicated sub-cultural terrain, environmental pressures, "grass roots" movements among order members, and structural changes all had an impact on the process. Leaders had a role to play, but that role included none of the individualized heroics of the leader-centered Integration accounts of change. Instead, a limited form of lead-ership was exercised by the provincial governing bodies who—as a group—enabled options to be expressed and actions taken.

> They did not contribute very much to the content of the process: order members who held the perspectives very strongly did that. But they did legitimize the different per-spectives, and they did carry out some actions, such as encouraging order members to live in provinces outside their own, which fostered the evolution of the new structure. (Bartunek, 1984, p. 370)

In these Differentiation studies, subcultures respond to a jolt from a usually stable environment. In the cases of the silver futures market and the religious order, there is some evidence that the environment is conceptualized in seg-mented terms; different subcultures within the market or the church seem to be responding to pressures from different segments of the environment. In these Differentiation accounts, the organization appears to be tightly coupled to the environment, as changes in the environment affect the organization, directly and severely. Within the organization, however, subcultures appear to be loosely coupled with each other, sometimes cooperating and sometimes acting on the basis of conflicting interests.[39]

A Differentiation account of cultural change implicitly draws attention to the ways internal loose coupling can dampen the flow of information within an organization. For example, subcultures at the periphery of an organization may not share information fully with subcultures at its technical core.[40] Subcultures can experiment and respond to segments of the environment, knowing that the effects of their interpretations and actions will be localized and that, in most cases, the organization as a whole will be buffered from the repercussions of their actions.

Although this loose coupling among subcultures may have beneficial effects (for example, permitting havens for experimentation and facilitating appro-priately localized responses to environmental demands), it may also cause prob-lems for some constituencies. For example, subcultural segmentation may inhibit the top-down planned change programs examined in Integration studies. Top managers would have to cope with loosely coupled information channels and subcultural differences in willingness to comply. In addition, subculturally seg-mented organizations may find it difficult to transmit, on an organization-wide basis, the lessons learned from localized, incremental responses to environmental pressures. *To summarize, when change is viewed from a Differentiation perspec-tive, it appears localized, incremental, and triggered (if not controlled) by pres-sures from a segmented environment.* The Differentiation view of change stands in stark contrast to the traumatic, organization-wide collapse of a world view described in Integration accounts of the change process.[41]

Whereas most Integration studies discuss managerial control of the change process, few Differentiation studies explore the ways employees could influence the cultural change. This lack of discussion is not surprising in those Differentiation studies that are explicit about their disdain for encouraging intense commitment to producing "high-salt, high calorie junk food" or selling "hearts and souls for the production and sale of soap, aspirin, entertainment, research, or computers." However, Differentiation studies that focus on the perceptions and unfulfilled needs of lower-status employees could offer prescriptions for collective action for subordinated groups, rather than higher-ranking managers. If Differentiation studies of cultural change were to draw on research in industrial relations, social movements, and collective behavior, a different and potentially useful kind of cultural change study might emerge.

METHODOLOGICAL CRITIQUES

Differentiation research, like Integration research, generally assumes an objectivist stance, assuming that careful methods will produce an objectively accurate picture of a cultural configuration. Criticizing Differentiation research from within this objectivist tradition, three methodological dilemmas are described below: depth versus superficiality; emic versus etic; and systematic versus convenience sampling. Qualitative and quantitative Differentiation studies have resolved these dilemmas differently.

Qualitative Differentiation Studies

Qualitative Differentiation research seeks to "penetrate the front" of managerial rhetoric and monitored compliance to managerial directives. In order to obtain an in-depth understanding of employees' thoughts and feelings (as well as their more observable and controllable behaviors), many qualitative Differentiation studies have used classic, long-term participant-observations of field settings. Other qualitative Differentiation studies have used unstructured interviews, developing ideas in a way that approximates inductive, "grounded" theory development.

This kind of research allows respondents' categories, rather than researcher preconceptions, to shape the conclusions which emerge. For example:

> No homogeneous units or specific characteristics of culture are defined a priori, but rather those groups and processes recognized by native participants are discovered and studied "in their terms" during the research. (Gregory, 1983, p. 366)

These qualitative methods attempt to describe a culture from the point of view of a cultural insider (an "emic" view), rather than from the perspective of a cultural outsider such as a researcher (an "etic" view). Emic studies rely on cultural members, rather than researchers, to generate descriptions of the culture and draw the relevant subcultural boundaries. Thus qualitative Differentiation studies usually emphasize an emic point of view and stress the importance of an in-depth understanding.

These are arguably strengths, but they are purchased at a cost. Qualitative Differentiation studies have been criticized, using standards usually reserved for quantitative studies, for having many of the same sampling deficiencies as qualitative Integration studies. Although sampling procedures are unfortunately seldom fully described in qualitative Differentiation studies, in most cases it is reasonable to infer that the time required for an in-depth interview study or participant-observation makes it difficult to study large numbers of organizations and large samples of employees. Furthermore, sampling procedures are usually unsystematic and based on convenience.

These samples are therefore potentially biased in several ways. The organizations studied tend to be rigidly stratified (large bureaucracies and manufacturing plants, for example). The work groups investigated tend to be relatively low status, with concomitant low pay and intrinsically less satisfying tasks. Informants may be deviants—for example, unusually garrulous and more likely to express discontent. Qualitative Differentiation studies seek a point of view that is different from that espoused by top management. They look where they are most likely to find it.

Quantitative Differentiation Studies

Quantitative Differentiation studies, such as Friedman's careful examination of corporate subcultures, have a different set of strengths and weaknesses.[42] Procedures for sampling organizations and individuals can be, and are generally, more systematic and more fully described. These studies offer primarily an etic (outsider) point of view in that the researcher formulates the questions to which the subjects respond. The researcher also selects the variables that are expected to be associated with subcultural differences (usually based on occupation or location in hierarchy). Employees' responses are then used to determine if these expected between-group differences are statistically significant. This way of drawing subcultural boundaries considers, for example, both within-group variances and between-group mean differences. This quantitative precision is purchased at a high price—the use of relatively superficial, specialized measures of culture. In addition, this approach does not detect subcultural boundaries that don't correspond to the boundaries expected by researchers.

Combining Qualitative and Quantitative Approaches

In an attempt to avoid some of these problems, Martin, Sitkin, and Boehm combined qualitative and quantitative approaches in a study of a small electronics company (selected for convenience reasons).[43] In the qualitative phase of this study, several months of observation and unstructured interviewing revealed that employees frequently and spontaneously referred to three boundaries that might indicate subcultural differences: tenure (''old salts'' versus ''wild-eyed guys''), hierarchical level (top management versus everyone else), and functional area (e.g., marketing, finance, etc.). In the quantitative phase of this study, these possible subcultural boundaries were used to stratify a random sample of seventy-one employees. These employees were asked (using a structured, open-ended interview format) to describe and interpret the meanings of ten events they each thought had "made the company what it is today." Their answers were then content analyzed. All themes mentioned by more than two employees were coded, for a total of more than 600 variables. These content analysis data were then statistically analyzed.

There were statistically significant differences in the historical accounts of employees at different levels of the hierarchy and in different functional areas, suggesting these boundaries represented subcultural differences. Contrary to the expectations of both researchers and employees, no statistically significant differences between "old salts" and "wild eyed guys" were found. Because this method retained the content of the histories generated by the employees, the substantive meanings of these differences, and absence of difference, could be discussed.

This method, then, may be a useful compromise between qualitative and quantitative approaches, for those who prefer an objectivist approach to studying culture.[44] Systematic sampling is also possible. A predominantly emic (insider) focus can be maintained, as employees generate the historical accounts and the subcultural boundaries which are subsequently statistically analyzed. The content analysis retains the content of the historical accounts, the codes are developed in a manner specific to this cultural context, and trust between researchers and employees can be facilitated during the qualitative phase of the project. For these reasons, some of the usual superficiality of quantitative cultural measures can be avoided. However, this approach cannot offer the depth of long-term participant-observation or the statistical sophistication possible with continuous (rather than nominal) data. In addition, the content analysis method, like most statistical methods, excludes from consideration all material that is ambiguous, in effect defining culture in terms of that which is clear:

> The method requires that we banish ambiguity and hence implicitly assumes that the absence of ambiguity is a quality of the phenomena being measured. (Morgan, 1983, p. 394)

This hybrid qualitative–quantitative study, like most Differentiation studies, systematically included employees from lower levels of the hierarchy. Because of this sampling focus, both qualitative and quantitative Differentiation studies are likely to encounter points of view that differ from those of top management. This sampling procedure alone could account for much of the discrepancy between the Integration and Differentiation perspectives.

Methodological debates about depth versus superficiality, emic versus etic viewpoints, and systematic versus convenience sampling are only a small component of the difficulties that critics of Differentiation research have pointed out. Most of these problems are substantive.

SUBSTANTIVE CRITIQUES

As was the case with the Integration views of culture, improved methods can only partially alleviate the limitations of Differentiation research. No change in methods can "fix" a study that asks the wrong questions, of the wrong people, for the wrong reasons. A fervent advocate of the Integration perspective, like the Integration protagonist in the culture fight with which this book began, might object to Differentiation research in the following terms: At the heart of the Differentiation view there is ultimately a supreme indifference to the fate of actual people in real organizations.[45] If there was a genuine interest in these people's fates, then this would lead to wanting to know how to make their organizational lives better. This in turn would require pursuit of the effectiveness questions (such as improved productivity and profitability) which most Differentiation studies avoid. In addition, exploration of these issues would end the intellectual isolationism of the Differentiation perspective and force these kinds of studies to consider the mainstream theory and research which they largely ignore.

For example, the environment features prominently in most mainstream organizational sociology, yet culture studies from both the Integration and Differentiation perspectives have tended to focus primarily or exclusively on internal organizational functioning. The next section of this chapter steps out of the three-perspective framework to resolve the cultural uniqueness questions raised by both Integration and Differentiation research, explore environmental influences on culture that both perspectives have underemphasized, and reconceptualize culture in a more complex fashion, opening the way for the third, Fragmentation perspective.

NEXUS: BRINGING THE ENVIRONMENT IN

The Uniqueness Paradox

As detailed in Chapters 4 and 6, many Integration and Differentiation studies, and more than a few cultural members, claim cultural uniqueness. For example, Young reports that both management and machinists agreed that the machinists' shop floor subculture was unique:

> "Oh I'll tell you, it's a unique little world of its own down there. They all have their own little events which they organize, and they've got their own lot of interests. You should see them all wearing roses on St. George's Day." (production director, quoted in Young, 1991, p. 93)

> "All that stuff over on the Board [a bulletin board containing pictures of members of the Royal family], that's all the old biddies really. They all do that. It's their way of sayin' 'ow special they think they are; 'ow they've been 'ere longest an' all that. Just sort of tryin' to put all the others down." (machinist, quoted in Young, 1991, p. 102)

There is considerable evidence that cultural uniqueness claims are misleading. Martin, Feldman, Hatch, and Sitkin found that employees in a wide range of organizations illustrated their claims of cultural uniqueness by telling variations of the same seven stories (e.g., the "Rule Breaking" story told in Chapter 4).[46] Trice and Beyer observed that the same kinds of rituals (i.e., initiation, enhancement, degradation) were enacted in small nonprofit organizations, corporations, the military, and universities.[47] Bockus reviewed thirteen separate qualitative case studies of the cultures of large corporations. All had a subset of the same content themes found in Martin, Anterasian, and Siehl's content analysis of the annual reports of 100 large corporations.[48] These studies indicate that *cultural members often claim uniqueness by referring to manifestations that are not in fact unique. This is the uniqueness paradox.*

If culture is defined as that which is unique, and if little is in fact unique, then there may be no such thing as organizational culture. Gregory claims that the phrase "organizational culture" is a misnomer.[49] When she studied the occupational subculture of programmers in several organizations in the "silicon valley" in California, Gregory observed that programmers had a similar subculture in each of the organizations she studied. She concluded that organizations do not have cultures. Instead, an organization is an arbitrary boundary around a collection of occupational subcultures that cross organizational boundaries. A cynic might argue that Gregory simply picked a geographical area and an occupation known for "company-hopping." However, it would be worthwhile for culture researchers to take this fundamental challenge seriously. Some Differentiation researchers do so, overtly disavowing claims of uniqueness. For example:

We note, then, that organizational entities may not be possessed of a distinctive and uniquely unified culture. (Turner, 1986, p. 111)

The phrase "organizational culture" suggests that organizations bear unitary and unique cultures. Such a stance, however, is difficult to justify empirically. (Van Maanen and Barley, 1985, p. 32)

Three resolutions to this debate about cultural uniqueness are described here. Each resolution retains some level of concern with uniqueness, but acknowledges substantial limitations to what is unique in a given organizational context.

First, researchers could follow the recommendations of those who define culture as unique, and focus only on that which is distinctive to a particular context. For example, Gregory defines culture as that which is unique and implies that very little that goes on within an organization's boundaries is unique to that context. This first approach, then, would narrow its focus to only a small portion of what goes on in a given organizational context.

A second alternative draws on the evidence cited above to conclude that employees may erroneously believe that certain aspects of their culture are unique. This belief suggests that culture includes aspects that are truly unique, erroneously believed to be unique, and correctly believed to be not unique. Researchers and members will find it hard to develop firm estimates of the size and contents of these three aspects of culture, but this second approach would permit researchers to study two out of the three (the truly unique and the erroneously believed to be unique), thereby escaping some of the narrowness of the first approach.

A Nexus Solution to the Uniqueness Paradox

A third, better approach starts from the premise that in many ways, an organization is a microcosm of the surrounding societal culture. Many external cultural influences will therefore permeate the organization's boundary and be enacted within it:

> The point is made that people do not leave their cultural perspective at the gates of organizations, they enter with them and that this has an important bearing upon organizational perceptions. (Mills, 1988, p. 355)

For example, the Trust for Public Land is a small nonprofit organization that uses charitable donations of money and land to transfer ownership of undeveloped tracts to the national and federal park systems. A Differentiation view of this organization is presented in Figure 6-1. In a study of the subcultures at this organization, in addition to hierarchical and functional differentiation, two more unusual subcultures were observed: accountants and Hispanics.[50] The large staff of in-house accountants thought of themselves as, in effect, an orthogonal, professional subculture. These accountants identified primarily with other accountants from outside the organization. This was a transorganizational, occupational subculture like Gregory's programmers. In addition, many of the secretarial staff were Hispanics, a heritage they shared with a few of the professional staff. From time to time, these Hispanics would function as a counterculture within the firm. This last subculture, then, cross-cut hierarchical and functional boundaries within the organization, as well as the external boundary between the organization and its environment. Louis labels such extraorganizational influences "feeder cultures."[51]

The possibility of feeder cultures suggests a better resolution to the uniqueness dilemma. Acknowledgment of the influence of feeder cultures permits a redefinition of "organizational culture," so that an organization is seen as a nexus where a variety of cultural influences come together within a boundary. A few of the cultural elements within that boundary will be truly unique to the organization. Other elements (some of which will be erroneously believed to be unique) will reflect cultural influences external to the organization. *What is unique and "organizational," then, is the way a particular mix of cultures combines and interacts within a given organization's boundary.*

For example, Meyerson viewed the occupational culture of social work as a nexus of institutional forces, including the ways different kinds of hospitals were structured and the ways different helping professions were educated to approach health care.[52] These institutional forces combined in different mixes in different hospitals, transforming the experiences of social workers in each context. This nexus approach to understanding organizational culture is illustrated in Figure 6-2.

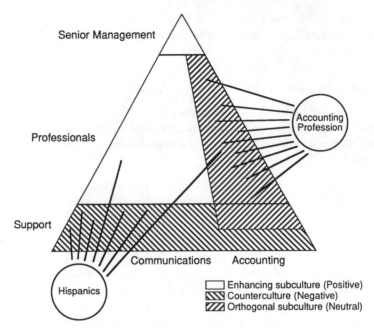

Figure 6-1. Trust for public land: differentiation perspective.

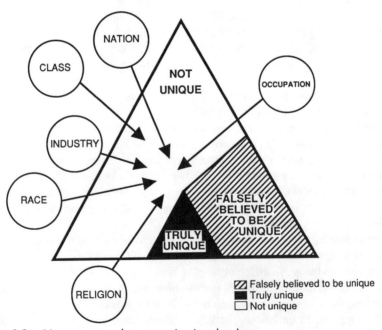

Figure 6-2. Nexus approach to organizational culture.

The nexus approach has several advantages. Only a small proportion of cultural manifestations are likely to be truly unique to a given setting. The conceptual breadth of the nexus approach maximizes the potential for offering insights into more aspects of organizational life. Furthermore, the breadth of the nexus approach more closely approximates the breadth of cultural members' viewpoints, as they are unlikely to restrict their attention to what is unique in a particular context.

Bringing the Environment In

Another advantage of the nexus approach is its acknowledgment of the environment. Organizational culture research has been very slow to acknowledge environmental influences.[53] For example, the editors of a special issue of the *Administrative Science Quarterly* criticized the studies submitted because they tended "to stress the internal, rather than to look to the external, societal, cultural context within which organizations are embedded" (Jelinek, Smircich, and Hirsch, 1983, p. 338). In contrast, the nexus point of view brings the environment to the forefront of cultural studies. This approach is congruent, for example, with a greater focus on demographic influences on cultural functioning, as when societal norms of sexism or racism are enacted within organizational boundaries. In addition, the nexus approach draws attention to international differences in organizational functioning.[54]

If a nexus view is not adopted, organizational culture researchers are taking what Keesing has labeled a *mosaic* approach. Although Keesing was referring to anthropological studies of tribal societies, the organizational analogy is easy to see:

> In this view, small-scale tribal societies . . . constitute a kind of mosaic of cultures. Each culture is seen as a separate and unique experiment in human possibility—as if each were a differently colored separate piece in a mosaic of human diversity to be studied, and valued, in its own right. . . . If we look at the tribal world as a mosaic of cultural variation. . . . we are led to attribute a spurious separateness and self-containment to these "cultures," to overlook the way peoples were tied into regional systems to trade, exchange, and politics, through which ideas as well as objects flowed. (Keesing, 1981, pp. 111–113)

The existence of inter- and extraorganizational connections does not mean that a given context has not also developed some truly unique cultural elements. It does mean that it is misleading to deny the influence of the environment on the content of cultures in organizations. The implication, of course, is that *we cannot understand what goes on inside an organizational culture without understanding what exists outside the boundary.*

By bringing environmental concerns into the domain of cultural studies, the nexus resolution to the uniqueness debate complicates what is meant by the term *organizational culture* or, more accurately, *cultures in organizations.* Once feeder cultures are considered, cultures in organizations must be seen as multiple, overlapping, and nested within each other. Boundaries of the organization must be viewed as permeable and, in a sense, arbitrary. This challenges usual notions of what an organization includes and excludes, opening new topics for study by organizational scholars, such as the unemployed and the family.

The unemployed, almost by definition, exist "beyond the pale" of organizational life, except in so far as they come into contact with public sector agencies, for example, in the role of a "client" receiving unemployment benefits, breaking the law, or claiming bankruptcy. The unemployed are the ultimate organizational culture deviants. Their existence personifies the threat implicit in an organization's request for compliance with formal procedures and informal behavioral norms. For these reasons, the unemployed (and perceptions of the unemployed) deserve study.

Families are also "not part of" organizations. This exclusion is reified in the distinction between the public and the private domains. The public domain (of the marketplace, the political arena, and the legal system) is contrasted with the "closed and exclusive sphere of intimacy, sexuality, and affection characterizing the modern nuclear family."[55] This dichotomy, of course, is false.[56] The public and private domains cannot be separated in this way. Most families do not fit the classic nuclear model. Furthermore, what happens at work affects the "family" and what happens in the "family" affects what happens at work.

For example, because most women carry a disproportionate share of domestic responsibilities, working women are more likely to have to find time during business hours to take a sick family member to the doctor, meet with a teacher, and so on. Because few organizations provide on-site day care, and because work hours are usually not restructured to allow family members' needs to be met, these conflicts take time away from work. Many working women, therefore, operate at a competitive disadvantage with comparable men. In these and other ways, the concerns of the private domain are inextricably intertwined with life at work.[57] For these reasons, studies of cultures in organizations should examine the ways domestic arrangements support how organizational jobs are usually structured. As these examples indicate, a nexus approach brings environmental concerns into the study of culture and opens new arenas of exploration.

NEXT STEP: FRAGMENTATION

This last section of Chapter 6 has stepped outside the three-perspective view of culture to offer a nexus resolution to the dilemma created by claims of cultural uniqueness. This resolution is incomplete in that it leaves an important difficulty unexplored. Both the Integration and Differentiation views of culture do not do a good job of acknowledging the inescapable ambiguities of organizational life. Both, for example, assume that we can define the edges where organizations end and environments begin. Since these boundaries are permeable and fluctuating, their placement is debatable. It is therefore difficult to define where a culture or subculture begins or ends.

The third, Fragmentation view of culture focuses on ambiguities such as this one. Rather than being a coherent entity contained within clearly defined boundaries, the Fragmentation view conceptualizes a culture as "a differential network, a fabric of traces referring endlessly to something other than itself, to other differential traces."[58] Lest this introduction to the third view of culture seem too ephemeral or abstract, the next chapter returns to the employees of OZCO as they describe their practical concerns about the ambiguities that pervade their working lives.

NOTES

1. Ortner (1974), p. 79.

2. Feminist theory has extended this argument by focusing on the ways the halves of dichotomies that are associated with the traditionally feminine (i.e., emotional, passive, etc.) have been devalued. For example, see Irigary (1985), Kristeva (1980), and Moi (1985).

3. For an empirical exploration of this observation, see Tversky (1977).

4. For other versions of this argument, see Argyris and Schon (1978) and Christensen and Kreiner (1984).

5. Siehl (1984).

6. Meyer and Rowan (1977).

7. See, for example, Jermier, Slocum, Fry, and Gaines (1991) and Kunda (1991a).

8. See Martin, Anterasian, and Siehl (1988) and Siehl and Martin (1990).

9. Young (1991).

10. This classification was originally offered by Louis (1985, p. 82), but the labels have been changed in this book.

11. McDonald (1991).

12. See, for example, Gregory (1983) and Van Maanen and Barley (1984).

13. Fernandez (1982), Kanter (1977).

14. See, for example, Ferguson (1984) and Weston and Rofel (1984).

15. After Meyerson (1991b). Sometimes a Differentiation study will claim to encompass ambiguity. For example, Rosen uses the word *ambiguity* to explain that a manifestation can have different interpretations (1985, p. 33). Simply because a manifestation can have more than one meaning, and those meanings may be inconsistent, is not an indication of ambiguity (in the sense of lack of clarity).

16. Louis (1983a), p. 43.

17. Van Maanen and Barley (1985), p. 33.

18. Bell (1990).

19. Feldman (1985).

20. Hochschild (1983).

21. Jermier (1985).

22. Many of these researchers have defined culture differently in different texts and in different parts of the same text.

23. See also Yanow (1982).

24. A few Differentiation researchers respond to inconsistencies and subcultural differences by distinguishing different types of culture. For example, because externally and internally espoused content themes may be inconsistent, Christensen and Kreiner (1984) find it useful to distinguish the firm's "organizational aura" from its "corporate culture." An organization's "aura" (which economists refer to as its "reputation") is the concept

held by the environment about the organization. The "corporate culture" is initiated and controlled by top management (in some ways, this is congruent with an Integration view). A third type of culture defined by Christensen and Kreiner is labeled "culture in work." This is quite similar to the work-group subcultures depicted in the Differentiation studies described in Young (1991) and Van Maanen (1991). These are potentially useful distinctions, but there is a danger in reifying them. Externally visible and internally enacted cultural manifestations do not always differ. Although top management may articulate a coherent vision of "corporate culture," Differentiation research suggests that this vision seldom generates organization-wide consensus. Finally, although work group subcultures often resist top management's demands (like ride operators at Disneyland), others may be enhancing subcultures that firmly support a managerial point of view. These complications suggest that a more flexible conceptual framework may be desirable.

25. Blau (1955), Chandler (1962), Lawrence and Lorsch (1967).

26. Rosen (1991).

27. Sunesson (1985), p. 244.

28. There are studies that do not fit easily within either the Integration or the Differentiation perspectives. For example, Walter (1985) described the conflicts experienced when two different integrated cultures come together, because of a merger or an acquisition, into a new organizational structure. Selsky and Wilkof (1988) described two internally integrated organizations which had difficulty developing a nonconflicting relationship. Since Walter focused on the creation of a new organization that must somehow find a way of living with conflict, his study seems to be closer to a Differentiation view. Because Selsky and Wilkof focused on ways the two, internally integrated cultures can better understand each other, this study remains closer to the Integration perspective. Both studies, however, are good examples of research that does not easily fit within the three-perspective classification scheme.

29. For other discussions of women and minorities as deviants within white male organizational cultures, see Bell (1990), Ferguson (1984), Fernandez (1982), Kanter (1977), and Martin (1990). To the extent that subcultural support might be helpful to women and minorities in this situation, these results suggest that clustering demographically similar individuals might be more helpful than scattering them, as solos, across a hierarchy. Discussion of the advantages—and dangers—of this clustering policy can be found in Pettigrew and Martin (1987).

30. For example, see Sahlins (1976), p. 206.

31. Van Maanen and Kunda (1989), p. 75.

32. See Barrett (1985), Clegg and Dunkerly (1980), Farley (1985), and Reed (1985).

33. Brunsson (1986).

34. Van Maanen (1986).

35. Meyer (1982).

36. Abolafia and Kilduff (1988).

37. Pfeffer and Salancik (1978), Weick (1976, 1979a).

38. Bartunek (1984).

39. This interplay between tight coupling with the environment and loose coupling within an organization has been described, for example, by March and Olsen (1976) and March and Simon (1958).

40. See, for example, Meyer and Rowan (1977), Scott (1981), Thompson (1967), and Weick (1976).

41. The Differentiation view of change as incremental and localized is, in some ways, similar to the "first order," changes studied, for example, by Watzlawick, Weakland, and

Fisch (1974). It also bears a resemblance to Kuhn's (1970) vision of the small contributions made by "normal" science.

42. Friedman (1983).

43. Martin, Sitkin, and Boehm (1985).

44. This mixed qualitative–quantitative approach can be criticized from a subjectivist point of view by asking such questions such as: How do the employees' accounts circumvent, ignore, and mask problematic aspects of the company's history? How can we be sure the use of the same phrases entails the same meanings for different people? Similar questions could be used to critique any Differentiation study from a subjectivist viewpoint.

45. This argument is loosely paraphrased from Donaldson's (1989, p. 250) critique of Reed's approach to organizational research.

46. This section's discussion of uniqueness is summarized from Martin, Feldman, Hatch, and Sitkin (1983).

47. Trice and Beyer (1984).

48. Bockus (1983), Martin, Anterasian, and Siehl (1988).

49. Gregory (1983).

50. Student group project, Graduate School of Business, Stanford University. Authors' names lost.

51. Louis (1985), p. 79.

52. Meyerson (1991a).

53. One exception is Schein, who has consistently stressed the importance of environmental influences on culture. However, Schein (1985, p. 9) conceptualizes an organization's environment and its culture as two distinct "variables"; they can affect each other, but they remain separated by an impermeable conceptual boundary. This view is quite different from the nexus approach to conceptualizing intra- and extraorganizational cultural influences.

54. Examples of relevant Integration studies include Lincoln and Kallberg (1985), Ouchi (1981), and Pascale and Athos (1981). Differentiation studies of multinational corporations include Jaeger (1979).

55. Benhabib and Cornell (1987), pp. 6–7.

56. Deconstructions of the public–private dichotomy that is taken for granted in so much organizational research include Frug (1986), Keohane (1988), Martin (1990), Nicholson (1986), and Olsen (1983).

57. Evidence supporting these claims regarding working women can be found in Berk (1985) and Hess and Ferree (1987). The few men who accept half the domestic responsibilities entailed by a partnership operate at a similar disadvantage. Pleck (1985) examines these same issues, focusing on men in dual-career marriages.

58. Derrida (1976).

OZCO: A Fragmentation View

Studies conducted from a Fragmentation viewpoint focus on ambiguity as the essence of culture. The clear consistencies characteristic of the Integration perspective, and the clear inconsistencies characteristic of the Differentiation perspective, are rare. No stable organization-wide or subcultural consensus is seen. Instead, issues temporarily generate concern, but that concern does not coalesce into shared opinions, either in the form of agreement or disagreement. In this chapter, OZCO employees speak of their concerns regarding the three content themes (egalitarianism, innovation, and concern for employee well being) that were the focus of Chapters 3 and 5. In this description of OZCO, these content themes are seen as sources of confusion, a variety of interpretations of any cultural manifestation seems plausible, and uncertainty is pervasive. In this culture, ambiguity is inescapable.

EGALITARIANISM?

OZCO management clearly states its commitment to egalitarianism, but some employees find the company's practices confusing in this regard. For example, resources and nonfinancial rewards are supposed to be distributed at OZCO in a relatively egalitarian fashion. However, how one actually obtains a better office space, a nicer desk, or a newer computer (or any other physical object that can have status connotations) is not clear to some employees. Need, status, power, and tenure all seem to come into play, but some employees can see no policy, even within a division.

Some are also confused about OZCO's much-touted commitment to open office spaces. There has long been some private discussion about whether or not open office spaces are "a good thing." This has become such a hot topic that a formal meeting was held, so that the costs and benefits of the open plan (as well as the financial costs of changing to a closed plan) could be debated. During this meeting, two kinds of confusion emerged. It was not clear whether the open offices were achieving the stated objectives of promoting informal communication and equalizing status differences. Perhaps more important, employees were confused about whether these objectives were a top priority, or even appropriate. Some employees were concerned about privacy or work efficiency, while others put greater priority on minimizing status differentials. No consensus about priorities emerged from this meeting. Some employees remained confused about how these conflicting objectives should be, and would be, prioritized. Possibly, these employees said, these objectives are incommensurable or irreconcilable.

Ambiguity also pervades some discussions about the difficulties of getting things done within the OZCO bureaucracy:

> There are a number of layers. The charters of different divisions often overlap. If you are going to impact other divisions then it's very difficult. Because rules and procedures differ across divisions, much confusion results when policies have to move across divisional boundaries. (Dan, product marketing)

Some employees are confused about how to get things done. They say that the ambiguity they perceive is exacerbated by the company's emphasis on low-level, consensual decision-making practices. For example, because of the size of the company, these employees say it is difficult to know what's going on outside one's own level of the hierarchy and division:

> Products have to work together. [They] can't work in isolation. They're not set up to do this. OZCO is a lot of little companies. (Bob, marketing planner)

Some employees feel that consensual decisions are sometimes based on little (and often erroneous) information. These employees claim that "no one" can make a decision because decisions are supposed to be pushed to the lowest level. And, if a decision involves other divisions, the decision must also move up and across the hierarchy. Getting decisions moved around in this way seems, to some, to be a very ambiguous process:

> It seems that when one moves beyond the division level to the group level there is a problem. When there is no way the divisions can coordinate on their own, then, a group manager is called in to "fix it." How far up to coordinate a project is unclear. These things come to people's attention where we choose to measure our results. When divisions are having trouble, when they've lost some sales because of lack of links, then they go to the group level to "fix it." (Stuart, marketing engineer)

> Coordination starts low . . . If [consensus] is not reached at the low level [then it] escalates. The escalation process is not well defined. . . . You just identify where there's a bottleneck, then try to resolve it by escalating. (Tom, marketing engineer)

For some employees, a similar confusion surrounds OZCO's lateral promotion policy, whereby top performers are supposed to receive "promotions" that are horizontal (same level, different functional area) before they are moved up the hierarchy. Lateral movement is often encouraged, but some employees feel confused about how to go about transferring, how to get interviews with other divisions, and how to get the support of their boss for a transfer:

> [Employees] can move around, although I really don't know how one does this. During a hiring freeze especially, I don't know how to get support for a transfer. (Bob, marketing planner)

Some employees wonder if transfer difficulties might be deliberately planned:

> Well, there is a kind of a problem there, too, because some divisions—I've heard of
> people getting—having a lot of trouble transferring. They blacklist you or something,
> virtually. You just can't go anywhere. They say, well, he is a rotten individual when
> they call up to get the recommendation from the previous boss. And things like that have
> also happened to me. (Joan, operations clerk)

Foreign transfers are seen by some employees as particularly problematic, as
indicated by this organizational story:

> Jim was transferred to Germany as an expatriate for a few years. He was doing a great
> job, so he stayed and consequently broke ties with the division he came from. Later, it
> was decided that he ought to return to the U.S. No one [was honest with him about this]
> and so, even though he was a capable guy, he ended up leaving the company. (adapted
> from Wilkins, 1978, interview data)

The reasons for the difficulties associated with foreign transfers are unclear.
Personnel staff offer a variety of explanations for these difficulties, sometimes
attributing a person's transfer problems to that individual's poor performance
before the transfer and, at other times, to a group's reluctance to match high
overseas salary levels:

> Coming back to the U.S., there have been a number of occasions where the individual's
> salary was high and, even though the individual might have been a capable individual,
> he wasn't in a particular group and there was no obligation for any particular group to
> pick up on the individual when he came back. And we kind of just let the individual
> hang. (Jerry, personnel staff)

In any one foreign transfer case, it would be difficult to determine whether this, or
some other explanation is valid. Some employees doubt the espoused reason for
such horizontal transfers (as a reward for good performance). They wonder if this
ambiguity is sometimes deliberately fostered, so that the unpleasant job of giving
negative performance feedback can be postponed or avoided.

Organizational stories at OZCO suggest that some employees are unaware that
lateral, rather than vertical, promotions are supposed to be the norm. For example:

> A very competent woman for two and a half years had been working in corporate
> personnel on the workforce restructuring project. She was passed over for a job that she
> would have been a natural for. Later, she was told that if she wanted to move ahead she
> had to come up [laterally] through the divisions. This was the first she had heard of this
> policy, even though she had been working on workforce issues for two and a half years.
> It wasn't clear to her. (Sally, human resources consultant)

In addition to portraying the ignorance of a single employee, this organizational story pinpoints a number of sources for the ambiguity that some see as
surrounding the company's lateral promotion policy. Was this woman never told
of the policy because her chances of promotion were nil? Or, were her chances of

promotion nil because she was not smart enough to realize the importance and personal relevance of the lateral promotion policy when she heard about it? Or, are women and minorities less likely to be coached by the informal "old boy" network of line managers who watch for "promotable" subordinates? Or, was the woman in the story, who was in personnel, seen as not having the skills that make a person "promotable"? Some employees observe that line managers tend to have engineering, rather than personnel backgrounds.

According to some employees, even apparently clear polices are implemented in a confusing fashion. For example, the implementation of the across-the-board pay cut caused considerable confusion:

> In certain divisions you were expected to come in anyways, for whatever reasons. In other divisions, it was less clear. You were just told that you were expected to get the job done and if it could be done in two days less, fine: otherwise, work. So, in a lot of cases it was a pay cut disguised. But it affected everybody differently, depending on their division and supervisor. (Denise, product marketing)

In summary, although OZCO management clearly states a commitment to egalitarianism, some employees are confused. The company's practices—financial and nonfinancial reward allocations, open office spaces, consensual decision-making, lateral promotion and transfer policies, and the across-the-board pay cut—are seen, by some employees, to demonstrate ambiguities associated with OZCO's commitment to this value.

INNOVATION?

In order to encourage the innovation of marketable new products, OZCO announced that it would reorganize. The new structure emphasized centralization and coordination, as a means of overcoming the divisions' tendencies to operate too autonomously. Announcements were vague about the extent and content of the structural changes to be made:

> Changes [will be made] only as needed. Details of how the marketing and sales sector will be organized at the various levels will be developed and communicated over the coming months. (internal newsletter)

Subsequent, supposedly "detailed" announcements failed to resolve some employees' confusion. The divisions were separate profit centers, proud of their autonomy. It was not "the OZCO way" to take an organization-wide perspective and declare that the appropriate solutions to any problem consisted of a centralized policy and the sacrifice of much-vaunted divisional autonomy. Even after the "reorganization" was implemented, according to some employees, much remained unchanged. They claimed that some "slack" due to excess resources remained structurally hidden and that redundancies in products, people, and projects were sometimes unintentionally undetected or deliberately protected.

The reorganization relied heavily on liaisons to coordinate divisional product development and marketing. Even some of these liaisons felt overwhelmed with confusion:

> My problem is that I don't understand half of these divisions and what they do. . . . I'm the liaison with the [a subdivision] from my division. . . . No one takes the time to explain how the divisions interrelate, what roles are expected of me, and what my relationship is to the other divisions. It's so decentralized that you have to learn by mistake. For example, [another] division developed a product that I'm supposed to market, yet I didn't even know about it until I heard about it from [a third] division. (Denise, product marketing)

This liaison assumes that her confusion is due to a lack of information from her superiors: "If only they would take the time." Other employees suggest that supervisors have not "explained" because they do not know the answers.

According to some employees, confusion impairs the efficiency of product development and perhaps even the quality and quantity of new products developed. Redundant and "dog" products, these employees claim, are often introduced. In part, this may be due to ambiguities in OZCO's performance appraisal system:

> Some of the products we have are dogs. My manager doesn't know if she is being evaluated on how well the products are doing or how many new products we introduce. So, we keep introducing new dog products. . . . I kept asking, "How am I evaluated?" My manager would just respond, "You're doing OK." When I ask for criteria my manager tells me not to worry, and that I am doing a fine job. (Denise, product marketing)

> What you might think is due to you or is coming to you is not necessarily so. . . . You can really knock yourself out and nothing is ever said, but you mess up once and you're called on the carpet. . . . It's just very frustrating when you see these things happen and you know it can happen to anyone and you can't do anything about it. (Joan, operations clerk)

Part of the perceived ambiguity in performance appraisal may stem from the fact that employees are compared with others at the same level in the hierarchy, within other divisions and functional areas. This method of comparison seems ambiguous to some employees who are uncertain about what factors, other than merit, influence the process:

> I'm not well versed in the ranking process because it's done by first line managers and up. I know pay increases are based on merit, but merit really depends on your job. . . . Since different jobs are compared to each other it's difficult. It's difficult to compare apples to oranges here and I don't know how they do it. . . . I'm a product marketing engineer here and I'm ranked against a lab engineer. (Tom, marketing engineer)

> Managers of each division argue for rank criteria that will favor their own division. The managers don't know what other division members even do. One product manager says evaluation is based on new product development. Another says they don't know. Another says growth. (Denise, product marketing)

Some relatively mundane tasks, related to the product development effort, require little creativity. Even in the context of these tasks, the process of administratively supporting innovation seems ambiguous to some:

> If I'm introducing a new product to a new source, I'm supposed to fill out a new product introduction form. This depends a lot on information which no one seems to know. The first couple of months I had to do it by being told what was wrong. I only learn when I'm told I'm wrong. I don't even know the steps necessary, or the questions to ask. It's not like I choose not to do it right. I don't even know what right is. Then, management gets frustrated because it's never right, so I get chewed out. There is no documented process, and there couldn't be, because it changes all the time. No one knows what the forms mean. I try to understand what the responses to the questions on the forms mean—the codes I use—and no one knows. It's just how you fill it out; there doesn't seem to be any meaning to it. They just seem like random numbers I fill the blanks with. (Denise, product marketing)

These employees attribute the ambiguities they experience to diverse sources: incomplete communication about the details of the reorganization; their supervisors' (perhaps deliberate) unwillingness to share knowledge; constant changes in procedures; and procedures that are inherently confusing or (apparently) improperly implemented. These attributions all assume that clarity is possible. Although some of this ambiguity may be inherent in, and specific to, the innovation process, ambiguity is perceived by some employees in other domains as well.

CONCERN FOR EMPLOYEE WELL-BEING?

Some employees describe widespread ambiguities in the company's policies regarding employee well-being. For example, after working some time on a "workforce rebalancing" task (OZCO jargon for voluntary functional and geographical relocation), Sally read an article in a local newspaper describing how some companies, as part of their personnel policy, help the spouses of relocated employees search for jobs, homes, and schools in their new neighborhoods. OZCO was one of the companies featured prominently in the newspaper article. As Sally recounts the incident:

> I was unaware of any such OZCO policy, so I called the Personnel Director to make sure. He had never heard of the policy, and said, "Well, we have some systems." When I asked what these systems were, he shuffled through a loose leaf notebook and responded, "Well, that page is missing." He knew that OZCO had some policies and procedures, but he apparently had no idea what they were or even how to find out where and what they were. (Sally, human resources consultant)

It does seem unlikely that the director of personnel would be unaware of a spouse relocation policy. Is there a lack of communication between personnel and top management, or between personnel and whomever talked to the newspaper reporter? Or, is there a spouse relocation policy that, for some reason, the personnel director is reluctant to tell Sally about? If so, is this reluctance due to Sally's official involvement in relocation tasks or is it because of something about Sally personally? Part of the ambiguity inherent in this incident is due to the multiple interpretations that are plausible.

Personnel's lack of information about this policy may be indicative of a relative lack of power within OZCO. The company's espoused concern with employee well-being suggests that personnel should be a centrally important area of function. Thus when evidence of personnel's powerlessness is pointed out, some employees feel confused about OZCO's commitment to its employees' well-being. Personnel staff jobs at OZCO are not particularly respected by some group and divisional employees, some claim, because

> staff decisions are often undercut, without appropriate official authority, by corporate employees. (Sonia, corporate staff)

This makes practices that are perceived as ambiguous, such as the lateral promotion policy, even more confusing because some employees feel they cannot get answers to their questions. Other employees believe that the personnel staff do care and would like to provide answers, but cannot because they are powerless. Consider the experience of a low-level employee, who went to personnel for help in dealing with his supervisor:

> And it was actually kind of sad because here I am in this big, beautiful company with all of these wonderful propaganda lists that they put out: we will do this for you and we will do that for you. And I thought—I saw the people in personnel and I, like I said, I've never been so disappointed in my whole life with anything. I mean, they just couldn't do anything. It was just a hopeless cause. . . . Well, they [the personnel staff] were a good sounding board. And they said, "Oh, yes, yes," and patted you on the head. In fact, the people in personnel told me that six or seven other people had had the same experience and the same things had happened to them. . . . They have one guy down at—down there and that is Bob in personnel and he is just fantastic. I mean, he'll do anything for you and I—the problem is that personnel is there but they have no power behind them. (Ron, operations staff)

Other people (or the same people at other times) say that the personnel staff simply do not care and so they act in an ambiguous fashion because they want to sweep difficult problems "under the rug":

> I'm beginning to wonder if they really care. I don't know. Well, the thing is, from my experiences and from other peoples' experiences that I know of, when you try and take it high up, it seems to be—everybody seems to try and hush you up and pass it by you and say, "Yes, we'll look into it." And then you start hearing all the different stories that everybody is telling and it never really gets told as it is. . . . I mean all the stepping stones you're taking it through, because everybody is responsible to everybody else down the line and they don't want to, I guess, admit that they're letting this happen. It's all just pushed aside. (Ron, operations staff)

OZCO's concern for its employees is often described in terms of a "family," but some employees express confusion about the meaning of this metaphor:

> I guess I hired on with the company just by their reputation. . . . They treated their employees very well and it had a type of family atmosphere, and that once you were hired on at OZCO, you were almost like one of the family and you never got thrown out of the company. They treated you very well. They cared about you—that sort of thing. And I must admit, I don't hear that today. Yes, I think you hear good things about OZCO, but not in the same way: that you are an individual, that you are cared about, [that] type of thing. I think basically that if you're here at OZCO and you do a good job you will be rewarded. But, you don't have that feeling of closeness. . . . When a company is allowed to grow too large—I am not saying it is too large—ahm, as it grows larger, that things, I've found, become more impersonal from a business side. . . . Then, of course, my thing is that I'm not quite sure whether my experiences that I'm seeing are just a matter of different personalities, or whether it is the growth of the company. (Aida, personnel clerk)

Some long-term employees have experienced a change from a small "family" to a big company atmosphere, and this has caused considerable confusion. Some wonder, "Does the company care about its employees, or are the changes I've experienced unique to me? Did they care when I was first hired, or was it my imagination, or was it some kind of corporate propaganda that I believed?" Because of contradictions between past and present experiences, these employees feel that the meaning of the "family" metaphor has become ambiguous.

Although virtually everyone at OZCO has heard the rhetoric about employee well-being, some employees say that even the president seems unsure how this espoused value is translated into action. For example, at the public panel discussion where Jim was asked about OZCO's concern for women employees with children, his first response was "I'm not sure." He then went on to restate the company's concern for the personal well-being of women employees, as described in Chapters 3 and 5, by telling the Caesarean story. (The ambiguities implicit in that story are dissected in some detail in the next chapter.) Jim went on to say that the company had decided not to enter the business of providing or supporting childcare; instead, employees' informal, self-help efforts to find adequate childcare were to be "facilitated" by management.

Some employees react to the company's refusal to provide or support day care with confusion. They do not understand if the company's espoused commitment to employees' personal well-being is getting translated into concrete policies and practices. For example, some employees interpret the president's vague commitment to facilitate informal day-care referrals as an attempt to cover his ignorance about whether OZCO has a company-wide policy regarding day care:

> The truth is that he has no clue. Each division has their own policy, maybe, and Jim Hamilton has no idea because there is no central policy. (Sally, human resources consultant)

Some employees regard the company's attitude about day care as a sign of managerial confusion and ignorance, rather than overt hypocrisy or a deliberate refusal to help employees who choose not to have one parent remain home with children. OZCO policies that have direct relevance to working women are interpreted by some employees as ambiguous, rather than as clear indicators of discriminatory intent. Perhaps because of these perceived ambiguities, senior women with policy-making responsibilities have not formed, according to some employees, cohesive subcultures. For example:

> The senior women don't support each other or the rest of the women. They seem competitive and cut throat. (Sally, human resources consultant)

Clear subcultures may not emerge in part because potential subcultural members may have little communication with each other. For example, senior women are scarce at OZCO and may seldom have a chance to talk. According to some employees, lack of communication is an endemic problem at OZCO; they claim that peers talk frequently, but superiors seem reluctant to communicate:

> Communication is bad. When the two course developers left, they hired two people and I ended up introducing myself to both of those people. The one guy in the Xerox room said, "Hey you probably noticed I've been hanging around for two weeks and talking to Jim Strathmore a lot." And I said, "Yeah." And he says, "I'm Sam Johnson and I'm going to be working here. I'm so-and-so's replacement." Well, I didn't even know they had hired anybody and I just thought that was kind of tacky. But they should have sent out a memo. And that's happened a lot. It happened a lot when I was in the production line. They make these big changes that are going to affect you. I mean, at least it's somebody working with you and you ought to know that and they don't tell you. You find it out from somebody else and usually your supervisor didn't think about it and that's one of the things that's bad. 'Though it's—everybody's on the whole pretty friendly, communication seems to be a problem. I don't know if it's because it's so big or if the managers don't really feel that the people lower than they really need to know. (Terry, personnel clerk)

This employee is confused first, by the lack of information, and second, by not knowing the reasons for that lack. Various explanations for the communication block are offered, but it is not clear which, if any, are correct.

Sometimes "bottom-up" communication is clearly encouraged, but even then, some employees remain confused, wondering if the encouragement is simply a "passing thing":

> About a year or so ago, all of us in our department were having some problems with our manager. So we were called in by his supervisor to kind of have each one talk to him and, I guess, tell their personal problems related to them, probably, and also relating their problems to the department. Now then, when we all got back, everybody said, "Oh, I was very honest" and "I was very truthful" and "I said just what I thought or felt like saying." The thing is, if everybody did this, we didn't see any significant changes in the department—either in the manager or with any of the other things that we

had brought out. So, I guess my feeling on that was: What was the purpose of that? Was it a—kind of like a pacifying thing that they did? I never did realize why. Why did he take his time to talk to all of us if really nothing was to be done? (Aida, personnel clerk)

LAYERS OF AMBIGUITY

According to this Fragmentation view, OZCO's culture is riddled with ambiguities. Employees are confused and uncertain about the company's commitment to egalitarianism, innovation, and concern for employee well-being. Formal and informal practices, as well as a variety of cultural forms, are interpreted (or in some cases, reinterpreted) in a variety of ways. Employees are uncertain about whether all, none, or some of these interpretations are correct.

Table 7-1 presents this Fragmentation view in the form of a matrix. Cell entries are interpreted in an ambiguous manner and bear an ambiguous relation to each other. Clear consistencies and inconsistences between cell entries are rare. Rather than expressing consensus on an organization-wide or subcultural basis, employees ask a variety of questions about the three content themes that have served to organize the presentation of the OZCO data in this book. A drawing of this Fragmentation view of OZCO is included in Figure 5-1. In this figure the Fragmentation perspective view of OZCO shows that employee well-being is a concern of some individuals, particularly those in the production and engineering divisions. Although these individuals are concerned about well-being, they do not perceive it similarly and do not have similar opinions about the company's approach to it. Figure 5-1 also shows that innovation is a concern of a different cluster of individuals, primarily those in the engineering division. These employees do not perceive innovation similarly or have similar attitudes about it. Egalitarianism is a concern of some other individuals, particularly those with lower-status jobs, but this issue also is perceived and interpreted in a variety of ways. From a Fragmentation perspective, ambiguities are so prevalent that OZCO employees' perceptions and evaluations do not coalesce in any detectable or stable clusters of consensus or conflict.

If more of the OZCO material, expressive of ambiguity, had been included in this chapter, additional themes would have emerged. Reliance on only three themes creates the mistaken impression that the Fragmentation perspective stands in dichotomous opposition to one or both of the other perspectives. Instead, as will be seen in the next chapter, the Fragmentation perspective offers a unique approach to understanding what cultures are and how they change.

Table 7-1 OZCO: A Fragmentation view

Content themes		Practices	
External	*Internal*	*Formal*	*Informal*
	Confusion about egalitarianism	Performance evaluation process and criteria unclear	Norms of distributing "perks" unclear
			Confusion about consensual decision making process
			Confusion about lateral promotion and foreign transfer
			Implementation of across-the-board pay cut unclear
	Confusion about innovation	Unclear performance evaluation criteria	Confusion about restructuring
		Ranking process compares "apples with oranges"	Confusion about liaisons' responsibilities and divisional relationships
		Confusion about product introduction process	
	Confusion about concern for employee well-being	Unclear relocation policy	Confusion about "family"-like caring
		Lack of clear policies regarding women with children	Personnel is powerless and unpredictable
			Commitment to female employees and families well-being unclear
			Lack of cohesive subcultures
			Poor communication causes confusion

		Forms	
Stories	_Ritual_	_Jargon_	_Physical arrangements_
Foreign transfer story			Goal and effects of open offices unclear
Ignorance about lateral promotion policy story			

"Dogs"

8

The Fragmentation Perspective: Multiplicity and Flux

The Fragmentation perspective[1] brings ambiguity to the foreground, rather than excluding it or channeling it outside a realm of cultural or subcultural clarity. This perspective abandons the clarity of consistency, as well as the clarity of inconsistency. Instead, the Fragmentation viewpoint explores the complexity of relationships between one cultural manifestation and another. Rather than seeing consensus within the boundaries of a subculture or a culture, the Fragmentation viewpoint presents a multiplicity of interpretations that seldom, if ever, coalesce into a stable consensus. These defining characteristics of the Fragmentation perspective (*focus on ambiguity, complexity of relationships among manifestations, and a multiplicity of interpretations that do not coalesce into a stable consensus*) are explored in more detail here.

Perhaps because it focuses on ambiguity, the Fragmentation perspective is difficult to discuss with clarity. Furthermore, this is the newest of the three perspectives and, so far, relatively few studies have been conducted from this viewpoint. Although these studies are scarce, however, it is already clear that the Fragmentation perspective will expand our understanding of cultural phenomena in ways that the other two perspectives do not.

This chapter is organized somewhat differently than the chapters that reviewed the Integration and Differentiation literatures. This chapter begins with a general description of the ambiguities that pervade contemporary industrial society and, more specifically, organizations. This description is followed by a brief summary of some Fragmentation studies that, in accord with the first defining characteristic of this perspective, make the experience of ambiguity the primary focus of their cultural descriptions. Next, the concept of ambiguity is elaborated and defined and the mode of thinking characteristic of this perspective is described. Whereas the Integration perspective seeks similarities and the Differentiation perspective relies on an oppositional mode of thinking, the Fragmentation perspective focuses on delineating multiplicities. After this mode of thinking has been explained and its methodological implications outlined, the chapter reviews studies that illustrate the other two defining characteristics of the Fragmentation perspective. The remainder of the chapter follows a familiar sequence, covering such topics as effectiveness and change and concluding with a sampling of methodological and substantive critiques.

A WORLD WITHOUT SIMPLICITY, ORDER, AND PREDICTABILITY

Contemporary life inside and outside organizations is permeated with ambiguities. In part, these ambiguities stem from societal problems that we do not fully understand and we cannot seem to solve. Such problems include, in the United States, the drug epidemic, poverty, pollution, crime, racism, and the threat of nuclear destruction. Technological change also brings ambiguities, partly because this kind of change is so rapid that few can understand and anticipate its repercussions. These problems and changes affect how people think about their experiences and surroundings. Juxtapositions of symbols, people, issues, policies, and actions are poorly understood, perhaps random. As possible interpretations multiply, and the discontinuities of change become transformed into ceaseless flux, ambiguities seem inescapable and pervasive.

Some scholars use the term *postmodernism* to characterize this view of contemporary society:

> Postmodernism is often represented by the anti-organic figure of pastiche, random accumulation, and mere contiguity. Thus [one emblem of postmodernism] is Los Angeles, the city of Angels and Dodgers, with its super-luxury multinationally financed megahotels rising on the plain of Spanish-speaking ghettos, the sprawling city of sentimentality and spectacle without center. Clearly, in such an arena—if this is the world of the future—any universal, totalizing theory may miss most of reality. (Gagnier, 1990, p. 23)

A world pervaded by ambiguity is not a world without pain. Just as the lack of a city center does not mean the absence of a ghetto for Spanish-speaking Los Angelinos, so life in contemporary industrialized societies entails suffering for many:

> This anarchy is not merely an intellectual matter. Families are torn by violence, cities plagued by crime and countries paralyzed by terrorism. (Taylor, 1987, p. 3)

Contemporary organizations can be seen as an analogue, on a small scale, of this description of Los Angeles. Many organizations lack a clear center. Organizational boundaries are often unclear, as temporary and part-time employees, contractors, and customers blur clear distinctions between insiders and outsiders. Personal ties among employees are often attentuated by physical or social distance. Even face-to-face interactions among organizational members are often fleeting and superficial. Many connections among employees can only be explained by sheer contiguity or random effects.

Technological innovations intensify these aspects of organizational life. For example, the connections that constitute an organizational subculture can be activated with the speed of a telephone call or a computer's parallel processor.

These same connections are often ephemeral, deactivated instantly as other issues and other individuals enter the foreground of attention. The speed of (dis)connection, the plethora of information and problems to be solved, and the difficulty of resolving any one issue for long—these complexities bring cognitive overload.

Demographic and international sources of diversity within organizations mean that contacts among employees are mediated by ethnic, racial, social, religious, and age differences, by geographical distance, and by other disjunctions of interest and experience that are only incompletely understood. In addition, some employees at the lowest levels of hierarchies (and their family and friends who may be unemployed) experience a material suffering that is incommensurable with the life experiences of higher-status executives. Taken together, these factors create an organizational world characterized by distance rather than closeness, obscurity rather than clarity, disorder rather than order, uncontrollability rather than predictability.

The Fragmentation perspective brings these sources of ambiguity to the foreground of a cultural description. Building on the complexities introduced by the nexus approach to understanding culture, Fragmentation studies see the boundaries of subcultures as permeable and fluctuating, in response to environmental changes in feeder cultures. The salience of particular subcultural memberships wax and wane, as issues surface, get resolved, or become forgotten in the flux of events. In this context, the manifestations of a culture must be multifaceted—their meanings hard to decipher and necessarily open to multiple interpretations. From the Fragmentation viewpoint, both the unity of Integration studies and the clearly defined differences of the Differentiation perspective seem to be myths of simplicity, order, and predictability, imposed on a socially constructed reality that is characterized by complexity, multiplicity, and flux. When culture is viewed from a Fragmentation viewpoint, the Integration and Differentiation perspectives seem to deepen confusion and misunderstanding by misrepresenting the complexities of living in an inescapably ambiguous world.

Like the other two perspectives, the Fragmentation viewpoint is not just an intellectual position. When researchers exclude ambiguity from the study of culture, they are making a moral judgment about the ambiguous aspects of contemporary life:

> Many anthropologists have a kind of temperamental preference for the simplicity, order, and predictability of less complicated societies, in which everyone knows what everyone else is supposed to do, and in which there is a "design for living." If you share that preference, then you can turn culture into an honorific term by denying it to those social arrangements which do not "deserve" it, thereby making a disguised moral judgment about those ways of life. But that leaves a good part of modern life . . . out of the culture sphere altogether. (Becker, 1982, p. 518)

From this point of view, if theory and research are to be relevant to problems of contemporary organizational life, the exclusion of ambiguity cannot be an option.

BEYOND EXCLUSION AND CHANNELING:
THE CENTRALITY OF AMBIGUITY

Some organizational researchers, such as Weick, Daft, Starbuck, and March and his colleagues, have long stressed the importance of ambiguity, although usually without a particular focus on culture. Weick lists various sources of organizational ambiguity that these researchers have explored:

> They include things like high mobility of people among positions, faulty memories, attempts to cope with overload by lowering the standards of acceptable performance, public compliance undercut by private deviation, sudden changes in authority or job descriptions, merging of odd product lines, and the like. (Weick, 1985, p. 117)

Fragmentation studies follow in this tradition, bringing ambiguity to the foreground of a cultural description. For example, textbook publishing has been described as a business riddled with ambiguity. According to Levitt and Nass, what makes a good textbook, why one succeeds and another fails, even what makes an editor have a successful career—all these critical factors are unclear:

> The editors consistently described their work in gambling terms, such as "a lottery with bad odds," "an attempt to hedge one's bets," or "a crapshoot." . . . The sense of confusion experienced by participants inhabiting this haphazard and unpredictable universe is captured in the following comment from a sociology editor: "Editors can become schizophrenic. You think a manuscript is good and it doesn't make money. Then you get a manuscript that you think is bad, and it makes money—but not always." (Levitt and Nass, 1989, pp. 191–192)

Social work has also been portrayed as an occupational culture permeated with ambiguity. According to Meyerson, there is no clear definition of what constitutes social work:

> Boundaries seem unclear because the occupation of social work includes a wide range of tasks and responsibilities, many of which are performed by members of other occupations. In a hospital, social work can include everything from concrete discharge planning—such as placing an individual in a nursing home—to less well-defined clinical work with patients and families. Yet nurses also plan discharges; psychologists counsel; and members of the clergy coordinate community resources. Thus, insiders, as well as outsiders, hold diffuse ideas about what social work is and about who is and is not a social worker. In addition, technologies seem ambiguous because what one does as a social worker (e.g., talk to clients) seems loosely related to what results (e.g., how clients behave). (Meyerson, 1991a, p. 136)

These social workers used metaphors to express the pervasiveness of ambiguities in their work lives. For example:

> One day I was feeling real scattered and I was trying to get a good image of what that meant for me. Tom said, "It sounds like you're trying to find a place to stand in the

middle of a kaleidoscope." And he just captured what I was feeling. (social worker, quoted in Meyerson, 1991a, p. 137)

Similarly, Feldman sees ambiguity as a central attribute of the work of policy analysts at the Department of Energy in Washington, D.C. In this cultural context, as in social work, metaphors were used to describe the experience:

Another claimed that he had "never really perceived the department as a thing or an entity. [It] is an amorphous collection of things—parts that fit together only in a rather rudimentary way and without an obvious sense of order." (policy analyst, quoted in Feldman, 1983b, p. 229)

According to these researchers, no adequate cultural description of textbook publishing, social work, or policy analysis could exclude ambiguity. However, to include ambiguity requires a new approach to thinking about culture.

DEFINING AMBIGUITY

Before this new approach can be described, some clear definitions of ambiguous phenomena are needed. Ambiguity is subjectively perceived; its meaning is interpreted.[2] Something is judged to be ambiguous because it seems to be unclear, highly complex, or paradoxical. A lack of clarity occurs because something seems obscure or indistinct, and therefore hard to decipher. Silences and absences can also create a lack of clarity. Something is highly complex because a plethora of elements and relationships makes it difficult to comprehend in any simple way. Both a lack of clarity and high complexity can sometimes be resolved with more information or a fresh insight, making the ambiguity disappear. Paradoxes are not so easily resolved. A paradox is an argument that apparently derives contradictory conclusions by valid deduction from acceptable premises.[3] *Ambiguity is perceived when a lack of clarity, high complexity, or a paradox makes multiple (rather than single or dichotomous) explanations plausible.*

It is helpful to distinguish these three aspects of ambiguity (lack of clarity, complexity, and paradox) from external sources of and internal reactions to ambiguity. External sources of ambiguity stem from conditions external to the person perceiving the ambiguity. For example, uncertainties in an organization's environment, such as an unexpected environmental "jolt," can cause the perception of ambiguity. Structural variables can also be an external source of perceived ambiguity, as when an organization's technical core is loosely coupled with the facade it presents to the outside world.

Such external sources of ambiguity should be distinguished from the various internal reactions people can have to ambiguity. These internal reactions range from disgust and antipathy (because many individuals do not tolerate ambiguity well) to joy and elation. Internal reactions to ambiguity, then, can be negative (e.g., a reaction of debilitating confusion or action paralysis) or positive (e.g., a reaction of feeling free of unhelpful constraints or able to innovate).

INTRODUCTION TO FRAGMENTATION: MODES OF THINKING

These definitions of ambiguity raise several questions: How is it, or is it, possible to think about multiple interpretations in a manner that is different from the oppositional modes of thinking characteristic of the Differentiation perspective? Furthermore, if there is a different mode of thinking characteristic of the Fragmentation perspective, what use is it? That is, what new kinds of understandings can emerge from this mode of thinking that would be, in a sense, "unthinkable" from the other two perspectives?

These questions must be answered in order to understand how Fragmentation studies conceptualize variations on the themes of consistency and consensus. Some of the more thoughtful answers come from postmodernism, an intellectual movement that was developed by philosophers, literary critics, feminist theorists, and anthropologists, among others. Particularly in the United States, postmodernism is controversial because it challenges the widely held assumption that theory and research can increase knowledge by bringing us closer to understanding objective truth. Most Fragmentation studies do not adopt a postmodern framework, although those that do offer insights inaccessible to those who rely on more traditional approaches.[4] Because the postmodern approach is fundamentally incommensurable with the assumptions of most of the research reviewed in this book, the implications of postmodernism will be discussed separately, in Chapter 10. *The few postmodern ideas introduced in this chapter can be understood and utilized without making postmodernism a necessary foundation for working within the Fragmentation perspective.*

Shortcomings of Oppositional Thinking

Before describing alternatives, it is important to understand why these alternatives are needed. In other words, what is wrong with the oppositional modes of thinking, such as dichotomies, that are used in Differentiation research? Studies conducted from a Differentiation viewpoint use oppositional thinking to distinguish subcultures, such as labor versus management, support versus professional staff, men versus women, blacks versus whites. Usually, subcultures represent ends of a dichotomy, and one of these dichotomous alternatives is viewed as having a higher status than the other. This emphasis on superior-subordinate relations may not be simply a reflection of how organizations are structured; some scholars argue that any kind of dichotomous thinking is inevitably hierarchical:

> Thus, whites rule Blacks, males dominate females, reason is touted as superior to emotion in ascertaining truth, facts supersede opinion in evaluating knowledge, and subjects rule objects. Dichotomous oppositional differences invariably imply relationships of superiority and inferiority, hierarchical relationships that mesh with political economies of domination and subordination. (Collins, 1986, p. 520)

One problem with dichotomous thinking is that it oversimplifies and misrepresents the attributes and viewpoints of members of lower status groups. When differences between groups are defined using dichotomies or other forms of oppositional thinking (as detailed in Chapter 6), the terms of these definitions are usually based on the characteristics and viewpoints of the dominant group; the attributes of the subordinated groups are considered only when they are different from the dominant group on these particular dimensions:

> For example, the terms in dichotomies such as black/white, male/female, reason/ emotion, fact/opinion, and subject/object gain their meaning only in relation to their difference from their oppositional counterparts. (Collins, 1986, p. 520)

An example may demonstrate the importance of these observations. When oppositional thinking is used to discuss racial differences in organizations, what it means to be black in a given organizational context has meaning only in so far as being black is seen as being not-white. Racial differences are assessed within an established hierarchical system that begins with dimensions of comparison relevant to the dominant group. Thus, not surprisingly, on these dimensions whites are seen as having more status and greater value than blacks. In this kind of oppositional thinking, attributes of the subordinated group that are unique to that group, and might be valued differently, fall outside the established hierarchy reified by the dichotomy and are ignored:

> Thus difference has always been construed and perceived through a set of binary oppositions that leaves no room for an authentic difference set outside of the established system. (Feral, 1985, p. 89)

Furthermore, dichotomies do not consider similarities or "mixed" attributes that fall "in between" polar opposites. The result is that oppositional thinking does not value diversity—in all its complexity. To continue with the racial example, black versus white is a dichotomous racial classification that does not capture the mixed racial backgrounds of many people. To complicate matters further, it is essential to recognize that not all members of a particular group react to their racial identities in the same way or have similar experiences. Class and gender differences among blacks, for example, challenge assumptions of homogeneity within a group of blacks. For example, the reactions of a black woman raised in poverty in the south, first in her family to earn a college degree, may well have little similarity to the responses of a college-educated black man raised in a prosperous suburb. As these examples indicate, when oppositional thinking is applied to the relationship between subcultures, vital concerns of subordinated groups are omitted and variations within both groups are ignored.

Often, the pernicious effects of these exclusions are invisible to members of a dominant group. For example, white men used to working primarily with other white men, may come to believe that they are working in a sexually or racially neutral world, rather than a world where white men dominate. Thus, when women are not present, gender is often not perceived as relevant—as if women have a gender, but men do not.[5] Similarly, many whites are blind to the advantages given to them by their race, as if they lived in a racially neutral world except in situations when blacks are present—as if blacks have a race, but whites do not.[6]

Perhaps for this reason, organizational research often does not mention women, blacks, or other members of subordinated groups. They are notable by their absence or, if present, by their silence. Differentiation studies are more likely than Integration studies to focus on members of subordinated groups. However, even Differentiation studies sometimes do not report how members of subordinated groups react to the actions of dominant group members. For example, in their bakery study, Bartunek and Moch drew attention to a "Kotex" joke told by white male machinists, reporting that "those listening . . . would nod and smile in approval." Were these listeners men? Were the women unaware of the joke or did they have a reaction that is not reported? What thoughts did the black bakery employees have when their gathering place was remodeled, by these same white machinists, into a non-smoking area for all employees? In a second example, at the advertising agency discussed in Chapter 6, there was no dress code for women "business" employees, presumably because most of these employees were men. Even in Differentiation studies that are sensitive to race and gender, silences, omissions, and absences are often the only traces of members of these subordinated groups.

Not all lower-status groups, of course, are demographic minorities. At OZCO, for example, marketing had less status than engineering. Unlike many demographic subcultures, however, members of both these groups were outspoken about their differences, perhaps because both had managerial or professional status. In contrast, members of other lower-status subcultures, such as clerical workers, cleaning crews, and assembly-line workers, were much less willing to articulate their feelings about the company, in part (they said) because they feared they would lose their jobs. In addition, much of what members of these lower-status groups did have to say was not relevant to the three themes used to structure the presentation of the OZCO material. Their concerns, in contrast, were multiple and not just simply the opposite of the concerns expressed in the Integration and Differentiation views of this company.

The focus of the OZCO case on three themes that were spoken about from all three perspectives meant that many of the concerns of lower-status groups were excluded from this cultural analysis. In this sense, the three-theme, three-perspective focus of the OZCO case is itself an example of the way oppositional thinking excludes and silences the voices of those at the bottom of an organizational hierarchy. These shortcomings are not inherent in the Fragmentation perspective itself, simply in the way it was operationalized in the Fragmentation view of OZCO, with only one matrix and only three, oppositional themes.

As the research quoted in this chapter illustrates, a Fragmentation study need not, and should not, rely on oppositional modes of thinking about difference. What then are the alternatives? We need to conceptualize difference in a way that legitimates it, does not reduce it to opposition, and does not include only those dimensions of comparison salient to a dominant group. We also need a means of detecting viewpoints that have been silenced. For example, how can we find traces of women and blacks in ostensibly gender- and race-neutral theory and research that mention neither? How can we find traces of the views of blue-collar and clerical employees in studies that report only managerial points of view? In more general terms, how can we study culture in ways that retain sensitivity to differences within oppositionally defined groups? Postmodernism suggests resolutions to these problems.

Differance: Difference Without Opposition

It is difficult to imagine writing or speaking without employing binary oppositions, as these are inherent in language itself. Derrida, one of the founders of postmodernism, seeks to undermine and subvert oppositional ways of thinking about difference by examining "differance." (Derrida spelled this word with an *a* to differentiate it from *difference* in French. It can be translated as both "difference" and "deferral" in English.) Differance is a mode of thinking that allows for the fact that there is only one way to be the same, while there are many ways to be dissimilar. When dissimilarities are framed as binary oppositions, analysis can reveal how these oppositions undercut and destabilize each other.

Differance is a difficult concept. It is a context-sensitive approach to examining differences in interpretation. Moi, a literary critic, introduces the idea by focusing on the process of deciphering the meanings of language. She starts with

> Saussure's concept of the *phoneme,* defined as the smallest differential—and therefore signifying—unit in language. The phoneme can in no way be said to achieve signification through binary opposition alone. In itself the phoneme /b/ does not signify anything at all. . . . /b/ only signifies in so far as it is perceived to be *different* from say /k/ or /h/. Thus /bat/:/kat/:/hat/ are all perceived to be different words with different meanings in English. The argument is that /b/ signifies only though a process that effectively *defers* its meaning on to other differential elements in language. In a sense it is the *other* phonemes that enable us to determine the meaning of /b/. (Moi, 1985, p. 106)

To restate Moi's ideas in the context of cultural studies, a cultural manifestation, like a ritual, cannot be understood out of the context in which it is enacted, perceived, and interpreted. It also cannot be understood without taking into consideration the position and history of the individuals doing the enacting, perceiving, and interpreting. Thus when two cultural members agree (or disagree) on a particular interpretation of, say, a ritual, this is likely to be a temporary and issue-specific congruence (or incongruence). It may well not reflect agreement or disagreement on other issues, at other times. Subcultures, then, are reconceptualized as fleeting, issue-specific coalitions that may or may not have a similar configuration in the future. This is not simply a failure to achieve subcultural consensus in a particular context; from the Fragmentation perspective, this is the most consensus possible in any context.

Furthermore, any judgment about agreement or disagreement must involve a context-dependent comparison to other issues, times, and individuals. Any individual's judgment cannot be understood out of the context of other interpretations of other manifestations by other individuals at other times. Judgments about what is similar, and what is not, are therefore endlessly deferred; consistency and consensus never rest, as an objective truth, in the relationship between any two manifestations or the degree of agreement between any two individuals. Something is the same or different only in relation to the context which surrounds it, as the consonants surround the phoneme in Moi's example.

Differance also stresses that the categories used in oppositional thinking are subjectively perceived and socially constructed. The boundaries between and contents of a category emerge in a context. Because contexts change, these categories can and should be endlessly disputed.[7] For example, the placement of boundaries between and contents within a subculture is never fixed. It is and should be continually debated. Such a debate cannot be taken out of a larger context, as subcultural boundaries have meaning only in so far as one subculture is perceived as being different from other possible alternatives. Thus, no cultural manifestation, no interpretation, and no subcultural configuration can be studied in isolation. *Differance allows for the complexity, multiplicity, and flux that are the hallmarks of the Fragmentation perspective, overcoming many of the shortcomings of more simplified, oppositional modes of thinking.*

From Modes of Thinking to Methods of Analysis: "Reading" Silences

Differance is a useful mode of thinking because it reveals understandings that would be excluded or ignored by the patterns of thought characteristic of the Integration and Differentiation perspectives. *Differance implies that meaning emerges from a process of deferral. Therefore, something is understood in a certain way because of what it (apparently) is not. Presence is understood, in part, by an analysis of what is absent.*

The usefulness of these ideas may be clarified by an analogy. Those who appreciate Japanese gardens study the space around a rock, for example, as much as the shape and texture of the rock itself. The space, as well as the rock, is to be "read." Thus, in a study of cultures in organizations, meaning is to be read in absences as well as presences. For instance, many organizations have a prodigal son story concerning a high-ranking executive who left the organization under some kind of cloud, but was later welcomed back and forgiven. At General Motors (GM), there are no prodigal son stories, presumably because executives who leave the organization are seldom, if ever, welcomed back.[8]

Whereas the absence of a prodigal son story has been noted in studies of GM, the possibility of a prodigal daughter is never mentioned. To understand this absence requires reference to a larger context. Both occupations and domestic life tend to have gender-segregated roles. It is likely that few women at GM have held an executive job with sufficiently high rank to qualify for the prodigal role. And if a woman did attain this role and then ran into trouble, it is not clear that her transgressions would be interpreted or forgiven in the same ways as the actions of a man in the same position. A study of the stories that people do not tell reveals aspects of a cultural context that would not be made visible in a study of stories they do tell.

This way of analyzing the absence of a prodigal son/daughter story begins to illustrate how a Fragmentation study might examine meanings:

The interplay between presence and absence that produces meaning is posited as one of *deferral:* meaning is never truly present, but is only constructed through the potentially endless process of referring to other, absent signifiers. The "next" signifier can in a sense be said to give meaning to the "previous" one, and so on *ad infinitum.* There can thus be no transcendental signified where the process of deferral somehow would come to an end. (Moi, 1985, p. 106)

In this way, the postmodern approach challenges all claims to have found a single objective "truth" that transcends all other interpretations.

If meanings lie in absences, and multiple interpretations can be made, how is a researcher to proceed? Integration and Differentiation studies exclude or channel ambiguity from the domain that is labeled culture, in effect excluding from analysis all that which cannot be explained. Yet

how could we ever discover the nature of the ideology that surrounds us if it were entirely consistent, without the slightest contradiction, gap or fissure that might allow us to perceive it in the first place? (Moi, 1985, p. 124)

Only a definition of culture as fragmented—marked by gaps, slides, and silences—would enable cultural theory to explain how even the most homogeneous cultures generate their own lacunae.[9] Eagleton makes a similar point, speaking of Macherey's view of textual analysis:

It is in the significant *silences* of a text, in its gaps and absences that the presence of ideology can be most positively felt. . . . The text is, as it were, ideologically forbidden to say certain things; in trying to tell the truth in his own way, for example, the author finds himself forced to reveal the limits of the ideology within which he writes. He is forced to reveal its gaps and silences, what it is unable to articulate. Because a text contains these gaps and silences, it is always *incomplete.* Far from constituting a rounded, coherent whole, it displays a conflict and contradiction of meanings; and the significance of the work lies in the difference rather than the unity between these meanings. (Eagleton, 1976, pp. 34–35, quoted in Moi, 1985, p. 94)

The problem then is how to "read" gaps, slides, and silences.

An example may help address this problem and also clarify the difference between a Differentiation and a Fragmentation analysis. A picture was engraved on the Pioneer spacecraft. The image showed a nude man and woman, with the man's arm raised in greeting. Anderson analyzed this image by offering two dichotomous interpretations of the raised arm: it could mean goodbye or hello. In a subsequent analysis of the same image, Owens offered other possible interpretations, including

the same gesture could also mean "Halt!" or represent the taking of an oath, but if Anderson's text does not consider these two alternatives that is because it is not concerned with ambiguity, with multiple meanings engendered by a single sign; rather two *clearly defined but mutually incompatible* readings are engaged in blind confrontation in such a way that it is impossible to choose between them. (Owens, 1983, p. 60)

Owens castigated himself for initially not noticing other interpretations:

I had overlooked something—something that is so obvious, so "natural" that it may at the time have seemed unworthy of comment. It does not seem that way to me today. For this is, of course, an image of sexual difference, or, rather, of sexual differentiation. . . . For in this . . . image, chosen to represent the inhabitants of the Earth for the extraterrestrial Other, it is the man who speaks, who represents mankind. The woman is only represented; she is (as always) already spoken for. (Owens, 1983, pp. 60, 61)

The first interpretation of this image, by Anderson, offers two opposing interpretations (hello and goodbye). This is the oppositional thinking characteristic of a Differentiation viewpoint. In the second analysis, Owens draws attention to the complexity of a seemingly simple image and delineates a variety of ways its message could be interpreted. He also notes an absence: the woman does not raise her hand in greeting, as the man does. In this analysis, Owens is working from a Fragmentation perspective, seeing a cultural manifestation as ambiguous and offering multiple interpretations of its meaning. Owens's analysis also illustrates the dynamics of power working through silence (in this case, about gender). Differance is not purely a cognitive strategy for analysis; it reveals the power inequalities implicit in absences, the suppressed ideology that slips "between the lines" of a text or drawing.

To summarize, a Fragmentation study uses analysis of differance to explore multiple meanings, paying attention to absence as well as presence. This is a mode of thinking that is particularly useful for understanding variation within groups and revealing the ways contexts influence interpretations. Although this section of the Fragmentation chapter has relied primarily on gender and race as examples, most Fragmentation studies do not focus on these particular group identities. However, when within group variation, contextual determinants of behavior and absences are seen as important sources of understanding, the silenced voices of demographic minorities are more likely to be heard.

The next section of this chapter describes how Fragmentation studies utilize versions of this mode of thinking about differance to bring ambiguity to the forefront of a cultural analysis, reconceptualizing what is meant by the absence of consistency and consensus.

BEYOND CONSISTENCY AND INCONSISTENCY TO COMPLEXITY

Integration studies describe the relationship between one cultural manifestation and another as consistent. Differentiation studies describe these relationships as clearly inconsistent; the interpretation of one manifestation directly contradicts the interpretation of another. Fragmentation studies move beyond clear consistencies or clear inconsistencies to reconceptualize these relationships in multivalent terms, as partially congruent, partially incongruent, and partially related by tangential, perhaps random connections. In some Fragmentation studies, this reconceptualization of (in)consistency includes a rudimentary exploration of differance. For example, one of Meyerson's social workers saw her work in shades of gray, rather than in the black and white oppositions favored by the Differentiation perspective:

> When they [other social workers] come to me for a simple, clear solution, I tell them: "Life is grey. If you want black and white go to Macy's. Black and white are in this year." (social worker, quoted in Meyerson, 1991a, p. 138)

This next section of this chapter traces patterns of differance across and down matrices. Rather than seeing relationships among cultural manifestations as either consistent or inconsistent, the relationships appear, from a Fragmentation perspective, to be unclear and multivalent. Three kinds of relationships are examined here. On a matrix these would appear horizontally between themes and practices (action ambiguity), horizontally between themes and cultural forms (symbolic ambiguity), and vertically among content themes (ideological ambiguity).

Action Ambiguity

Fragmentation studies often begin with an idealized vision of how things ought to be. These themes are then shown to bear an unclear relationship to observed practices. For example, some OZCO employees were confused about the relationship between the company's espoused values regarding employee well-being and its formal benefits policies. Sometimes this confusion arose simply because particular employees were ignorant of the relevant policies, as when the personnel director could not answer a question about spousal relocation benefits. And sometimes confusion arose because the policies themselves were so complex. Whether the relationship between espoused values and practices was unclear because of complexity or lack of information, these OZCO employees reacted with confusion and sometimes action paralysis: they simply did not know what to do.

Action ambiguity was also observed at the Department of Energy:

> Analysts are supposed to analyze relatively well defined problems and produce solutions that can be implemented by politicians (Feldman, 1989). . . . [But] analyses do not lead to positions that are promoted through politics. Analyses do not even support positions chosen by politicians. Analyses are being produced, but it is not clear for what or for whom. (Feldman, 1991, pp. 154–155)

This description of analysts' decision making bears some resemblance to the "garbage can" model of decision making. Cohen, March, and Olsen describe this model in terms of streams of loosely coupled problems, decision makers, choice opportunities, and "solutions" entering (and leaving) the organizational context according to a temporal, rather than a rational-causal logic.[10] Some problems attract others, some choice opportunities never happen, some decision makers enter or leave the decision making context, and some "solutions" get attached to new problems, while others go unheeded.

Organizations where garbage can decision making is the norm have been labeled *organized anarchies*.[11] In these organizations, confusion and paradox are the rule, rather than the exception. Patterns of connection are diffuse, membership and participation in decision making is fluid, and coordination is hard to come by. When it does occur, it does so often on one level (perhaps agreement on a policy), but not on another (how to implement that policy or why that policy is desirable).[12]

The U.S. military has been described as an organized anarchy. The U.S. military bureaucracy includes the Department of Defense, the Office of the Secretary of Defense, the Joint Chiefs of Staff, and the various arms of the military. Although the government appointees and military officers in charge do what they can to see that decisions are made in a structured, "rational" manner,

> information still becomes lost in the system, directed to the wrong people, or both. Similarly, during a crisis, the wrong people may try to solve a problem because of their prowess at bureaucratic gamesmanship, or the right people (because of mismanagement or oversight) may be overlooked or sent elsewhere. (Sabrosky, Thompson, and McPherson, 1982, p. 142)

When decision-making practices differ so profoundly from the rhetoric about how such decisions are supposed to occur, the rhetoric provides no guide for action and and so patterns of response have to be developed.

Weick provides a listing of these kinds of reactions to action ambiguity:

> A loosely coupled system is a problem in causal inference. For actors and observers alike, the prediction and activation of cause-effect relations is made more difficult because relations are intermittent, lagged, dampened, slow, abrupt, and mediated. Actors in a loosely coupled system rely on trust and presumptions, are often isolated, find social comparison difficult, have no one to borrow from, seldom imitate, suffer pluralistic ignorance, maintain discretion, improvise, and have less hubris because they know the universe is not sufficiently connected to make widespread change possible. (Weick, 1979a, p. 122)

It is worthwhile to contrast Weick's description, written from a Fragmentation view, with the clear inconsistencies of Meyer and Rowan's discussion of loose coupling in school systems. Where Weick sees ambiguity, Meyer and Rowan describe clear inconsistencies between the school's formal practices (visible to the external constituencies of the school) and the informal practices of the teachers in the classrooms. Meyer and Rowan's teachers know what do do and loose coupling simply buffers them from outside interference. In Weick's description, actors are more confused about what they should do and what effect their actions will have and loose coupling makes everything more difficult to figure out.

A Fragmentation study seldom offers clear and comforting prescriptions for action. When an organizational situation is ambiguous, it is difficult to know if action is called for, which actions would be inappropriate, and what their consequences might be. The frequent result is inaction.[13]

Fragmentation studies that focus on action ambiguity often assume that the experience of ambiguity is noxious. This can be seen, for example, in the descriptions of OZCO in Chapter 7 and in parts of the studies of the military and the Department of Energy, described earlier. A negative reaction to ambiguity is also evident in Weick's study of the factors that complicated decision making one night at the Tenerife airport. The fog was exceptionally thick, one flight crew (due to flight time regulations) was in a rush, and it was very difficult to turn around large airplanes (like the two KLM and Pan American 747 jets waiting for instructions) on the small runways. In addition,

> controllers at Tenerife were also under pressure because they were shorthanded, they did not often handle 747's, they had no ground radar, the centerline lights on the runway were not operating, they were working in English which was a less familiar second language, and their normal routines for routing planes on a takeoff and landing were disrupted because they had planes parked in areas they would normally use to execute these routines. (Weick, 1991, p. 122)

The stress on both controllers and flight crews was severe that night, amplifying the ambiguity they perceived:

> As stress increases perception narrows, more contextual information is lost, and parameters deteriorate to more extreme levels before they are noticed, all of which leads to more puzzlement, less meaning, and more perceived complexity. (Weick, 1991, p. 129)

The Fragmentation studies quoted in this section, including Weick's study of Tenerife, echo Katz and Kahn's assumption that ambiguity is noxious and potentially a threat to effective performance:

> Such research began with the assumption that ambiguity frustrates the human need for clarity and structure in the environment, accordingly regarded it as a stressor, and sought evidence of resulting strain and performance decrement. (Katz and Kahn, 1978, p. 206, quoted in Meyerson, 1989, p. 2)

Ambiguity can also be reacted to with neutrality, as an unavoidable aspect of organizational life that is tolerable, not dangerous, and only moderately stressful. For example, the textbook editors and social workers studied by Levitt and Nass were generally very aware of the ambiguity that pervaded their working lives, but relatively few expressed strong negative reactions to it.

There is a final possible reaction that is virtually absent in these Fragmentation accounts: ambiguity could be embraced with joy. A social worker came closest to this perspective:

> The social worker is really like the bastard who could go in anywhere. The social worker gets in between them all and can do it all. That's one of the advantages. It's certainly not a limitation. It is a flexibility that is phenomenal. (social worker, quoted in Meyerson, 1991a, p. 142)

Although few of Feldman's policy analysts expressed the unmitigated enthusiasm of the social worker quoted above, one analyst did acknowledge the possibility of joy in ambiguity, describing the Department of Energy as "a vehicle that can be ridden for awhile with great joy." He went on to say that the vehicle could also just "be endured. One would hope it's a vehicle that can be steered—though a lot of able people have dashed their hopes on that one." (policy analyst, quoted in Feldman, 1991, pp. 150-151)

In contrast to this analyst's half-hearted observations about joy, other scholars seem to revel in ambiguity. For example, Barthes advocates taking joy in ambiguity:

Imagine someone . . . who abolishes within himself all barriers, all classes, all exclusions, not by syncretism but by simple discard of that old specter: *logical contradiction;* who mixes every language, even those said to be incompatible; who silently accepts every charge of illogicality, of incongruity. (Barthes, 1975, p. 3)

Imagine a cultural description focused on paradoxes, grounded in the idea that "the center does not hold," that things are neither consistent nor inconsistent, that it is not even clear what consistency would mean in a world so confusing that oppositions, congruencies, and orthogonalities cannot be deciphered. Few Fragmentation studies of culture revel in ambiguity with this kind of enthusiasm, but they could do so—perhaps capturing a previously unexplored aspect of life in organizations.

Symbolic Ambiguity

From a Fragmentation point of view, there are no clearly consistent or clearly inconsistent relationships between themes and cultural forms (such as physical arrangements, jokes, and organizational stories). At OZCO, for example, egalitarian values seemed to bear no clear relationship to the physical arrangements of the open office plan; some effects of these arrangements were apparently egalitarian, others seemed inegalitarian, and still other effects were difficult to decipher. Physical arrangements[14] also seemed to bear an unclear relationship to espoused egalitarian values in Tom's study of the Women's Bank in New York City:

Of the trainers, only Elaine has an office of her own. . . . All other trainers and trainees work in open areas. Some trainees are assigned desks of their own when their jobs require that they have a permanent work place. Many trainees do not actually belong in any one place at all but must sit where they can find a place close to the task they are performing. All trainers have desks of their own, usually somewhat larger than the trainees' desks. In general, the assignment of space is confused and fluid. People often lose things that they leave sitting in a space they had carved out for themselves when someone else appropriates the space. People use others' desks when they are vacant, and it is not uncommon for Elaine to be forced to vacate her office. (Tom, 1986, pp. 58, 62)

In this discussion, acknowledgment of ambiguity does not prevent the dynamics of status differences from surfacing. However, differences between groups do not appear as clear cut or as static as in a Differentiation account.

Some Fragmentation studies interpret cultural forms in terms that show awareness of and ambivalence toward paradox. For example, according to Meyerson, social workers found cynical humor a helpful response to unresolvable dilemmas:

> Cynicism defused the felt ambiguity that erupted from seemingly unsolvable problems (e.g., when a patient refuses to cooperate with his rehabilitation), from irreconcilable differences (e.g., when the attending physician ignores seemingly essential emotional factors), and most frequently from situations in which social workers lacked the clarity or authority to take action (e.g., when they are faced with incomprehensible "red tape"). By acknowledging and suspending the ambiguity with a cynical remark, the cynic enabled the conversation to proceed without premature closure: allowing unsolvables, irreconcilables, and untenables to remain unresolved. (Meyerson, 1991a, p. 141)

There is a striking contrast between this cynical ambiguity acknowledgment and the clear hostility between groups reflected in the "Kotex" and "egg in the hard hat" jokes in Differentiation studies.

A similar cynicism was found in some of the self-deprecating jokes told by traders working in the chaos of Wall Street investment banking firms:

> What's the difference between a Wall Streeter and a pig? Not even a pig would stoop so low. What's the difference between a bond and a bond trader? A bond matures. Did you hear about the new Drexel bond? The maturity is twenty to life. (Abolafia, 1989, p. 14)

These jokes involve a play on difference that has echoes of differance. They are funny because of the similarities (e.g., between a greedy Wall Street trader and an omnivorous pig), as well as the differences between the two concepts in each joke. The fact that this similarity is not mentioned sets up awareness of other silences (e.g., A bond gets more worthwhile as it ages—does a trader? A greedy pig makes better eating, etc.). These jokes are popular, in part, because their silences reverberate; the cumulation of unspoken similarities and differences between the two juxtaposed concepts ultimately leaves each intact and unclassifiable: neither the same or different.

Organizational stories provide particularly rich data for this kind of analysis. The Fragmentation view starts from the premise that a story has multiple meanings:

> We can also see how the very same surface reality may embody many different meanings, some of which may be complementary and others contradictory, as when an action signifying genuine friendship on one occasion may on another be hollow and perfunctory, and on yet another, be used as a manipulative ploy. (Morgan, 1983, p. 388)

> *All* meaning is contextual. . . . A text can be taken to have any number of contexts. Inscribing a specific context for a text does not *close* or *fix* the meaning of that text once and for all: there is always the possibility of reinscribing it within other contexts. (Moi, 1985, p. 155)

For example, when the "Rule Breaking" story recounted in Chapter 4 is regarded from the Fragmentation perspective, the meanings of this story can vary, depending on the context in which the story was told, who was telling it, the audience listening, and so on.[15] One person might conclude the boss in this story was admirably obeying the rules; another might say he was self-consciously setting an example. A third might wonder why he sent someone else back for the badge he had forgotten rather than getting it himself.

The silences in this story are also eloquent. For example, the story is worth telling only because of an unstated assumption that most top executives don't obey company rules. In addition, the story is silent about gender differences. The story recounts the shock experienced by the men observing the confrontation between the low-ranking woman and her male boss. Why is the story silent about the woman's reaction to the situation? Would the story have the same shock value if a man, holding the subordinate position, challenged the boss? Why, in so many versions of this story, is the woman described as short and lightweight? Why is the boss never a woman? The absence and presence of such "unnecessary" details suggest a deeper, silenced level of meaning in this story.

A Fragmentation analysis can also illuminate reactions to the "Caesarean" story (recounted in full in Chapter 3) told by the president of OZCO. When he was asked what OZCO was doing to "help" women employees with children, the president said:

> We have a young woman who is extraordinarily important to the launching of a major new [product]. We will be talking about it next Tuesday in its first worldwide introduction. She has arranged to have her Caesarean [operation] yesterday in order to be prepared for this event. (Martin, 1990, p. 139)

A Differentiation analysis of this story would examine what the story says, focusing on the inconsistency between the president's claims to be helping women, in accord with OZCO's commitment to employee well-being, and the fact that this woman is being praised for altering the timing of her Caesarean operation to fit OZCO's product introduction schedule, rather than the baby's maturational needs. Rather than "helping" the woman and her baby, a Differentiation analysis would conclude that the company is helping itself at the woman's and baby's expense.

A Fragmentation analysis of this story would not disagree with the points raised by the Differentiation analysis above, but it would go deeper. A Fragmentation analysis would focus on multiple interpretations of the story's language—including what is not said. Martin used deconstruction (a postmodern analytic strategy for systematically examining texts) to analyze the Caesarean story.[16] This deconstruction focused on the connotations of metaphors and puns, as well the implications of silences, revealing unstated assumptions and sexual taboos implicit in the story's language. For example, the first phrase in the story, "we have a young woman," could have been restated as "we employ a young woman." The choice of the verb "have" in this sentence implies an extraordinary degree of corporate control, in excess of the rights and duties inherent in the usual employment contract. The phrase "having a young woman" also is a sexual pun which has male heterosexual connotations that are repeated in other sexual puns throughout the story.

In a subsequent part of this Fragmentation analysis, Martin revealed hidden assumptions of the story by examining the effects of two small changes in the text. Instead of a woman undergoing a Caesarean birth, the central character was rewritten to be a man undergoing a coronary bypass operation. This small change had massive ramifications. The story's structure, its use of metaphor, and the nature of its sexual puns, no longer "made sense"; the hidden workings of gender-biased ideology were revealed.

As these examples indicate, when the language in this story (its unstated assumptions, silences, metaphors, puns, etc.) is deconstructed, we can read "between the lines," finding traces of what has been suppressed by a dominant ideology. The workings of power and the interests of members of relatively powerless groups (in this story, a woman) can be exposed in this kind of Fragmentation study.

As illustrated in this analysis of the Caesarean story, a Fragmentation study offers a highly complex portrait of the relationship between espoused values and the multiple meanings inherent in a cultural form. In some Fragmentation studies, the relationship between espoused values and cultural forms is attenuated even further, so that these two types of cultural manifestation become decoupled and the forms loose their meaning. For example, Schultz describes how forms have become

> a hard and repetitious outward show without any underlying system of meaning. The rituals, stories, metaphors, etc. of the culture appear isolated from the fragments of meaning created by the members of the organization. . . . The same basic values are repeated perpetually: In speeches and annual reports, advertisements for recruiting staff, press releases and manuals for the personnel, on ceremonial occasions, speeches of thanks and appointments. . . . The same stories are told perpetually: In the canteen to new members of the staff, in nostalgic moments while drinking coffee in the afternoon. (Schultz, in press)

According to Schultz, these meaningless slogans, endlessly repeated stories, and empty rituals are perpetuated, carrying a seductive promise that is never fulfilled.

Fragmentation studies offer a complicated view of the relationship between content themes and cultural forms. Sometimes this relationship is hard to decipher because it is obscure or indistinct. In other instances, the relationship is difficult to comprehend because of the complexity of relevant factors. In still other cases, hidden traces of the suppressed interests of members of subordinated groups complicate interpretation, or empty cultural forms are perpetuated even though they have become decoupled from their meanings. From the Fragmentation viewpoint, symbolic interpretation is not simple.

Ideological Ambiguity

Given the ambiguities discussed above, it should be no surprise that Fragmentation studies also see ambiguity in the relationships among content themes. In accord with this point of view, March has long argued that tastes, values, and preferences are seldom clearly consistent or inconsistent with each other. For example:

> Choices are often made without respect to tastes. Human decision makers routinely ignore their own, fully conscious, preferences in making decisions. They follow rules, traditions, hunches, and the advice or actions of others. Tastes change over time in such a way that predicting future tastes is often difficult. (March, 1978, p. 596)

If content themes operate like March's description of tastes or values, cultural perceptions should not be organized in any way that would be recognized by the consistency-seeking Integration study or the inconsistency-seeking Differentiation study.

In a Fragmentation study of cultures in organizations, themes do not provide a clarifying ideology. Instead, ideology is as ambiguous as other aspects of working life. For example, the female management of the Women's Bank attempted to provide benefits for women from all class backgrounds by instituting a bank teller training program for mothers who had previously been receiving welfare payments. The management staff who served as trainers in this program saw the trainees as immature and ungrateful, with poor working habits and inadequate mothering skills. These complications created unresolvable ideological tensions for the trainers:

> They speak vaguely of equal opportunity for women, building women's financial "presence" and sophistication, and offering a "chance" to trainees. This vaguely-felt sense of purpose offers the trainers little defense when faced with some of the contradictions of their organization—such as explaining the Bank's refusal to grant joint checking accounts to women and their husbands when some of them prefer such accounts and go to another bank to get them. (Tom, 1986, p. 93)

In Tom's study, both trainers and trainees encountered tensions that ideology did not help them resolve.

Meyerson reported that social workers also experienced ideological ambiguity. For example:

> One social worker mentioned that being "the elbow in the system's side" was her professional responsibility. Others viewed themselves as the patient's advocate. However, because social workers work in organizations in which they have little formal power, they must comply with and even become exemplars of the system to gain legitimacy. Some admitted that their job was to uphold, even "grease" the system. . . . Thus, although some social workers believed that their role was to change or resist the status quo, they also believed that to be effective they must work within and thereby perpetuate the status quo. Social workers must simultaneously advance reforms and preclude them, critique the medical model and enforce it. (Meyerson, 1991a, p. 140)

This is a paradox—an ambiguity that is unlikely to be resolved, once and for all, by a fresh insight or more information.

When a Fragmentation study moves beyond consistency and inconsistency it sometimes encounters a type of paradox that is a logical "dead end." Such a paradox (sometimes called an *aporia*) exposes a system riddled with irreconcilable ideological difficulties. For example, organizational behavior professors (like myself) are often horrified at the ways students demand simple, unambiguously "correct" answers to the complex problems of management:

> It was then suggested to the student that for managers to be decisive in the manner being advocated there had to be an assumption that the managers concerned actually knew what to do. This was received with a cry from another student of, "Managers are paid to know what to do," followed by an aside from a further student of, "It's your job to teach us." . . . This seemed to reflect a rather worrying conceptualisation of management as, being-told-what-to-do. (Golding, 1987, p. 3)

Although as organizational behavior teachers, we often expect our students to recognize and accept ambiguity, we do not hold ourselves to the same standards when we do research on organizations. We do not often admit, when we write about our research findings, what we do not or cannot know.[17]

A few academics and more than a few managers have confronted this difficulty, observing that organizational research does not capture context-specific complexities of the problems managers face.[18] This creates Starbuck's paradox:

> Prescriptions for managing organizations have to be simple in order to be understandable. When prescriptions describe methods and strategies which are easily translated into actual behaviors, these prescriptions oversimplify, they ignore contingencies, and they state half-truths. When prescriptions specify methods and strategies applying to complete, complex systems, these prescriptions read like poems that express verities but that have obscure applications to actual behaviors. (Starbuck, Greve, and Hedberg, 1978, pp. 122–123)

Starbuck's paradox implies that helpful advice from academics (and others) is always going to be hard to come by. The practitioner is left in the lurch, and teachers and researchers face an aporia: they cannot do research or teach in a way that is complex enough, and simple enough, to be both comprehensible and useful.

In summary, the Fragmentation view offers no comfort to those—academics or practitioners—who long for clarity. Truth claims are seen as invalid bids for domination, ideologies become false dogmas that conceal their opposites, and ambiguities multiply endlessly.

BEYOND CONSENSUS TO MULTIPLE, FRAGMENTED INTERPRETATIONS

The Fragmentation perspective reconceptualizes consensus in a manner which acknowledges that cultural members sometimes change their views from moment to moment as new issues come into focus, different people and tasks become salient, and new information becomes available. Group identities (such as gender, race, or job classification) do not form stable subcultures in a Fragmentation study. Instead, multiple interpretations and reactions are always possible. For example, when OZCO employees acknowledged ambiguities in Chapter 7, some of them worried, others were apathetic, a few confessed ignorance, and many felt dismay. No clear organization-wide or subcultural consensus was evident in this Fragmentation view of OZCO.

Multiplicity of meanings can have extremely important practical consequences. For example, at Tenerife airport:

> After the KLM plane made the 180 degree turn at the end of the takeoff runway, rather than hold as instructed, they started moving and reported, "we are now at takeoff." Neither the air traffic controllers nor the Pan Am crew were certain what this ambiguous phrase meant, but Pan Am restated to controllers that they would report when they were clear of the takeoff runway, a communique heard inside the KLM cockpit. When the pilot of the KLM flight was asked by the engineer, "Is he not clear then, that Pan Am?", the pilot replied "yes" and there was no further conversation. The collision occurred 13 seconds later at 5:06 P.M. (Weick, 1991, pp. 118–120)

Five hundred and eighty-three people were killed when the KLM jet tried to take off and hit the Pan Am airplane in its path. The Spanish government conducted a postcrash investigation that, in part, analyzed the multiple interpretations and misunderstandings implicit in the conversation reported above. In addition to these cognitive confusions, the government investigators were sensitive to the power dynamics implicit in gaps and silences. The report focused on the silence that occurred after the pilot replied with an emphatic "yes":

> Perhaps influenced by [the pilot's] great prestige, making it difficult to imagine an error of this magnitude on the part of such an expert pilot, both the copilot and flight engineer made no further objections. The impact took place about 13 seconds later. (Spanish Ministry of Transport and Communication's report on the crash, p. 71, quoted in Weick, 1991, p. 121)

In this analysis of discourse, as in Martin's deconstruction of the Caesarean story, an analysis of the ambiguities of silences brings the hidden dynamics of power inequality into focus, illuminating why widespread consensus is unlikely.

Fragmentation studies often portray goals as unclear, making consensus very difficult to achieve. For example, in the study of the military:

> No consensus exists on either the proper means of assuring the common defense, or the preferred intermediate goals one ought to pursue. Without agreement on goals and general force types, there can be no agreement on programs. And without agreement on the definition of acceptable goals and adequate forces, "progress" toward either cannot be measured readily. (Sabrosky, Thompson, and McPherson, 1982, p. 142)

Lack of consensual understanding can also be seen in one of the few Fragmentation studies to mix quantitative and qualitative methods. Krackhardt and Kilduff used constructs generated by employees in open-ended interviews, so their data are less superficial and have fewer of the researcher-generated constraints of many other quantitative studies of culture. After a series of statistical analyses, the authors conclude:

> The results demonstrate that individuals in a joint enterprise can construe the same interpersonal reality in completely different ways on constructs that capture the main dichotomies in the organization. The puzzle of how people with different perspectives succeed in enacting roles toward each other in organizations has partly been explained by the finding that the diversity of attributions is patterned by the network of personal friendships. (Krackhardt and Kilduff, 1990, pp. 18–19)

The language in the last sentence is important. The heterogeneity is explained only in part by the friendship network and that network is more a matrix of pairwise relationships than it is a set of subcultures.[19] This is a quantitative image of an absence of organization-wide consensus. From a Fragmentation viewpoint, this study's absence of consensus does not indicate an absence of culture, but rather the presence of a Fragmented culture. This conclusion is, in part, an effect of how culture is being defined.

DEFINING CULTURE FROM A FRAGMENTATION PERSPECTIVE

The definitions of culture offered in Integration and Differentiation studies often bear relatively little relationship to what is actually studied. In contrast, Fragmentation studies often abstain from defining culture at all. The exceptions, however, are informative and directly relevant to the conclusions of this kind of research.

A reviewer of one of my papers suggested that I seemed to be defining culture in these terms:

> Culture is a loosely structured and incompletely shared system that emerges dynamically as cultural members experience each other, events, and the organization's contextual features. (anonymous reviewer, 1987)

This definition does not exclude ambiguity from the domain of culture and it captures the sense of constant flux that is implicit in many Fragmentation studies.

However, this definition leaves open a question that is particularly relevant for organizational researchers: Given this ambiguity, how do people engage in coordinated action? How is this definition a socially constructed reality, rather than a collection of unique individual views? Meyerson has one answer to this dilemma:

> Members do not agree upon clear boundaries, cannot identify shared solutions, and do not reconcile contradictory beliefs and multiple identities. Yet, these members contend they belong to a culture. They share a common orientation and overarching purpose, face similar problems, and have comparable experiences. However, these shared orientations and purposes accommodate different beliefs and incommensurable technologies, these problems imply different solutions, and these experiences have multiple meanings . . . Thus, for at least some cultures, to dismiss the ambiguities in favor of strictly what is clear and shared is to exclude some of the most central aspects of

members' cultural experience and to ignore the essence of their cultural community. (Meyerson, 1991a, pp. 131–132)

Feldman offers an issue-specific response to the same dilemma:

As others have noted (Martin and Meyerson, 1988; Van Maanen and Barley, 1985) culture does not necessarily imply a uniformity of values. Indeed quite different values may be displayed by people of the same culture. In such an instance, what is it that holds together the members of the organization? I suggest that we look to the existence of a common frame of reference or a shared recognition of relevant issues. There may not be agreement about whether these issues should be relevant or about whether they are positively or negatively valued. . . . They [may] array themselves differently with respect to that issue, but whether positively or negatively they are all oriented to it. (Feldman, 1991, p. 154)

This issue-specific focus is essential to understanding how the Fragmentation perspective defines culture. A focus on specific issues addresses one of the problems inherent in the Differentiation approach to understanding culture. In a Differentiation study, clear dichotomies and clearly defined subcultures cut up and constrain the ways we see a culture, making unintelligible all the issue-specific complexities that "fall between the cracks" of this way of thinking. In contrast, the Fragmentation perspective sees issues as connecting individuals in temporary, issue-specific coalitions. Other individuals and other issues are linked in different, overlapping, temporary patterns of connection.[20]

One metaphor for this approach to understanding culture is a web:

Individuals are nodes in the web, connected by shared concerns to some but not all the surrounding nodes. When a particular issue becomes salient, one pattern of connections becomes relevant. That pattern would include a unique array of agreements, disagreements, and domains of ignorance. A different issue would draw attention to a different pattern of connections—and different sources of confusion. Whenever a new issue becomes salient to cultural members or researchers, a new pattern of connections would become significant. (Martin and Meyerson, 1988, p. 117)

Sometimes these issues can be content themes. For example, the Fragmentation view of OZCO presented in Chapter 7 focused on three content themes: egalitarianism, innovation, and employee well-being. Connecting concerns can also be more specific—a particular problem or a shared set of tasks. *From a Fragmentation perspective, then, an organizational culture is a web of individuals, sporadically and loosely connected by their changing positions on a variety of issues. Their involvement, their subcultural identities, and their individual self-definitions fluctuate, depending on which issues are activated at a given moment.*

A jungle metaphor for the Fragmentation view of culture captures some of the complexity evident in the web metaphor and also retains more of an emphasis on the unknown and the unknowable. In Chapter 4, culture was defined, from an Integration perspective, as that which is clear, "an area of meaning cut out of a vast mass of meaninglessness, a small clearing of lucidity in a formless, dark, always ominous jungle.''[21] Rather than denying or channeling ambiguity, the Fragmentation perspective accepts it and makes it the focus of attention. In this view, culture is no longer the clearing in the jungle; it is the jungle itself. Table 1–1 in Chapter 1 contrasts the characteristics and metaphors used to define culture in Fragmentation studies to those in Integration and Differentiation research.

FRAGMENTATION AT DIFFERENT LEVELS OF ANALYSIS

Some critics have argued that a Fragmentation view reduces culture to an individual level of analysis because this perspective sees no stable organization-wide or subcultural consensus. This is a misunderstanding. The Fragmentation perspective offers a distinctive approach to the subcultural, individual, and organizational levels of analysis, as described next.

Fragmentation at the Subcultural Level

At the subcultural level of analysis, a Fragmentation study avoids the clear group boundaries and the clearly defined subcultural relationships (enhancing, conflicting, orthogonal) of the Differentiation perspective. Instead, a Fragmentation view of subcultures portrays boundaries as permeable, subcultural membership as fluctuating, and relations among subcultures as multivalent. In other words:

Group alliances look like affinities or coalitions rather than identities, and they are characterized by fluidity, the ability to mobilize and disperse. Some theorists call them microresistances. (Gagnier, 1990, p. 23)

When subcultures are regarded from a Fragmentation rather than a Differentiation perspective, an examination of *differance* replaces an oppositional mode of thinking. A Differentiation study of gender subcultures, for example, would start with a men versus women dichotomy. In one such study, Millman and Kanter observe that men often fail to see that gender-segregated groups exclude women:

When male sociologists (or men in general) look at a meeting of a board of trustees and see only men, they think they are observing a sexually neutral or sexless world rather than a masculine world. (Millman and Kanter, 1975, p. xiv)

This is a Differentiation analysis because it makes a generalization about men in tacit, binary opposition to women. It assumes that all male sociologists are "essentially" the same, with unified interests that stand in opposition to the interests of an equally homogeneous grouping of women.[22] Thus, all male sociologists would see an all-male board of trustees in sexually neutral terms, while presumably all female sociologists would not.

In contrast, a Fragmentation study would offer a far more complex analysis of this situation. Such an analysis would not deny the bias inherent in seeing a sex-segregated world as sexually neutral. Both Differentiation and Fragmentation studies work from the premise that people notice what they are comfortable noticing; inequities from which they benefit will be ignored. However, a Fragmentation study would go further, analyzing how Millman and Kanter's generalization masks important differences between and within groups.

A Fragmentation analysis might begin by observing that Millman and Kanter do not mention the race of the trustees and the sociologists. Are the trustees all white? If so, why is this not mentioned by the male sociologists or by Kanter and Millman? Are all these researchers white? Next, gender and race might be considered simultaneously. Would black male sociologists tend to be sensitive to racial segregation among the trustees, but perhaps blind to sexual segregation? Would black female sociologists tend to be sensitive to both?

Finally, the possibility of variation within all these groups might be considered. Millman and Kanter imply that because the male sociologists are members of the dominant gender, they are blind to the gender segregation of the all-male group of trustees. However, membership in a dominant group does not necessarily mean that one is blind to the exclusion of subordinate group members. Some male sociologists might notice the gender segregation of the trustees group. Furthermore, some female sociologists might be gender-blind, seeing the trustees in sexually neutral terms. Similarly, some whites might be sensitive to racial segregation, while some blacks might not focus on this issue.

The complications revealed by a Fragmentation analysis are not merely "error variance" that can be easily dismissed as trivial compared with group averages. For example, women have different ethnic, class, and racial backgrounds and these sources of diversity mean that women can see things very differently, have similar or conflicting interests, and benefit from diverse and possibly diverging paths of social action. Similar diversity exists for men. In addition, denying differences within a subordinated group can further the subordination of minority members within that group. And denying the differences within a dominant group can mean the disregard of potential allies for those who are subordinated. These observations are as relevant for other groups (based, e.g., on occupation or hierarchical level) as they are for demographic groupings. Generalizations based on dichotomous statements about between group differences can often mask differences that are critical for understanding inequality or working toward change.

A Fragmented View of the Self

This approach to the study of subcultures also has implications for the individual level of analysis. When differences within categories are acknowledged, the boundaries of subcultures become diffuse, permeable, and fluctuating. Because these boundaries are subjectively construed and socially constructed, one person sees them differently than another. Subcultures overlap, they are nested within each other, and they intersect in the individual:

> One might plausibly keep dissecting levels of subcultures until one reaches the level of the individual. Each individual does, in fact, live in at least a slightly different subculture or intermeshing of subcultures. (Sternberg, 1985, p. 1116)

When regarded from a Fragmentation viewpoint, the Integration view of the self as centered, autonomous, and unitary seems unlikely. Equally unlikely is the Differentiation view of a divided self, pulled between clear, conflicting allegiances. Instead, a fragmented self constantly fluctuates among diverse and changing identities, pulled by issues and events to focus on one aspect of the self rather than another—temporarily. The self is fragmented by a variety of nested, overlapping identities, external influences, and levels of consciousness:

> The perceiving subject, deluded by imagined notions of its unity and coherence, is in actuality split in such imponderable ways by the unconscious that it might be conceived of as a vacancy mirroring Other(s) whose "space" creates its experience of being a conscious subject. (Gelpi, 1990, p. 7)

Members of subordinated groups have vividly articulated variations on this sense of a fragmented self. They must know the ways of the dominant group in order to survive, but it can be deadly to have only this knowledge. In the United States, for example, the dominant ideology asserts: "equal opportunity is available; economic and social status is allocated by merit; so, if you are not prosperous, it is your own fault." If members of subordinated groups are to avoid blaming themselves for outcomes beyond their control, they must develop and maintain identities that are different from those suggested by the dominant ideology. Since these alternative identities are often multiple, so these "selves" become fragmented. For example:

> The new *mestiza* (a person of mixed ancestry) . . . copes by developing a tolerance for contradictions, a tolerance for ambiguity. She learns to be Indian in Mexican culture, to be Mexican from an Anglo point of view. She learns to juggle cultures. She has a plural personality, she operates in a pluralistic mode—nothing is thrust out, the good the bad and the ugly, nothing rejected, nothing abandoned. Not only does she sustain contradictions, she turns the ambivalence into something else. (Anzaldua, 1987, p. 79, quoted in Rosaldo, 1989, p. 216)

> For women, then, existing in the dominant system of meanings and values that structure culture and society may be a painful double dance, clicking in, clicking out—the divided consciousness. (Du Plessis, 1985, p. 149)

Fragmented identities, however, are not the exclusive preserve of women and minorities. A middle-class man may be trained as an engineer, have a nontechnical managerial job, a large family, a working wife, a commitment to serving on the Town Council, strong religious faith, and an enthusiasm for environmental conservation. In Walt Whitman's words: "Do I contradict myself? / Very well then, I contradict myself, / I am large, I contain multitudes."[23] According to this Fragmentation view, an individual's identity is a fluctuating composite of partial allegiances:

> More a busy intersection through which multiple identities crisscross than a unified coherent self. (Rosaldo, 1989, p. 194)

Some researchers have taken this view of the self one step farther, denying individual uniqueness in terms that echo the nexus approach to understanding culture. An individual is seen as a fragmented composite of external influences:

> It does not matter how "unique an individual" we think we are, we are nothing but the discourses through and in which we live. In a sense we are nothing more than traversing points in networks of discourses. Thus, when you (or I), "unique individual," think, or speak, or write, or read, who is doing it? Your (or my) "unique words"—or our inherited discourses and view of the world as they may be said in our times? (Calas and Smircich, 1987, p. 22)

Fragmentation at the Organizational Level of Analysis

This Fragmentation view of the subcultural and individual levels of analysis has implications for the organizational level of analysis. The salience of particular issues for given individuals fluctuates, realigning the salience of subcultural identities and creating transient issue-specific coalitions. At the organizational level of analysis, then, the Fragmentation perspective reveals a constantly fluctuating morass of allegiance. All is heterogeneous and in flux. No static, totalizing, organization-wide interpretation is possible.

A FRAGMENTED VIEW OF EFFECTIVENESS

There are many studies of ambiguity in organizations. Some of these are a variant of the Integration perspective; everyone in the organization is described as seeing the same ambiguities and having the same reactions to them. In these Integration studies, "everyone" agrees about the positive (or negative) "effects" of ambiguity.[24] Other studies of ambiguity are written from a Fragmentation perspective, and, in these portrayals, organizational members vary in the kinds of ambiguity they see and in their reactions to it. These Fragmentation studies sometimes, but not always, include a variety of opinions about whether ambiguity has positive or negative effects on performance.

A rosy view of the link between ambiguity and effectiveness usually emphasizes the freedom ambiguity brings. When expectations, preferences, and evaluation criteria are unclear, there is no apparent right or wrong outcome. Negative consequences of actions, as well as their causes, are difficult to detect and assess. Because there is less risk of being wrong, ambiguity brings individuals a sense of psychological safety. With that safety, comes autonomy for acting, playing, and experimenting.[25] Political maneuvering can proceed with less constraint, professions can create an aura of mystery to protect their technical monopolies, and the freedom to deviate can flourish.[26] Causal explanations and preferences can be allowed to emerge retrospectively, after actions have occurred.[27] Without the constraints of prospective planning and rationalization it becomes easier to innovate. Fragmentation studies which stress the benefits of ambiguity do not usually argue that it should be controlled. Rather, a manager is told how to "capitalize" on the potential advantages of ambiguity, for example, by creating an atmosphere where the unexpected does not disrupt a smooth (and rigid) routine, creativity is fostered, and the unpredictable can have unanticipated benefits.[28]

Other studies of the relationship between ambiguity and effectiveness are less sanguine. For example, Weick's study of the Tenerife air disaster was focused on effectiveness issues; its goal was to enable people " to detect a potential problem; to anticipate and forestall disasters."[29] Perrow also explores the negative effects of ambiguity with a focus on disaster.[30] Analyzing the Three Mile Island nuclear reactor incident, Perrow concludes that such accidents are "normal" (i.e., unavoidable) in centralized, tightly coupled systems where warnings or training cannot prevent or correct complex faults. A better alternative, Perrow argues, is reliance on decentralized, loosely coupled organizational designs: simple to understand, simple to fix, and with low risk of the negative synergy that can cause devastating accidents.

Perrow is offering a contingency argument that echoes Weick's recommendations for developing "organic" and "under-organized" systems:

> If Burns and Stalker's organic system is treated prescriptively as an arrangement capable of dealing with uncertainty, we would expect to see organizations pressured by ambiguity to demonstrate more use of specialized professional skills (high complexity), continual redefinition of individual tasks (low formalization), development of more ad hoc centers of authority located closer to the source of a problem (low centralization), and movement toward a network structure (this list is adapted from Gerwin, 1981, p. 6). (Weick, 1985, p. 125)

This description of an organic system is similar to Sabrosky, Thompson, and McPherson's portrait of the military bureaucracy. According to these researchers, the military depends heavily on specialized professional skills (high complexity). In spite of a rigid and explicit ranking of titles, individual tasks are redefined constantly because the military employee is expected to be "ready to take on any assignment" (low formalization). Authority is shared with the President, the Joint Chiefs of Staff, the Secretary of Defense, the National Security Council, Congress, and so on (low centralization). The structure is more like that of a network or web than the "triangle" of authority and reporting relationships that constitutes a traditional hierarchy. This study sees a link between ambiguity and the effectiveness of the military. For example:

> The existence of bureaucratic inertia, fragmentation of authority, and relative lack of efficiency may be a collective blessing in disguise in certain circumstances. Elected and appointed officials are not always paragons of intelligence and wisdom, and the inability of the military bureaucracy to execute rapidly some radical (or reactionary) executive proposals could have some inadvertent utility (Rourke, 1972, p. 52). (Sabrosky, Thompson, and McPherson, 1982, p. 149)

Nevertheless, the authors conclude that the dysfunctional effects of ambiguity can also have serious negative consequences:

The consequences of such organized anarchy within the military bureaucracy entail unnecessary expenditures, wastage of scarce resources, or operational redundancy. Matters are far worse when that semi-anarchical state of affairs unnecessarily risks war, costs lives, and contributes to the loss of a war or the failure of an operation. (Sabrosky, Thompson, and McPherson, 1982, p. 147)

This study, then, suggests that a simple contingency version of the ambiguity-effectiveness argument may not be sufficient in some circumstances.

Other Fragmentation studies of culture abstain from arguing that there is a link between ambiguity and effectiveness. These studies implicitly argue that it is wrong to assume that ambiguity is positively or negatively related to effectiveness issues (i.e., make sense, be clear, generate commitment, increase productivity, facilitate control). According to this point of view, practices and forms do not exist to rationalize "reality" (as advocates of retrospective rationalization have argued) or to disguise it (as some Differentiation and loose coupling studies have speculated). Instead, these Fragmentation studies simply examine ambiguity as an inescapable, undeniable attribute of working life. This, for example, is the tone of Meyerson's study of social workers and Feldman's examination of the policy analysis process. From this viewpoint, arguing for a link between ambiguity and effectiveness is an exercise in futility. As these examples indicate, Fragmentation studies do not have a unified position on effectiveness questions.

FRAGMENTATION VIEWS OF CULTURAL CHANGE

In a Fragmentation account, power is not localized solely at the top of a hierarchy or at the subcultural level of analysis. Instead, power is usually seen as being diffused more broadly in the environment and among individual organizational members. In addition, from a Fragmentation perspective change is a constant flux, rather than an intermittent interruption in an otherwise stable state.

Many Fragmentation studies emphasize environmental sources of change. These studies, however, do not assume that people can control, or even influence, what happens. For example, some policy analysts described working in the Department of Energy as a

whole ball of yarn thrown up in the air making tracks we run on. Every once in a while a giant comes along and throws it up in the air rearranging the strands. (Feldman, 1983a, p. 230)

An organizational story about this agency focuses on one major environmental source of change: the policy alterations that come with the election of a new president. Once again, these changes are beyond the control of employees:

Employees had reluctantly become used to walking down dimly lit corridors, washing their hands in cold water, and sweltering in the Washington heat without adequate air conditioning. Then a new President was elected and energy conservation was no longer top priority. The lights came on, the water became hot, and the air conditioning actually did its job. Old timers were not surprised by the change; they called it the "New Administration Effect." (Feldman, 1983a, quoted in Martin, Feldman, Hatch, and Sitkin, 1983, p. 445)

Textbook editors also emphasize environmental control as they describe what happens to the books they publish:

This is a high-risk business, and it's also a demoralizing business. You think a book is solid and well-written, and it doesn't do well. It never got a chance, and you don't know why. Maybe the jacket was the wrong color. You think of it as the luck of the game. We have little control. You have to accept the things you don't have control over. (Levitt and Nass, 1989, p. 192)

A similar lack of individual control over events can be seen, for example, in Weick's description of the airplane crash at Tenerife and Perrow's account of the "normal" accident at the Three Mile Island nuclear reactor.

Other Fragmentation studies take a more activist stance, focusing on the ways individuals can have a diffuse and fragmented impact, undermining the usual ways of doing things, ultimately promoting fundamental cultural realignments. These Fragmentation accounts of change pointedly abstain from the "frontal assaults" of overt between-group conflict or the "totalitarianism" of top-down planned change. A Fragmentation study of the women's movement illustrates this point:

Power and authority are no longer vested in a central point. . . . Nor does resistance arise from a single point. For that reason, a very different form of political organization and struggle suggests itself, an alternative to the frontal attack on the state led by the One revolutionary subject. . . . What Leftists have criticized in the women's movement as fragmentation, lack of organization, absence of a coherent and encompassing theory, and the inability to mount a frontal attack may very well represent fundamentally more radical and effective responses to the deployment of power in our society than the centralization and abstraction that continue to plague Leftist thinking and strategy. (Diamond and Quinby, 1988, pp. 9–10)

Integration and Differentiation accounts of planned change emphasize conscious, goal-directed decision-making and ideological solidarity within a culture or a subculture. These aspects of organizing for change are fundamentally incompatible with the Fragmentation perspective's stress on negating clarities and disrupting shared assumptions. It is possible, however, to articulate an alternative view of change that is both activist and congruent with these aspects of the Fragmentation viewpoint. Foucault sees power as enacted, through discourse, in a multiplicity of everyday, taken-for-granted interactions (e.g., in the ways jobs are structured, performance is evaluated, pay is distributed, tasks are defined, etc.).[31] From this point of view, cultural change can be triggered by disrupting these everyday discourses, pointing out ruptures, absences, and breaks, thereby revealing contradictions in the symbolic order.[32] With this perspective, deconstruction (e.g., of the Caesarean story) could be considered one small part of a cultural change effort.

The Fragmentation perspective is difficult to translate into an action plan for either the powerful or the powerless. Because of the multiplicity of possible interpretations, any shared sense of "progress," "learning," or "improvement" becomes difficult to discern or attain. Environmental sources of change and individual attempts to promote change will be differently perceived and will cause a plethora of transient reactions. Furthermore, since change is perceived and enacted by individuals, change by one individual in one direction may well be counteracted by another individual moving in a different direction, resulting in little stable, net change on the group or organizational level of analysis. Certainly, coordinated change by large numbers of individuals—simultaneously and in the same direction—seems unlikely to happen spontaneously and difficult to trigger intentionally—except perhaps by poorly understood, somewhat random processes, such as contagion.

Given these difficulties, it is not surprising that the Fragmentation perspective offers few specific, well-articulated guidelines for those who would normatively control the cultural change process. Only one avenue to change is spelled out in any detail in the Fragmentation literature: there are explicit and useful guidelines for revealing, through deconstruction, the ideological underpinnings of discourse. Advocates of the Fragmentation perspective who are deeply concerned about cultural change (not all are) have written eloquently about the dangers of overestimating the importance of such intellectual work and underestimating the impact of material realities, such as the unequal distribution of power and money.[33]

There may be approaches to planned change that are potentially congruent with a Fragmentation perspective, but that have not yet been explored by cultural researchers. For example, if ambiguity is as pervasive as Fragmentation research implies, members of dominant groups (for reasons of intellectual honesty, if not social compassion) should abandon the comfort of believing there is only one—homogeneous—sense of how the world is put together. They should not try to impose homogeneity on others by seeking a unifying vision or shared values. From the Fragmentation perspective, seeking homogeneity is a futile effort, one that attempts to eliminate valuable variation. Members of dominant groups should therefore not exclude, assimilate (destroy), or distort (accept only parts of) others' differing points of view.

Instead, organizations might try to place greater value on employee diversity. This approach would entail a commitment to be uncomfortable, to admit the validity of other points of view, and try to interact without seeking to dominate. Members of dominant groups would have to become aware of and willing to abandon many of the ways they benefit from their dominance. In this effort, intellectual work might contribute by undermining deceptive myths and symbols of unity and homogeneity, destabilizing categories used to define boundaries and differences, and challenging assumptions about what is biologically determined, "natural," or otherwise objective and unchangeable.

Alternatively, change programs based on a Fragmentation viewpoint could focus on more material issues, such as experimental ways to restructure organizations. Some of these recommendations would be familiar; others not. For example, in a move to counter some of the debilitating effects of hierarchy, Ferguson advocates rotating leadership, using egalitarian authority structures, training lower-status employees, and avoiding specialized division of labor.[34] She also suggests structuring organizations around conversations, not rules, so that many voices are heard and all who wish, get a chance to speak. In this way, organizations could be conceptualized as public spaces, where all members are citizens and conflicts are resolved with primary emphasis on permitting people to grow.

These are inspirational ideas, but those familiar with the organizational literature on experimental organizations (including Ferguson) would predict that some of these innovations would not last long in the present competitive organizational environment.[35] To cite only one problem, such a change effort takes time, patience, and money. If such change programs were to succeed in any long-term fashion, some fundamental assumptions would have to change on a rather wide scale. For example, an experimental organization based on Ferguson's ideas would have little chance of survival unless there were widespread changes in the structure of markets and in the assumption that competitive efficiency is the primary criterion for survival.

Change recommendations derived from the Fragmentation perspective tend to be naive, in so far as they assume that society can be changed by changing the perceptions of individuals. Such change programs overestimate the power of ideas and underestimate material constraints on idea development, such as lack of education, time to read, or money to buy books. Most important, ideational, individual-level recommendations for change fail to deal with conflicts of interest between groups, the inequality of material resources, and other sources of power available only to members of dominant groups.

Organizational research outside the cultural domain has already examined some of the change recommendations congruent with the Fragmentation perspective. If these intellectual traditions could be combined, the noncultural theory and research could contribute a pragmatism (especially regarding power and self-interest) that might strengthen the critique of contemporary organizations implicit in Fragmentation research, contributing a material emphasis and practical expertise that currently is missing.

METHODOLOGICAL CRITIQUES

Like their Integration and Differentiation counterparts, these Fragmentation studies have a tautology problem: they seek evidence of ambiguity where they are most likely to find it. Virtually all Fragmentation studies are qualitative. In these studies, sampling procedures at the individual level of analysis tend to be systematic, relatively comprehensive, and fully described. The tautology problem emerges when an occupational or organizational context is selected for study. For example, some Fragmentation studies focus on occupations that are commonly seen as unusually ambiguous:

> I studied hospital social work because of the ambiguities that seemed to characterize this occupation. (Meyerson, 1991a, p. 132)

We were informed however, that college-text publishing simply represents "the poker game with the highest ante because of the high costs of production" and that the procedures for decision making are best described as "guesswork, intuition, and opinion." (Levitt and Nass, 1989, p. 192)

Qualitative Fragmentation studies also select organizational contexts for perspective-reinforcing reasons. For example, a crowded airport on a foggy night or a public bureaucracy serving multiple constituencies seem likely breeding grounds for ambiguity.[36]

A few Fragmentation studies use quantitative methods. These studies generally use systematic sampling procedures at the individual level of analysis, but select methods that are designed to elicit ambiguities. For example, it is interesting to contrast the content analysis techniques used by studies congruent with each of the three perspectives. Integration studies used content analysis methods that focused on similarities (e.g., Barley's study of funeral directors). Differentiation studies used content analysis techniques that tapped both similarities and differences (e.g., Gregory's study of programmers). Fragmentation studies require a content analysis technique that does not exclude ambiguities which are neither clearly similar or clearly dissimilar. One partial solution to this problem is the optimal matching technique. This method provides

a quantitative measure of the minimum extent of modifications in one sequence required for it to match the other. In optimal matching, the three basic types of modifications are (1) the substitution of one element for another at the same position in the sequence, (2) the deletion of an element from a sequence, and (3) the insertion of an element into a sequence. . . . Each modification is assigned a "cost," a real number greater than zero that reflects an a priori decision as to the severity of the modification; the less severe, the smaller the cost. . . . As the strings are converted until they match, the costs of the transformations are summed. (Levitt and Nass, 1989, p. 200)

Because this quantitative approach seeks both similarities and dissimilarities, it provides a measure of heterogeneity. It fails, however, to capture the full complexity of the Fragmentation view.

Most Fragmentation research is not quantitative because it is so difficult to capture modes of thinking, such as differance, with conventional statistical techniques. Quantitative methods have little affinity with the subjectivist, idiographic, context-specific, transient aspects of the Fragmentation perspective. Quantitative methods represent an

idealized rationality [that] leaves no loose ends, it reduces all conditions to binary states—consistent or inconsistent, true or false, existent or nonexistent. . . . Left alone, scientific rationality would assemble pristine structures of logical congruence, elegant in their parsimonious simplicity, and utterly at odds with almost all observable phenomena. (Starbuck, 1987, p. 71)

To the extent that fleeting changes in individual cognitions, attitudes, and behavior could be quantitatively measured, and to the extent that numbers could capture fluctuations in the ways these individual perspectives coalesce and fail to coalesce in clusters of temporary, issue-specific consensus, the fragmented and transient nature of these patterns would produce no statistically significant differences.[37] Although this absence of stable patterns would be congruent with the Fragmentation view, support for a null hypothesis has seldom generated much enthusiasm, for good reasons, among quantitative enthusiasts.

Fragmentation studies that utilize a postmodern approach would be even less enthusiastic about the use of quantitative techniques, although they would also have objections to the tone of the qualitative studies referenced in this chapter. Advocates of a postmodern approach would note with distaste, for example, Levitt and Nass's tacit assumptions about the "objectivity" of their approach, the unproblematic nature of their "facts," and their use of ideologically loaded language, such as "costs" and "real" numbers. Whether qualitative or quantitative, the Fragmentation studies of organizational culture, discussed earlier, make an implicit truth claim: "As an author, my (single) interpretation of these cultural members' (multiple) interpretations is correct." In contrast, postmodernism is adamantly opposed to truth claims, whether qualitative or quantitative methods are used.

The last chapter of this book explores the implications of this postmodern critique. Before proceeding, however, to an overview of the three perspectives and their postmodern faults, it is only fair to let some substantive criticisms of the Fragmentation perspective be heard.

SUBSTANTIVE CRITIQUES

To avoid redundancy, I will offer here only a few, particularly biting critiques of the Fragmentation perspective. The first is an Integration view of the scientific and practical dangers of focusing on ambiguity:

> [Better theory] requires the systematic elimination of ambiguity in causal explanation, not its consecration. The excitement of science and the reason for attempting to construct a social science is the possibility of seeing more clearly, and thus empowering action rather than paralyzing it by mere appreciation of tension and ambiguity. (Donaldson, 1989, pp. 250–251)

The Differentiation perspective, with its sensitivity to the difficulties encountered by disempowered groups, is troubled by the Fragmentation perspective's reluctance to acknowledge the reality and severity of human suffering and to suggest practical action plans to alleviate it. An acknowledgment of ambiguity and a commitment to political activism are not easy to combine. For example:

> We risk lapsing into boundless difference and giving up on the confusing task of making partial, real connection. Some differences are playful; some are poles of world historical systems of domination. [The difficulty] is about knowing the difference. (Haraway, 1985, p. 79, quoted in Gagnier, 1990, p. 30)

Finally, as this is the last of the three cultural perspectives to be delineated, a final word will be given to an advocate of the Fragmentation view. Rosaldo rhetorically raises and effectively counters some of the most powerful critiques of this kind of scholarship:

> Are there no standards? Where has objectivity gone? Can this be the advent of unbridled chaos that allows nihilism and relativism to walk hand in hand in a land where "anything goes"? In what follows, I argue, to the contrary, that dismantling objectivism creates a space for ethical concerns in a territory once regarded as value-free. (Rosaldo, 1989, p. 181)

At this point, this book has come full circle, back to Chapter 1's fierce debates among three incommensurable perspectives. So far, the Integration, Differentiation, and Fragmentation perspectives have been presented in separate chapters, and often in authors' own words, so that the integrity, convictions, and allegiances of each perspective could be presented with minimal interference from other points of view. This structure has tried to make the presentation of these views less like the fierce debate with which this book started, and more like a conversation, where each viewpoint gets a chance to speak at length, without interruption, and be heard.

In spite of these efforts to be fair and even-handed, my own views have unavoidably influenced the selection of quotations, the wording of conclusions, and the inclusion and exclusion of particular criticisms. Now is the time, then, to acknowledge the obvious: after listening to all the evidence, it seems to me that the Integration perspective presents a relatively unlikely scenario (consistency, organization-wide consensus, the absence of ambiguity), more reflective of the desires of top management than the realities of most employees' working lives. Undoubtedly, if a study goes deep enough, there will be some highly abstract ideas (e.g., about time) that most organizational members clearly understand and share. However, are these the most important things to know or do they tend to be, in Becker's words, "rather banal?" If a cultural theory focuses on a highly unlikely scenario and excludes much of organizational life, how useful to practitioners will recommendations be, based on that theory?

This is not simply a case of needing a better understanding of when the Integration perspective provides an accurate description of a cultural context and when it does not. Differentiation and Fragmentation studies have convincingly demonstrated that cultural descriptions which exclude conflict and ambiguity disproportionately silence the relatively powerless, particularly those men and women who hold low paid jobs or who are in some way demographically different. The Integration perspective, in effect, reifies existing power relationships in organizations, asserting that the opinions of the powerful few are shared by the many and refusing to incorporate the voices of those whose views differ. These inclusions and exclusions are neither trivial or innocent. For these reasons, *an adequate representation of any cultural context should include the insights of all three perspectives, not just one.*

The next chapter tries to demonstrate how a cultural context can be studied using all three perspectives, in a way that acknowledges their irreconcilable differences and permits them to inform each other—unassailed by pressures toward homogeneity, assimilation, or distortion. This overview focuses on the process of cultural change and attempts to portray that process from all three perspectives at once.

NOTES

1. Katrina Hackman suggested this label.

2. Meyerson (1991b) distinguishes ambiguity "itself" from the subjective interpretation of its meaning. See also Feldman (1991).

3. Definition adapted from *Webster's Seventh New Collegiate Dictionary* (1969), p. 611. See also Van de Ven and Poole (1988), p. 4. There are some commonalities between Daft and Weick's treatment of equivocality and these definitions of aspects of ambiguity. Daft and Weick (1984) distinguish between "ambiguity" that obtains when there are no clear interpretations or when meanings are vague, and "equivocality" which obtains when multiple interpretations are possible. Lack of clarity is roughly equivalent to Daft and Weick's definition of ambiguity, while the discussion of complexity and paradox includes many of the elements of equivocality. However, in this book, all three are labeled aspects of ambiguity and all three are seen, from a Fragmentation perspective, as creating the potential for multiple interpretations.

4. See, for example, Bjorkegren (1991), Jeffcutt (1991), Letiche (1991), Linstead and Grafton-Small (1991), Meyerson (1991b), and Willmott (in press).

5. See, for example, Millman and Kanter (1975).

6. See, for example, Collins (1986).

7. See Grafton-Small and Linstead (1987).

8. Wright (1979).

9. Moi (1985), p. 26, uses some of these phrases and ideas to describe the emergence of feminist theory.

10. Cohen, March, and Olsen (1972).

11. March and Olsen (1976). See also Brunsson (1985) and Hedberg (1981).

12. For example, see Brunsson (1985).

13. These conclusions are congruent with Latane and Darley's (1970) bystander intervention studies which found that people do not usually intervene in an emergency as long as the situation is ambiguously defined. Once the ambiguity is clarified, bystanders will help.

14. See also Meyerson (1990).

15. For an explication of context-specific interpretations of the multiple meanings of organizational stories, see Brown and Duguid (1991).

16. Martin (1990).

17. For a different treatment of this issue, see Meyerson (1991a), p. 144.

18. See, for example, Bonini (1963), p. 136.

19. Similar nonhierarchical networks have been found, for example, in studies of interorganizational relationships in Japan. However, these studies portray the networks in Integration terms, as a unified and coordinated source of cooperation for functional goals, and so these studies are more congruent with the Integration perspective than with a Fragmentation viewpoint.

20. Jaggar (1983), p. 367.

21. Berger (1967), p. 23, quoted in Wuthnow, Hunter, Bergesen, and Kurzweil (1984), p. 26.

22. For a critique of this position, see Collins (1986) and Spivak (1986).

23. Whitman (1921), p. 77.

24. Examples of Integration studies of ambiguity that emphasize effectiveness include Weick's (1983) portrait of universities and Eisenberg's (1984) description of the political uses of ambiguity.

25. For example, McCall (1977), Rogers (1961), Weick (1979a, 1985).

26. See, for example, Huff (1988) and Van Maanen and Barley (1985).

27. Studies of retrospective rationalization and ambiguity include Brunsson (1985), March (1976, 1981), and Starbuck (1983).

28. For example, see Cohen and March's (1974) study of college presidents and Mc-Caskey's (1988) examination of how to "manage" ambiguity.

29. Weick (1991), p. 117.

30. Perrow (1984).

31. Foucault (1977).

32. See, for example, Moi (1985), p. 170.

33. See, for example, Flax (1990) and Spivak (1986).

34. This summary is based on Ferguson (1984) and a series of her presentations at an National Science Foundation-sponsored conference of Feminism and Ethics, held in Alta, Utah, in October 1989.

35. See, for example, Rothschild-Witt (1979) and Kanter (1972).

36. In addition to the references cited in this chapter, other studies with some elements of the Fragmentation view include Bromiley (1985), March and March (1977), Sproull, Weiner, and Wolf (1978), Stinchcombe (1959), and Swidler (1979).

37. See, for contrast, Reinhardz (1985).

9

Cultural Change: Moving Beyond
a Single Perspective

The three perspectives view cultural change differently at the organizational, subcultural, and individual levels of analysis. Since they offer distinctive conceptualizations of the roles of leaders and environments, implications for practice differ accordingly. These contrasting elements of the three single-perspective views of cultural change, originally delineated by Meyerson and I, are explained in more detail in Chapters 4, 6, and 8 and are summarized here in Table 9-1.[1]

Each of these single-perspective views makes an objectivist assumption: that each view offers a correct interpretation of how change occured in a particular context, accurately reflecting what researchers have observed and what cultural members reported. An objectivist, single-perspective approach assumes that researchers can judge, by some objective standard, which one of the perspectives offers a more accurate description of a particular context at a given point in time.

The first half of this chapter discusses examples of this objectivist, single-perspective approach to understanding cultural change. Some of this research suggests that particular kinds of organizational cultures responding to particular kinds of environments should be more congruent with one perspective rather than another. Other studies offer a stage theory of change, whereby an organizational culture moves, for example, from an Integrated to a Differentiated to a Fragmented stage of development. Still other studies challenge the unidirectional, linear assumptions of stage theories, postulating tracks or oscillations as alternatives to a stage model. All these approaches to understanding cultural change make the objectivist, single-perspective assumption that an organization at a single point in time is more accurately described by one perspective rather than another.

In contrast, the OZCO case study illustrates the importance of adopting *a subjective, three-perspective view of any organizational culture. At any point in time, a few fundamental aspects of an organization's culture will be congruent with an Integration perspective—that is, some cultural manifestations will be interpreted in similar ways throughout the organization, so they appear clear and mutually consistent. At the same time, in accord with the Differentiation perspective, other issues will surface as inconsistencies and will generate clear sub-*

Table 9-1 Objectivist, single-perspective views of cultural change

	Perspective		
	Integration	*Differentiation*	*Fragmentation*
Role of leader	Leader-centered	Teams of leaders can have secondary influence	Power diffused among individuals and environment (hegemonic discourses)
Role of environment	Can have some influence, but is separate from culture	Environmental influences salient; can be external (jolt) or enacted (nexus approach)	Boundary between environment and organization permeable and is constant flux (nexus approach)
Organizational level	Inertia, active maintenance, or "revolutionary" replacement of one unity with another unity	Change may be localized in subculture or total subcultural configuration may be incrementally changed	Constant flux; change is localized and incremental
Subcultural level	Subcultures may assist, comply, or attempt to ignore change	Subcultures are prime movers of change effort	Constant, issue-specific flux of subcultural alignments
Individual level	Individuals may conform, internalize, or "creatively deviate" from change	Individuals submerged in subcultural identities	Individual is fragmented; issue-specific flux of iden-tities
Action implications	Top-down control by leaders, or seek culture-strategy fit, or question normative ability to control culture	Little direct advice to managers or subordinate groups	Individual seen as powerless or as able to contribute intellectually to undermining hegemonic discourses

cultural differences. Simultaneously, in congruence with the Fragmentation viewpoint, still other issues will be seen as ambiguous, generating unclear relationships among manifestations and only ephemeral issue-specific coalitions that fail to coalesce in either organization-wide or subcultural consensus. Furthermore, individuals viewing the same cultural context will perceive, remember, and interpret things in different ways.

No single perspective can capture this kind of complexity. In order to avoid the blindspots inherent in a single-perspective approach, a researcher must be able to study any cultural context from all three perspectives. In a longitudinal study of change, a context must be viewed from all three perspectives at one point in time before proceeding to a three-perspective study of the next point in time. *In order to adopt this multiperspective approach, a researcher has to abandon the objecti-*

vist assumption that one perspective will be correct, or more correct, than the others. Instead, the perspectives need to be seen as subjective frames—like lenses—that bring some aspects of a culture into focus while inevitably blurring others, not because of researcher carelessness, but because of the inherent limitations of any one perspective.

The second half of this chapter elaborates this subjective, three-perspective framework by explaining what was learned in an unusual seminar and what was experienced by Peace Corps staff and volunteers in Africa during the Kennedy and Nixon administrations. I discuss reasons why individuals sometimes prefer the insights offered by a particular perspective, referred to here as a "home" perspective. Because adopting a three-perspective approach is difficult (given the deep-seated reasons why these perspectives differ in the first place), examples are used to show how researchers and cultural members can move across perspective boundaries. The chapter concludes by examining the advantages of doing so.

TYPES OF CULTURES: AN OBJECTIVIST, SINGLE-PERSPECTIVE APPROACH

It is clear, from the preceding chapters of this book, that organizational culture studies have produced contradictory results. Extensive evidence, congruent with each of the three perspectives, has been found. One way to reconcile these contradictions is to argue that different kinds of organizations (varying, e.g., by age, size, structure, or purpose) have different kinds of cultures. This stance is an objectivist, single-perspective view. I do not agree with it, but many scholars do, so it is important to discuss it before offering a more complex, dynamic alternative.

Advocates of the three perspectives have tended to study different kinds of organizations. Extrapolating from these differences, some have argued that different types of organizations will have different types of cultures. For example, the Integration perspective will be more appropriate for small organizations founded by charismatic leaders and for larger organizations that face stable, nonsegmented environments. The Differentiation perspective will be more appropriate, for example, in firms with troubled labor relations or for organizations that face stable, segmented environments. The Fragmentation view will be more appropriate for public-sector organizations that serve multiple constituencies or high-technology firms that must innovate constantly in order to be responsive to a turbulent environment. Table 9-2 illustrates this objectivist, single-perspective approach, listing types of organizations and environments that might be congruent with each perspective.

This is implicitly a contingency approach to thinking about cultural change: an organizational culture will develop a certain set of characteristics in order to adapt to a particular internal and environmental configuration, in accord with the specifications of one cultural perspective rather than another. Such an approach is a relatively unsophisticated variant of "ecological functionalism," which explains particular cultural configurations "by the adaptive functions that its various ele-

Table 9-2   An objectivist, single-perspective view of types of organizational cultures

Most "appropriate" cultural perspective	Primary source of change	Most likely types of organizations	Most likely types of environment
Integration	Emphasizes leader response to environmental pressures	Small (ideology-or-founder-centered) or large and centralized	Stable and not segmented *Examples*: Small start-up company; large paper products manufacturer
Differentiation	Emphasizes collective action within organizational and environmental influences	Large and/or decentralized (functional, geographical, and hierarchical divisions)	Stable and segmented *Examples*: Catholic church; automobile manufacturer
Fragmentation	Constant change	Innovative organizations or public-sector bureaucracies with multiple constituencies	Turbulent *Examples*: Computer research laboratory; Department of Energy

ments fulfill."[2] Before discussing the shortcomings of this viewpoint, a variant of it merits discussion.

OBJECTIVIST, MULTIPERSPECTIVE VIEWS OF CULTURAL CHANGE

A more elaborated approach argues that organizations progress through stages of cultural development, reflecting one of the three perspectives at each stage. This approach assumes that any stage of development can be adequately described with a single perspective. For example, Jonsson and Lundin argue that cultures move through stages of organization-wide enthusiasm and subsequent discouragement focused on key ideas or "myths" about the meaning and necessity of certain organizational behaviors.[3] Widely shared enthusiasm for a myth makes action possible (Integration). Then crises begin to occur, bringing discouragement, the acknowledgment of ambiguity, and anxiety (Fragmentation). Action paralysis is often a by-product. In order to decide how to act, cultural members seek a return to clarity; a new "ghost" myth is formulated and substituted for the old (a new Integration). The process recurs.

Jonsson and Lundin's sequential portrayal of the organization-wide collapse and regeneration of a monolithic culture (clarity, the introduction of ambiguity, new clarity) echoes Schein's individual-level conceptualization of the socialization process (unfreezing, learning, refreezing).[4] In a sense, all of the stages described by Jonsson and Lundin are congruent with an Integration viewpoint because progress is defined as movement toward organization-wide consensus, consistency, and clarity.

Other stage theories of cultural change have been constructed, drawing on noncultural research which argues that organizations pass through predictable stages of organizational development.[5] To translate these ideas into the terminology used in this book, organizations might emerge from the chaos of a start-up period and achieve a founder-centered, organization-wide consensus around the founder's vision. Growth might bring subcultural differentiation; hierarchical and functional subcultures might start to emerge as the firm moved to a more "professional" management style and a more traditional bureaucratic structure. This progression is a Fragmentation-Integration-Differentiation sequence.

Another stage scenario of cultural change might begin with a stable integrated culture. An environmental jolt (e.g., a major unanticipated change in the market for the firm's products) might make resources scarce, exacerbating conflicts among subcultures. As economic difficulties increase, and the firm's survival in its present form becomes more doubtful, confusion and uncertainties should multiply. At this point, stability and a leader-centered cohesion might be welcome. This is a four-stage sequence: Integration, Differentiation, Fragmentation, and a new Integration.

A stage theory is implicit in a number of case studies of cultural change, although the particular stages vary from study to study. For example, Bartunek concludes, from her study of change in a religious order, that cultural change has a dialectical structure. An environmentally triggered crisis created ambiguity for the religious order:

> The crisis challenges the validity of the organization's interpretive schemes, suggesting that they are no longer adequate. During such crisis periods all organizations experience a loss of former certainty. (Bartunek, 1984, p. 364)

Subcultures in the order suggested conflicting alternative resolutions of the problems. Bartunek concludes that ultimately a new synthesis was achieved, reflecting power inequalities among the subcultures:

> Second order ["revolutionary"] change can be understood as occurring dialectically, with the original interpretive schemes as the thesis, other ways of understanding as the antithesis, and what will emerge from their interaction as a synthesis . . . (Watzlawick, Weakland, and Fisch, 1974; Kegan, 1982). Because this process is dialectical, it necessarily involves conflict . . . between groups holding the different perspectives. The resolution of the process will depend in part on the comparative power of these different groups to have their perspective heard. (Bartunek, 1984, pp. 364–365)

This is an Integration, Fragmentation, Differentiation, (new) Integration sequence. In Bartunek's study, subcultures influenced the content of the new organization-wide consensus. In other studies of change a transformational leader is given credit for the content of the new Integration.[6] Further examples of stage theories of cultural change could be given,[7] but what is important here is that they all assume a rationally explainable, unidirectional movement across stages.

Other views of cultural change question these assumptions of unidirectional, linear progression across stages. For example, Frederick describes a pattern of oscillation between the Integration and Differentiation perspectives.[8] He argues that culture restricts the response options of an organization. In order to accommodate changes in the environment, an organization must adapt, add, or substitute coping mechanisms, for example, by changing content themes or formal practices to adjust to changes in the marketplace. An organization will achieve requisite variety when each state of the environment is matched by an off-setting organizational reaction. The benefits of requisite variety are purchased at a cost: the consistency and consensus of the culture is undermined. According to Frederick, the more integrated the culture becomes, the more requisite variety will become a problem, creating a counterbalancing movement toward differentiation. When the complications of differentiation become too great, making predictability and coordination difficult, an organization should seek simplicity, thereby enhancing consistency and consensus. Frederick asserts that the alternation between these integrating and differentiating forces forms the basis for cultural change.

Frederick's oscillation approach is an objectivist view that, like stage theories, encompasses multiple perspectives—one perspective at a time. This oscillation approach could be expanded to include alternation between other pairs of perspectives. For example, at Apple Computer, technical personnel are sometimes assigned to project teams. While a project is underway, team members report intense commitment to shared values, intensified by long hours of hard work and informal socializing. When a project ends, and before another project team is constituted, technical employees often report that they "wallow" in ambiguity, asking questions such as: "Why do I work in such a crazy company?", "What happened to my personal life?", and "Is it worth it to work so hard?", "Am I in the wrong career?" Turnover during these lulls is high. As soon as a new project is assigned, however, technical employees return to the familiar levels of intense commitment. This alternation is an oscillation between Integration and Fragmentation.

Other scholars go beyond both the stage and oscillation approaches to allow a variety of "tracks," or sequences of perspectives to occur.

Not all organizations pass through transitions or the same set of stages, nor do they depart from similar positions or have common destinations. (Greenwood and Hinings, 1988, p. 303)

For example, Schein offers perhaps the most complex of the objectivist views of cultural change.[9] Although any summary risks oversimplification, this change theory combines stages with a variant of Greenwood and Hinings's "tracks"; that is, alternate scenarios are offered at each stage of the cultural change process. At some of these stages, subcultural conflicts emerge or ambiguities proliferate. Sometimes these conflicts and ambiguities are described in non-Integration terms, as strengths or solutions to problems,[10] but more often a successful resolution at each stage is conceptualized in terms congruent with an Integration perspective.[11]

Each of these views of the cultural change process has an objectivist premise:

that, at any time, there is only one correct way to view a culture. Next I explain why this is a problem and offer a resolution.

A SUBJECTIVE, MULTIPERSPECTIVE APPROACH

Any single perspective ignores or distorts crucially important aspects of an organization's culture. When cultural change is being discussed, an objectivist, single-perspective approach becomes even less adequate. For example, a Differentiation study of cultural change must cope with the possibility that a resistance movement might succeed (will they try to establish a new organization-wide consensus?) or fail (will the clarities of the conflict be eroded?). A Fragmentation study of change must acknowledge that some unity and clarity is necessary for most forms of coordinated action. An Integration study cannot ignore the conflicts and ambiguities that become evident during change. *Any cultural context can be understood more fully if it is regarded, at any point in time, from all three perspectives. To exclude any of these perspectives from the domain of organizational culture research would be to limit what we could try to understand.*

This is more than just an intellectual desire to deepen understanding. A three-perspective approach to studying culture has political implications. For example, Integration studies sometimes assert, on the basis of limited data, that all or most employees share the view of top management. The Integration perspective, used in this manner, reifies established authority and denies the existence of alternative points of view. These alternatives are most likely to be advocated by lower-status employees or members of demographic minorities. To the extent that these people (or others) have viewpoints that differ from a dominant view, the Integration perspective implicitly considers their thoughts, values, and feelings to be "irrelevant" to cultural theory and research. If the goal of cultural research is to provide a fuller understanding of life in organizations, it is essential that these often-ignored voices be incorporated into our work. Otherwise, cultural research is likely to recapitulate the managerial bias evident in so much organizational theory and research.[12]

For these reasons, a subjectivist, multiperspective approach to understanding culture is more informative. Such an approach rests on three propositions:

1. Any cultural context contains elements that can be understood only when all three perspectives are brought to bear.
2. A three-perspective approach to studying cultural change therefore offers insights unavailable from a single perspective.
3. Individual researchers can study a single context from all three perspectives, if they wish to do so.

The rest of this chapter explores these three propositions by discussing the results of three case studies: an unusual seminar on organizational research, the OZCO data summarized in this book, and cultural changes in Peace Corps/ Africa during the Kennedy and Nixon administrations.

HIDDEN PERSPECTIVES: THE AMBIGUITY SEMINAR

An unusual culture evolved in a popular doctoral seminar taught by a professor known for his research on ambiguity in organizations. Initially I was convinced that this culture could be fully understood by using only the Fragmentation perspective. According to students in this seminar, ambiguity wasn't just acknowledged—it was relished.[13]

At the first meeting of the seminar, the professor asked each student to write down, individually, what he or she wanted to learn and expected to contribute. No attempt was made to reach consensus on these issues. The professor then asked when and where the students wanted to meet and who wanted to lead the next class discussion. Confused, students desperately attempted to get him to define the topic of the course (listed in the catalogue as "organizational learning"). The students also asked for guidance: "What kind of student presentations should be given?" The professor consistently refused, with a smile, to provide this kind of structure. He was, however, agreeable to all the alternatives suggested. Finally, he was coerced into leading the second class session himself.

At the second class session, the professor led an open-ended discussion of two papers, one of which was titled "Organizational Learning." In subsequent classes, none of the student presentations followed this example. A few of these sessions seemed, according to the students, to have "no" relevance to organizational learning. When asked, the students said they were not disturbed by this lack of focus on the course's ostensible topic (i.e., "We didn't know what to expect, anyway"). Most students defined a bad student presentation as a "formal talk." The "best" presentation was made by a student who put three brief diagrams on the blackboard and started the group "playing around with ideas."

At the last class session, the professor announced, "I think this is an appropriate time to distribute the class syllabus." In a spirit of "How can I know what I am thinking until I see what I say?" the syllabus listed the readings assigned by the student presenters for previous class sessions. Many of the students smiled in appreciation of this gesture.

When asked to describe the seminar experience at the end of the quarter, many students used the word "ambiguous." Often their language was vague (i.e., "We came to the seminar as colleagues" or "We all came to learn"). The students felt they had learned a lot from the seminar, but each one had a different sense of what had been learned. Whatever they thought it was, it probably did not have much to do with "organizational learning."

I described this ambiguity seminar, using only the Fragmentation viewpoint, in my culture class. The students were quick to point out that I had missed evidence congruent with the Differentiation and Integration perspectives. According to these students (some of whom had also attended the ambiguity seminar), there had been a subcultural split between the research-oriented and applied students. The research-oriented students in the ambiguity seminar "reveled in confusion," and were delighted to ponder complexities and explore the unclear indefinitely. They were true-believers in the value of ambiguity.

According to the applied students, the research-oriented students were developing into navel-gazing experts, enveloped in the action paralysis that can come when ambiguity seems pervasive. In contrast, the applied students were excited by the diversity of backgrounds and interests of the ambiguity seminar participants and saw this diversity as a resource that could be utilized for practical purposes. The class presentations of the applied students tended to be case studies of problems they thought the class could help them solve. Each of the applied students remained a true-believer in an unambiguous view of the world. The seminar made these students more eager to experiment with new (unambiguous) solutions to old problems. These differences between the applied and research-oriented students were congruent with a Differentiation perspective.

Another student in my class observed that I had also missed evidence congruent with an Integration view. This student observed that if I walked into the room where the ambiguity seminar was held, one person would be considerably older than the rest, only one person would consistently have the group's full attention when he spoke, and only one would assign grades at the end of the course. This was a leader-centered seminar in spite of the professor's attempts to avoid a traditional leadership role. In addition, the seminar met regularly, in a university room, and students received credit toward a degree. These formal and informal practices suggested that the professor and seminar participants all shared some basic assumptions about how to teach and learn in university contexts.

I had fallen into the "trap" of regarding this seminar from only one perspective. Retrospectively, I could see that my informants had been drawn disproportionately from the research-oriented subculture. In addition, the professor who led the seminar, my key informant, and I had all done research congruent with the Fragmentation perspective. Furthermore, having been a professor for some time, I had come to take for granted certain potentially questionable aspects of the university's approach to teaching and learning. Perhaps because questioning practices such as grading or the authority of the professorial role challenged my own, I had suppressed my awareness of these issues when describing the seminar. The three-perspective interpretation of my students offered a fuller understanding of this context than my single, Fragmentation viewpoint.

OZCO, like the ambiguity seminar, is a context that is more fully understood when a three-perspective approach is used. Most previous studies of OZCO, cited in Chapter 2, have described this culture solely or primarily from the Integration perspective, portraying it as the epitome of leader-centered harmony and shared values. In contrast, the OZCO employees cited in Chapters 3, 5, and 7 spoke of the company in ways that are congruent with all three perspectives. Inconsistencies are evident and ambiguity is pervasive in many of their observations.

This seminar and this corporation are not unique. *Any cultural context contains elements that can be understood only if all three perspectives are utilized.*

THE DYNAMICS OF SUPPRESSION:
HOME AND HIDDEN PERSPECTIVES

Sometimes, however, a particular context seems to fit one of the perspectives more easily than the others. For example, I thought the Fragmentation perspective offered the most obviously relevant view of the ambiguity seminar. When the researchers cited in Chapter 2 studied OZCO, they used an Integration viewpoint. It is not correct to conclude, however, that the two excluded perspectives offered "less accurate" descriptions of these contexts. *When one perspective seems to be the "best" way to regard a context, the other two, forbidden perspectives may be particularly useful sources of insight.*

The three perspectives work in a manner that recapitulates the psychodynamics of suppression. The "home" perspective is the viewpoint that comes most easily to mind when a particular person regards a particular cultural configuration. It seems to be the most obvious, accurate, or appropriate way to view the culture. To draw an oversimplified analogy, a "home" perspective holds the position of the superego within Freud's view of a person's psyche.

In any context, at any time, the other two perspectives explain aspects of the culture that are ignored or misrepresented by the home perspective. Of these two suppressed perspectives, one is often fairly easily accessible. For example, "Oh, of course, I should have seen that" was my reaction to the subcultural analysis of the ambiguity seminar. This is analogous to the ego in a Freudian framework. Insights at this level are "preconscious" and can be retrieved with a little effort.

Material in the id, however, is unconscious. It has been repressed because its emergence would be threatening. [14] Understanding of this deeply hidden material is most difficult and most essential for therapeutic insight. For example, it was most difficult for me to acknowledge the implications of the Integration interpretation of the ambiguity seminar, in part because it made me aware that aspects of my position I had taken for granted (i.e., a teacher's giving grades) could be challenged and altered.

Over time, the relationship among the three perspectives may seem to change, so that the home perspective becomes suppressed and a different viewpoint surfaces in the home position. These ideas can be used to rethink the objectivist views of cultural change discussed earlier. For example, Table 9-2 postulates, in objectivist terms, a "fit" between single perspectives and particular types of organizations at one point in time. The ideas in this table should be reformulated as a prediction by showing which of the three perspectives is most likely to be the home perspective for viewing a particular type of organization.

It is possible, then, that a majority of cultural members or observers might agree that a particular perspective is the "home perspective," that is, the most appropriate way to view their organization. If the firm's management had attempted to promote this perspective, the employees' agreement would suggest that this promotion effort had been at least partially successful. However, this agreement cannot be interpreted as evidence that one perspective is objectively correct and the other two are wrong, or less accurate. A home perspective is a subjective viewpoint, not an objectively accurate description of the single, most accurate way to look at a culture. Any cultural context contains elements that can be understood only when all three points of view are utilized.

For example, OZCO is an organization that many researchers and managers have described solely from an Integration viewpoint. Some of these people, reacting to an earlier draft of the OZCO data presented here, argued that these data must represent a later stage in the company's development, when growth and a tough market had eroded the shared values that made this firm such an epitome of clarity, consistency, and organization-wide consensus. This objectivist view assumes that a stage of cultural development can be adequately described using a single perspective—in this case, an Integration viewpoint.

I would reframe these observations. At one time, the Integration viewpoint may well have been the home perspective of many OZCO managers and researchers (most of whom were white, middle-class men with professional or managerial jobs). However, at this or any other time period, some elements of the OZCO culture could only be understood from the (suppressed) Differentiation and Fragmentation viewpoints. Subsequently, when growth and a tough market made subcultural differences more obvious, the Differentiation perspective may have moved into the home position, with the other two perspectives being suppressed.

Figure 9-1 contains two other examples of a subjective, multiperspective approach to understanding cultural change. In this figure, a growing start-up company is shown using all three perspectives at three points in time; the home perspective moves from Fragmentation, to Integration, to Differentiation, with the other two perspectives at each time period being suppressed. In the second example, an environmental jolt hits an established corporation, moving its home perspective from Integration, to Differentiation, then Fragmentation, and finally a (new) Integration. In each of these four time periods, all three perspectives are included, but two are suppressed. In this figure cultural change is conceptualized as shifts between home and suppressed perspectives, so that all three perspectives are considered at each stage. Any other sequence of home perspectives is possible, although the stage theories of cultural change cited earlier suggest that these particular sequences will be frequently seen.

The word *seen* in the last sentence is carefully chosen. These perspectives, like culture itself, must be subjectively perceived. None is more accurate than the others—even the home perspective. There is no standard (even a majority vote among cultural members or expert observers) that can be used to determine the relative accuracy of these perspectives. Instead, like the superego, ego, and id in Freud's model of the psyche, all three perspectives make an essential contribution to understanding. In cultural research, as in psychoanalysis, the more the relevance of a particular perspective is suppressed, the greater the potential growth in understanding if that perspective can be accessed and utilized. Insights gathered from viewing a culture from the home perspective often are relatively obvious, while insights from the suppressed perspectives are more likely to be surprising.

A growing start-up company:

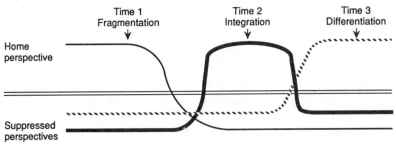

An environmental jolt hits an established corporation:

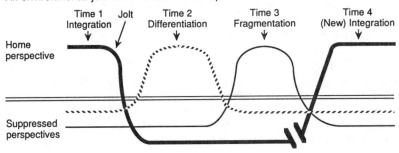

Figure 9-1.   A subjectivist, three-perspective view of cultural change: two examples.

A cultural framework is useful only when it exposes something previously unknown or unacknowledged. For these reasons, a three-perspective view of cultural change is more useful than any single perspective. Rather than collecting data to determine which cultural perspective is a more accurate description of one or many contexts, it is more informative to ask what can be learned from using all three viewpoints.

A THREE-PERSPECTIVE VIEW OF CHANGE: PEACE CORPS/AFRICA

The case studies of the ambiguity seminar and the OZCO employees do not focus on the change process. Therefore, a longitudinal example of the three-perspective approach might be useful here. Meyerson and I studied changes in the culture of Peace Corps/Africa at two time periods (during the Kennedy and Nixon administrations).[15]

In this account we tried to place equal weight on all three perspectives at both points in time (not specifying a home perspective), so the dynamics of suppression would not not give the insights of one perspective greater weight in any time period. In our writing, the perspectives were presented sequentially, so that each view could be expressed without "contamination" or dilution by the others. This sequential structure echoes the way the architect Venturi recommends walking around a building:

One contradictory meaning usually dominates another, but in complex compositions the relationship is not always constant. This is especially true as the observer moves through or around a building, and by extension through a city: at one moment one meaning can be perceived as dominant; at another moment a different meaning seems paramount. (Venturi, 1977, p. 32)

The Integration view of Peace Corps/Africa during President Kennedy's administration focused on the values that were espoused by Kennedy and top Peace Corps staff. Core values included the importance of international volunteer work, altruism, and open-mindedness, especially concerning the excitement of living in new environments. Peace Corps volunteers at this time were generally drawn from the middle class. Most were recent college graduates, often with a liberal arts degree. According to high-ranking Peace Corps officials, these volunteers fervently believed that, through these ideals, they could change the world. For example:

An idea, to conquer, must fuse with the will of men and women who are prepared to dedicate their lives to its realization. We had a sense twenty five years ago [at the Peace Corps' conception] that there were such men and women in America waiting to be called, impatient to carry the idea of service to mankind. As it turned out I think we underestimated both their numbers and their dedication. (Shriver, 1986, p. 18)

This is a monolithic view of the Peace Corps/Africa culture; it asserts that volunteers, staff, and leaders, like Shriver, all shared the same values.

A Differentiation view of the Peace Corps/Africa culture during the Kennedy administration would focus on the various subcultures that evolved. For example, the top staff (composed of the Peace Corps/Africa director, a director for each African host country, and assorted other managerial personnel) formed a relatively cohesive, enhancing subculture. In addition, volunteers assigned to particular countries tended to form rudimentary subcultures, in part because volunteers in countries with large, relatively wealthy, urban areas had very different living conditions than volunteers assigned to countries where poverty stricken, rural villages predominated. Although contact with volunteers in other countries was sporadic and difficult, a variety of project-oriented subcultures cross-cut national boundaries. For example, volunteers teaching English (education being the largest of these project subcultures) would discuss shared problems that were quite different from the difficulties experienced by volunteers assigned to sanitation and agriculture projects. This Differentiation view of Peace Corps/Africa during the Kennedy administration is illustrated in Figure 9-2.

A Fragmentation view of the Peace Corps/Africa culture under Kennedy, also illustrated in Figure 9-2, focused on the constant flux that accompanied the two-year turnover of most volunteers. There was considerable turnover of country directors as well. In addition, transient issue-specific interest groups often developed, although individuals involved seldom agreed about what the problem was, where it had surfaced, or how it should be resolved. For example, debates about the importance of teaching English, the appropriateness of love affairs, and problems due to unfamiliar illness all aroused much controversy, for short pe-

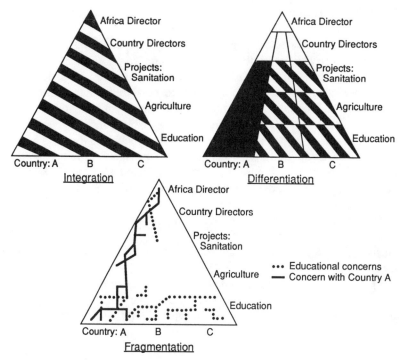

Figure 9-2. Peace Corps/Africa: three perspectives at time one. (Adapted from Meyerson and Martin, 1987)

riods of time. Some individuals became involved in a subset of these issues; others remained ignorant or uninvolved. Two transient issue-specific alliances, regarding an epidemic in Country A and a dispute about the relative importance of English instruction, are diagramed in the Fragmentation view of Peace Corps/ Africa in Figure 9-2.

At this time, each volunteer and each staff member had a unique set of experiences, often in isolated settings. Volunteers' contacts with staff members were infrequent and often considered (by volunteers) to be unnecessary. There was much confusion, even on the part of veteran volunteers, about how they were expected to deal with particular difficulties. An ability to live with ambiguity was essential for any member of the Peace Corps.

When Nixon became President, he decided that the Peace Corps had become a haven for those with suspect political views and a sinecure for middle-class liberal arts graduates with no marketable skills. An Integration view of the culture at this time focused on Nixon's leadership initiatives, in particular, the changes he made in the kinds of volunteers to be recruited. The "new" Peace Corps volunteer would be a senior citizen or a younger blue-collar worker with practical skills in areas such as construction, plumbing, and farming. There was to be more of digging ditches, laying pipes, and building bridges and less teaching of English (and liberal political values). According to this Integration perspective, illustrated in Figure 9-3, Nixon mandated a "new" Peace Corps with new personnel and a different mission.

A Differentiation view of Peace Corps/Africa at this time focused on how environmental factors had influenced subcultural composition. For example, a severe drought had spread to previously unaffected areas of Africa, bringing famine, increasing the flood of refugees into new areas, and creating political turmoil in several national governments. The countries participating in the Peace Corps changed, in part to keep volunteers away from politically motivated violence. Water-based sanitation projects became impractical and were discontinued in many areas. New drought-resistant crops and irrigation projects were introduced. As illustrated in Figure 9-3, subcultural configurations linked to these countries and projects were quite different than they had been under the Kennedy administration.

A Fragmentation view of the culture of Peace Corps/Africa under Nixon focused on the confusions caused by all these changes. Turnover was high, as the idealists quit and more diverse and pragmatic staff and volunteers took over. Budget cuts from Washington, D.C., suggested that the days of the Peace Corps might be numbered. Many staff and volunteers were demoralized and looking for other work. Although many staff and volunteers shared concerns about particular issues, there was little agreement about what should be done. For example, a

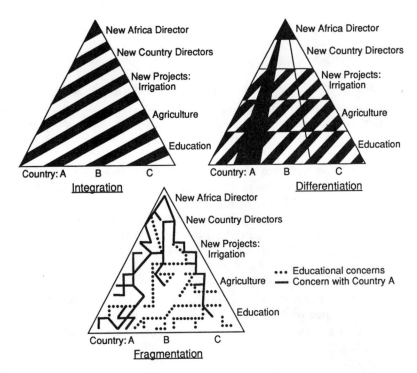

Figure 9-3. Peace Corps/Africa: three perspectives at time two. (Adapted from Meyerson and Martin, 1987)

wide range of volunteers (not just the English teachers, but also those introducing new crops or irrigation methods) were worried about effective education techniques. However, teaching children a new language was quite different from persuading a village council to adopt a new method of sewage disposal or convincing people to cook untraditional grains. As can be seen in Figure 9-3, the educational issue produced widespread, but loose and transient connections among the staff and volunteers during the Nixon administration. Volunteers and staff with past or present service in country A also shared a loose and transient concern with political violence in that country, although they disagreed about whether these upheavals represented progress or a deterioration in the country's governing structure.

Stepping back from this brief description, the limitations of each perspective's view of the cultural change process become evident. For example, an Integration view of Peace Corps/Africa, focusing on policy changes mandated by Nixon and the Peace Corps leadership in Washington, D.C., underestimates environmental factors that are the focus of Differentiation accounts of this time period, such as the drought or national political changes. In addition, project-related difficulties were crucial factors in the experiences of country staff and volunteers. Finally, both the Integration and Differentiation views ignore the ambiguities so central in the personal experiences of volunteers and staff working in rapidly changing, relatively isolated settings.

This brief analysis of Peace Corps/Africa illustrates how a three-perspective approach to the study of cultural change can offer insights inaccessible to any single perspective. The three-perspective approach has also been utilized, for example, in Jeffcutt's study of a temporary educational organization for unemployed women in England and in Baburoglu and Gocer's study of the privatization of Sumerbank in Turkey.[16] However, a multiperspective approach is impractical unless researchers can and do move from one perspective to another.

MOVING ACROSS PERSPECTIVES: POSSIBLE?

Both researchers and cultural members can move across perspectives, although not all do so.[17] For example, some OZCO members expressed opinions congruent with more than one perspective. Stuart, a marketing engineer, described the implementation of pay-cut-with-time-off policy in egalitarian language, congruent with an Integration view of OZCO:

> Everyone did it. It's like profit sharing, same concept: everyone takes the hit. Across the board at OZCO, everyone takes the good and the bad and spreads it around with only minor exceptions. (Stuart, marketing engineer)

Voluntary time off was another cost-cutting policy that was supposed to be available in an egalitarian fashion, but according to Stuart, particularly busy employees were unable to participate. This observation of inequality was congruent with a Differentiation perspective of this firm:

Voluntary Time Off sounds good, but if you have lots of work, then time off is a joke. It is really a pay cut when you have lots of work. If you don't, then the time off is really not voluntary. I guess it's my choice, but I have too much work to take time. In the last six months, I've only taken two days off. (Stuart, marketing engineer)

Denise expressed an egalitarian view of these policies, congruent with the Integration view:

I guess it's laid back and informal. Everyone has flex hours now. Everyone has a pay cut. (Denise, product marketing)

Denise also challenged these egalitarian interpretations:

In certain divisions you were expected to come in anyways, for whatever reasons. In other divisions, it was less clear. You were just told that you were expected to get the job done and if it could be done in two days less, fine: otherwise, work. So, in a lot of cases, it was a pay cut disguised. But it affected everyone differently, depending on their division and supervisor. (Denise, product marketing)

Stuart again vacillated between an Integration and a Differentiation viewpoint when he described the distribution of "perks" as both relatively egalitarian (based on job-related need) and inegalitarian (as determined by a boss' power):

If you have a reason, you get something better. Design people get better terminals. Sales people have cars, but they need them. I have a schlocky desk, but that's OK. I can still do my work. (Stuart, marketing engineer)

If my manager has extra money, after everything is taken care of, then we get some perks. (Stuart, marketing engineer)

Sally also expressed opinions consistent with more than one perspective. For example, she discussed the "family" orientation of OZCO in terms that acknowledged the positive affect generally characteristic of an Integration viewpoint:

OZCO is like a midwestern family: good, kind, fair, community folks. (Sally, human resources consultant)

Sally went on to note that power differences associated with traditional gender roles in families also reflected power inequalities between men and women at OZCO. These views are congruent with the Differentiation perspective:

Along with this very nice, humanitarian theme goes the midwestern mommy and daddy: daddy makes the decisions and takes care of the family and mommy does the supplementary stuff. (Sally, human resources consultant)

Like these OZCO employees who move across perspective boundaries, some cultural researchers have conducted studies that are congruent with more than one perspective. For this reason, the perspectives are used as descriptions of studies, not individual researchers. For example, Barley's description of funeral directors fits within an Integration framework, while his description of conflicts between radiologists and technicians in hospitals exemplifies a Differentiation viewpoint. Pettigrew's description of headmasters is a leader-centered, Integration view, while his longitudinal case history of a corporation is more congruent with the Differentiation and Fragmentation viewpoints. My early work on stories and scripts fits within the Integration perspective, my later work on countercultures and subcultures was conducted from a Differentiation standpoint, and my most recent work (the deconstruction of the Caesarean story) is congruent with a Fragmentation view. Other researchers whose cultural research has crossed perspective barriers include Smircich, Beyer, Trice, Weick, Brunsson, and Louis.[18]

Researchers can move across perspective boundaries because the three perspectives are not consistently associated with particular methodological preferences or epistemological positions. There are quantitative and qualitative (phenomenological, ethnographic, and hermeneutic) examples of cultural research that fit within each of the three perspectives. Even the Fragmentation view, which in its postmodern form eschews logical positivism and all other empirical roads to truth, has been associated with a variety of epistemological and methodological approaches. Therefore, these three perspectives are not fully developed *paradigms,* in the sense that Kuhn or Burrell and Morgan use this term. This methodological and epistemological eclecticism makes it easier for a researcher, with a particular set of skills and preferences, to move from one of the three perspectives to another.

MOVING ACROSS PERSPECTIVES: DESIRABLE?

Although it is possible for a researcher to adopt a multiperspective approach, many researchers consistently utilize only one perspective in their published culture studies. There are understandable reasons for this restraint:

> Scholars often make their mark in academia by becoming associated with a particular position and entering into frequent doctrinal debates while stubbornly defending their particular orthodoxy. After all, to the extent that academics measure their own and others' success by the number of entries in the citation index, it pays not necessarily to be right, but to be clearly identified with a particular position and then to be attacked and to counter-attack frequently. Academics often gain little from seeking commonalities among denominations or building bridges across sets. (Strober, 1990, p. 238)

There are other reasons for relying on a single perspective, beyond such pragmatic considerations as establishing a coherent intellectual reputation or offering a succinct account within the space limitations of a journal article. The three perspectives are not simply different ways to sort collections of superficial cultural manifestations. Each perspective offers a politically motivated pattern of interpretation of the manifestations included (and excluded) in a cultural portrait. By "political," I mean that each perspective takes a stance toward established authority. Those stances are dialectically related.

Each perspective, in some sense, denies the others. For example, the Differentiation view explicitly denies the Integration perspective's homogenizing claims of unity. The Integration view implicitly denies Differentiation claims concerning the importance of differences and the dynamics of power and oppression. Both the Integration and Differentiation perspectives deny the intrusions of ambiguity into "cultural" islands of lucidity. The Fragmentation perspective finds it difficult to acknowledge that some collective assumptions may be so fundamental they are tacit—and shared by almost all.

Politically motivated differences among the perspectives are reflected in their orientations toward authority, whether than authority is vested in an individual or a power structure. The Integration perspective encapsulates and enshrines an established authority. (Although Integration studies usually take the viewpoint of the top management of a hierarchy, it is also possible to offer an Integration view of a relatively nonhierarchical revolutionary social movement or a commune.) The Differentiation perspective inherently challenges an established authority, as it describes groups of people who hold differing opinions. The Fragmentation perspective undermines the truth claims of any established authority as well as any group challenging that authority.

The political motivations underlying this dialectical tension means that some researchers will not want to abandon their preferred perspective or undermine it, by temporarily utilizing other viewpoints. This may be short-sighted for reasons implicit in the adage "know thine enemy." For example, insights garnered from an Integration viewpoint can be invaluable to a critic working from the Differentiation perspective. An Integration study can map the terrain of an organization's dominant ideology, providing the critic with a clearly delineated set of themes to challenge. In addition, some members of subordinated subcultures believe in ideologies that legitimate their own subordination, as when blue-collar workers endorse some elements of conservative ideology or women express support for ideas about femininity that imply the inferiority of their gender. The Integration perspective can explicate this kind of belief, even if it is conceptualized (from a Differentiation perspective) as "false consciousness." Furthermore, if a Differentiation study examines strategies for collective resistance by subordinated groups, it will be helpful to know how those in power view the situation. For all these reasons, a Differentiation view is strengthened when it is coupled with a full analysis from the Integration perspective.[19] These examples illustrate that crossing perspective barriers does not necessarily involve abandoning one's political commitments.

A researcher who prefers an Integration perspective can also benefit from insights generated by utilizing the other two perspectives. As illustrated by the OZCO case study, an Integration study often underestimates employees' resistance to managerial directives and their confusion about what kinds of behaviors are wanted. Top managers might find it easier to implement policy changes if they could view their organization's culture from the Differentiation and Fragmentation viewpoints, so that pockets of resistance, ignorance, and confusion could be anticipated. To the extent that an Integration researcher wants to provide information useful for increasing consistency and consensus, knowledge gathered from the other two perspectives will help isolate problem areas.

Even a fervent advocate of a single perspective could benefit from taking a three-perspective approach. However, whether a researcher moves across perspectives reluctantly (seeking ultimately to bolster a single-perspective) or enthusiastically (seeking to maximize understanding from all three viewpoints), it is essential to keep each perspective separate:

> It would be pointless to seek a homogenization or reconciliation of all points of view: there can be, in this sense, no common world view. What is seen to constitute the social world, rather, is the nature of the relationships between different views from different social positions. . . . The essence of the comparative method is to make sense of differences, not to collapse them. (Strathern, 1987, p. 286)

Pressures toward assimilation would undermine a perspective's inherently oppositional stance toward the other viewpoints, threatening its conceptual and political integrity. A multiperspective view of culture must vacillate among the three viewpoints, presenting each in turn. When it is used in this way, a three-perspective approach is both possible and desirable.

NOTES

1. Meyerson and Martin (1987), Martin and Meyerson (1988).
2. Schein (1985), p. 309.
3. Jonsson and Lundin (1977).
4. Schein (1978). Other illustrations of this clarity-ambiguity-clarity version of the cultural change process can be found in Brunsson (1985).
5. See, for example, Kimberly and Miles (1980) and Kimberly and Quinn (1984).
6. These cultural change studies are similar to noncultural leader-centered theories of organizational change, such as Greiner's (1972) theory of organizational leadership, and leader-centered descriptions of organizational transitions, such as Kimberly's (1979) description of how a leader managed the founding of a medical school.
7. Similarly, some theories of organizational change observe fluctuations in configurations of strategy, structure, and (sometimes) "ideology" or "culture," that move from one integrated "gestalt" to another, passing through periods of ambiguity or conflict. See, for example, Miller and Friesen (1980, 1983), Morgan and Ramirez (1984), Torbert (1976), and Tushman and Romanelli (1985). To the extent that these studies include culture, they define it in a very limited way, generally excluding all formal practices, such as structure and pay. See the discussion, in Chapter 2, of the problems inherent in such specialized definitions of culture.
8. Frederick (1985).
9. Schein (1985).
10. See, for example, Schein (1985), p. 291.
11. Ibid., p. 273.
12. See, for example, Burrell and Morgan (1979), Calas and Smircich (1987), Jermier (1985), Roethlisberger (1977), and Stablein and Nord (1985).

13. Debra Meyerson was a particularly helpful informant.

14. Meyerson (1991b) discusses why the Fragmentation perspective is particularly threatening and therefore likely to be suppressed.

15. This case description is adapted from Meyerson and Martin (1987).

16. Jeffcutt (forthcoming) and Baburoglu and Gocer (1991). See Aldrich (in press) for an application of this three-perspective framework to other areas of organizational theory, such as institutionalism.

17. Although no research has been conducted on this issue, it seems reasonable to hypothesize that certain individual personality traits (such as tolerance for ambiguity) or patterns of experience (e.g., as a victim of obvious discrimination) might create a propensity for an individual to repress or utilize a particular perspective.

18. Other researchers have crossed perspective boundaries in a different way, by conducting cultural research congruent with one perspective and investigating concerns, normally associated with the other two perspectives, in their noncultural research. For example, as detailed in footnote 1 of Chapter 4, Schein's cultural studies are primarily congruent with an Integration perspective, but his noncultural research has examined topics such as deviance, process consultation, brainwashing, and the tension between an individual and an organization. These noncultural studies are more congruent with the Differentiation perspective's focus on conflict and the Fragmentation emphasis on ambiguity. Schein as an example illustrates well the dangers of using the perspectives to categorize researchers, rather than their studies.

19. Some elements of this argument for combining the Integration and Differentiation views are congruent with Differentiation perspective critiques of Integration research by, for example, Alvesson and Melin (1987), Rosen (1985), Turner (1986), and Young (1989).

10

Giving Up the Authority Game: A Postmodern Critique of the Three-Perspective Framework

OZCO was selected as a pseudonym in part because Baum's classic tale, *The Wizard of Oz*, captures much of the spirit of this multiperspective approach to understanding cultures in organizations. Dorothy's long journey on the yellow brick road ended at the gates of the Emerald City of Oz, where she hoped to find the Wizard and ask him to send her back to Kansas. The guard at the gate of the city would not let her enter until she had put on some spectacles. She was given a box of spectacles to choose from: all of which had green lenses.

Cultural perspectives can also serve as lenses, coloring what is seen, bringing some elements of a culture into focus, and blurring others. When Dorothy and her companions chose their spectacles, entered the city of Oz, and finally found the wizard, the following dialogue ensued:

"Who are you?"

"I am Oz, the Great and Terrible," said the little man, in a trembling voice, "but don't strike me—please don't!—and I'll do anything you want me to."

Our friends looked at him in surprise and dismay. "I thought Oz was a great Head," said Dorothy.

"And I thought Oz was a lovely Lady," said the Scarecrow.

"And I thought Oz was a terrible Beast," said the Tin Woodman.

"And I thought Oz was a Ball of Fire," exclaimed the Lion.

"No, you are all wrong," said the little man meekly. "I have been making believe."

"Making believe!" cried Dorothy. "Are you not a great Wizard?"

"Hush, my dear," he said; "don't speak so loud, or you will be overheard—and I should be ruined. I'm supposed to be a Great Wizard."

"And aren't you?" she asked.

"Not a bit of it, my dear; I'm just a common man."

"You're more than that," said the Scarecrow, in a grieved tone; "you're a humbug."

"Exactly so!" declared the little man, rubbing his hands together as if it pleased him; "I am a humbug." . . .

"I think you are a very bad man," said Dorothy.

"Oh, no, my dear; I'm really a very good man; but I'm a very bad Wizard, I must admit." (Baum, 1986, pp. 176–180)

In this chapter I step back from being an advocate of the three-perspective framework and analyze the various ways its attempt at wizardry is incomplete. This chapter makes an increasingly deep series of criticisms of the three-perspective framework, beginning with relatively conventional observations about the limitations of this way of looking at cultures in organizations. Reflexively, I clarify where I stand in the cultural debates that have been discussed. This chapter (and this book) end with a postmodern critique that raises serious questions about current research in this field and other social scientific domains. My objective is to outline an increasingly difficult and important series of problems that organizational culture researchers might be able to address.

A SEARCH FOR THE FOURTH PERSPECTIVE

Any time a categorization system is introduced, its boundaries become questionable. If presented with three categories, the question arises: Is there a fourth? The three perspectives have been defined in terms of three variables: the relationship among the cultural manifestations (consistency, inconsistency, or complexity); the degree of consensus (organization-wide consensus, subcultural consensus, or multiplicity of views); and orientation toward ambiguity (excluding it, channeling it, or focusing on it). Working within this framework, a fourth perspective would have to be defined in terms of these three variables. How can cultural manifestations be related to each other, beyond having a relationship that is consistent, inconsistent, or complex? What can be done with consensus, beyond the three alternatives outlined above? What can be done with ambiguity—in addition to excluding, channeling, and focusing on it? Even if these questions could be answered, would the attributes of the resulting "fourth perspective" cohere as an approach to studying cultures?

Within these limitations, I have not been able to come up with a fourth perspective. It may be possible, but I suspect that the three-perspective framework is a closed system, in the sense that a fourth perspective cannot be added without changing the three defining variables. A more effective way to critique this system might be to ask: What concerns have been blurred or ignored by this framework? What other variables might cross-cut these three?

OTHER WAYS OF CARVING UP THIS FIELD OF INQUIRY

There are a variety of other ways to "carve up" this domain of inquiry. Below I draw on several reviews of organizational culture research that suggest important limitations of the approach I have taken.

The three perspectives do not have distinctive orientations toward organizational effectiveness, methodology, or epistemology. Therefore, a different view might emerge if these variables were used to classify cultural studies. It might be helpful to distinguish cultural studies that examine different kinds of effectiveness, perhaps using the criterion, "Who benefits?": top and middle managers, shareholders, lower-ranking employees, or various demographic groups? In addition, effectiveness studies might focus on different aspects of culture than other kinds of cultural research.

It might also be useful to classify studies by methodology. Quantitative studies tend to be specialist, that is, focused on relatively few cultural manifestations. Understandably, the manifestations selected tend to be easily measured by quantitative scales, for example, self-reports of behavioral norms or espoused values. Hybrid quantitative–qualitative studies have developed innovative approaches to measuring interpretations of a wider variety of manifestations, but they still do not attain the breadth or depth of understanding of the best qualitative studies.

Ethnographic studies, in particular, are more able to "penetrate the front" of cultural members' attempts at impression management. An ethnographer who works in a cultural context for months, ideally years, copes with physical, emotional, and intellectual difficulties that presumably enable a deeper (more "emic") understanding of the culture. The few organizational culture studies that attain this intensity of involvement tend to arrive at different kinds of conclusions than studies that rely on more superficial approaches. These methodological issues are ignored by the three-perspective approach.

Turning to epistemological issues, there may be conceptual differences between, for example, phenomenological and hermeneutic studies of culture. Burrell and Morgan's research suggests that if organizational culture research were classified using epistemological criteria, the resulting categories might be full-fledged "paradigms," rather than preparadigmatic perspectives.[1]

Focusing on substantive rather than methodological or epistemological orientations, Smircich finds it useful to distinguish cultural studies that focus on cognitive, symbolic, and unconscious processes.[2] These distinctions are blurred in the three-perspective approach, as any manifestation can be interpreted, from any perspective, in cognitive, symbolic, or unconscious terms. An examination of these different substantive orientations might yield an analysis that is more sensitive than the three-perspective approach to variations in the conceptual depth of inquiry.

Stablein and Nord offer a political critique of organizational culture research.[3] They classify culture studies using Habermas's three-way typology of interests: technical (a structural-functionalist, managerial orientation), practical (the interpretive position of seeking to understand context-specific meaning), and emancipatory (seeking new ways of organizing that would be less oppressive). They find that most studies are conducted in a technical interest and advocate more emancipatory research.

It is possible to conduct emancipatory research from either a Differentiation or a Fragmentation viewpoint. A few Differentiation studies have focused on strategies that subordinated groups could use to make organizations less oppressive. Fragmentation research also can undermine attempts to establish hegemonic authority, through the deconstruction of managerial or intellectual discourse or other, more direct types of action.[4] Ideally, emancipatory Fragmentation research would create room for alternative points of view, enabling more tolerance of ambiguity. The three-perspective framework does not exclude the emancipatory research that Stablein and Nord advocate, but it also does not illuminate the difficulties inherent in doing this kind of work.

Other reviews suggest other ways of carving up the domain of organizational culture research, but there is a limited amount one can learn from variations in the classification of a relatively narrow set of studies. Perhaps the most important limitation of the three-perspective approach (and all the reviews discussed above) is a disproportionate focus on U.S. studies. When the citations congruent with the three perspectives are reviewed from an international perspective, it appears that the Integration perspective is favored primarily by U.S. researchers, that some British researchers seem to have an affinity for the Differentiation perspective, and that many Western European scholars gravitate toward the Fragmentation view. If international differences do exist, these might make an interesting study.

If I had been familiar with a different or broader sample of organizational culture studies by researchers from other countries, the proportion of studies assigned to the three perspectives, and probably the composition of those perspectives, might have been different. Several new organizational culture books by European authors have been or will soon be published.[5] Their ways of carving up this domain of inquiry are quite different.

So far, only relatively limited and conventional criticisms of the three-perspective approach have been presented. Postmodern critiques of the research reviewed in this book are far deeper—incommensurably so. Although a detailed presentation of postmodernism cannot be adequately made within the space constraints of a single chapter, when the three-perspective approach is critiqued from this point of view, useful insights emerge.

A POSTMODERN CRITIQUE OF THE THREE-PERSPECTIVE FRAMEWORK

Most of the research summarized in this book makes modernist assumptions: for example, that universal, scientific principles can lead to legitimate, authoritative statements of the truth about a cultural context—whether that context is viewed as the epitome of harmony and homogeneity or as a collection of subcultures with differing, sometimes conflicting viewpoints.[6] Of the three perspectives, the Fragmentation viewpoint comes closest to postmodernism in its acknowledgments of ambiguities and multiple interpretations. Whereas modernism is "associated with the removal of mystery and ambiguity from social life," the Fragmentation perspective, like postmodernism, celebrates "indeterminacy, heterogeneity, and ambivalence."[7] Nevertheless, most Fragmentation studies are written as if the author's presentation of cultural members' interpretations constituted an objectively accurate portrait. Postmodern thinking would concur with the Fragmentation perspective's emphasis on ambiguity and multiple interpretations, but would find fault with any account that failed to question deeply the author's inevitably inaccurate and incomplete representation of the viewpoints of cultural members.

Postmodernism would make similar criticisms of the three-perspective framework. Since that framework insists on the subjective nature of cultural knowledge and emphasizes ambiguity and the multiplicity of cultural interpretations, it is partially congruent with postmodern thinking. However, the three-perspective framework commits at least two postmodern sins: it is a meta-theory and it is presented in a way that fails to challenge, deeply, the authority of the author. Implications of both of these criticisms are discussed next.

Against the Imperialism of Meta-theories

Meta-theories attempt to encompass, and thereby surpass, predecessor theories. They encounter difference and contradiction by seeking absorption and assimilation. For example, an Integration view seeks unity by focusing only on similarities, consistencies, and agreement, moving to higher levels of abstraction until only these aspects are visible. A Differentiation perspective uses dichotomous thinking to focus on dissimilarities and inconsistencies, sometimes offering a dialectical synthesis that transcends differences. Both abstraction and dialectical synthesis are meta-theoretical moves.

Not surprisingly, postmodern theorizing is adamantly disdainful of meta-theories, labeling them "narratives of transcendence" because each claims to be better than its predecessors—more abstract and yet also closer to "the" empirical "truth." Lyotard, for example, views meta-theories as totalitarian attempts, by those who are or who wish to become dominant, to provide all-encompassing world views that silence diversity of opinion.[8] Postmodern scholars argue that attempts to create meta-theories are misguided and futile; fragmentation and multiplicity will flourish, in spite of attempts to make particular meta-theories dominant.[9]

The three-perspective framework is a modernist attempt to build a meta-theory. Its tripartite categorization scheme is based on a series of undeconstructed dichotomies that position the perspectives in opposition to each other. The difficulties usually associated with using categories, described in Chapter 1, have left their mark in the intervening chapters. I have ignored aspects of studies that straddled boundaries among the three perspectives, omitted unclassifiable research or relegated it to footnotes, and reserved treatment of issues that transcended these categories (such as methodology, epistemology, and political ideology) to this final chapter. Perhaps most important, by using these categories to classify studies, I cannot completely avoid reifying the perspectives and pigeonholing researchers. Such a use of categories is common scientific practice, but it can have deleterious effects on the ways knowledge gets "created" and scholarly work is and is not evaluated.

Furthermore, I have presented the three-perspective framework as a meta-theory that might, because of its supposedly greater inclusiveness or insightfulness, deserve to dominate other approaches to understanding cultures in organizations. I make a blatant truth claim: "I believe even the most fervent advocate of a single perspective could benefit from taking a three-perspective approach." I make this claim in the name of knowledge: a multiple perspective would offer deeper understanding of a cultural context. Furthermore, the three variables used to define aspects of all three perspectives (relationship among manifestations, degree of consensus, and orientation toward ambiguity) are the rudiments of a synthesis: they allude to similarities among the perspectives—common issues each perspective resolves differently. In these senses, the three-perspective approach is not just another theory; it is an attempt to build a meta-theory that transcends—through abstraction—the work classified within each perspective.

Gagliardi, as discussed in Chapter 1, makes this point when he describes the three-perspective framework as an attempt to establish a paradigm that would institutionalize this view of cultural research within the mainstream of organizational theory. Gagliardi, like Turner, views this development with understandable ambivalence, regretting the loss of excitement and creativity that accompanied the initial rise of interest in cultural approaches to the study of organizations.[10]

A postmodern view would anticipate the failure of this attempt to establish a meta-theory, in part because of any author's inescapable inability to present a theory as authoritative: the one truth. This is the crisis of representation that lies at the heart of a postmodern critique. Such analysis of author-ity must be reflexive, drawing attention to the limitations of the author's eye/I.

Deconstructing Author/ity

I have written this book in a style that attempts to present each perspective in a fair, even-handed manner. For example, I claimed to "respect the integrity" of each perspective by allocating a separate chapter for each and relegating the most explicit criticism to the chapter's conclusion. I have quoted extensively from studies representative of each perspective, so that researchers could speak "in their own voices." Perhaps most important, I have not attempted to resolve the dialectical tensions among the perspectives. In this way, I hoped to minimize pressures toward assimilation or distortion, stressing each perspective's antagonistic stance toward the others.

I have also tried to allow individual OZCO employees to "speak for themselves." By using extensive quotations and individual pseudonyms, I have tried to preserve the individuality of these informants in the text. In presenting the OZCO material, I have eschewed the seductions of narrative structure, minimized generalizations and interpretations (e.g., using such indeterminate modifiers as "some employees" and "sometimes"), and let the informants' emphasis on the three themes (egalitarianism, etc.) structure the presentation of this material.

This writing style implicitly presents the author (myself) as a neutral presenter of theories, as if I were "above the fray" of the war among the perspectives. Postmodernists, among others, would be quick to point out that no such neutral stance is possible. Although I admit my biases in Chapter 1, in the intervening chapters I have generally avoided using the personal pronoun, refrained from explicitly elaborating my own position, and utilized a series of traditional devices that draw attention away from my role as author. This absence of reflexive analysis hides weaknesses and silences in my argument that merit discussion.

Perhaps most obvious, I do not believe all three perspectives are equally valuable. I have tried to be even-handed in my presentation of each, but in some places in this book my preferences are evident. I am deeply suspicious of integrationist claims that all members of a culture see things the same way and share the same values. I believe that, even at the most fundamental level, assumptions, interpretations, and values can and do differ, especially in a contemporary organization composed of employees with different educational backgrounds, class positions, ethnicities, races, nationalities, and genders. My political concerns with the magnitude of economic inequality between some of these groups makes the Differentiation perspective my "home." However, I am entranced with the insights that can come from a Fragmentation perspective and find its emphasis on multiple interpretations and its inclusion of ambiguities congruent with my own experiences in organizations.

These, however, are choices and limitations specific to me and to this text. A deeper and more general critique offered by postmodernists is that any theoretical writing inevitably employs literary devices that enhance the authority of the author and increase the persuasiveness of a text in a manner that is not legitimated by any scientific canon. These issues have been articulated well, with direct relevance for the cultural problems that are the focus of this book, by postmodern critics of ethnography.

An author of an ethnography usually begins a text with a "fable of rapport" that details his or her physical, emotional, and intellectual suffering before being accepted as a protomember of the culture being studied. After this account of initiation, the author usually disappears from the text. The text then appears to focus on the culture as it is seen by cultural insiders (i.e., "The Balinese believe . . ."). When an author disappears, the voice that is speaking through the text becomes the impersonal, objective voice of scientific authority. If no person is doing the describing, then the description must be "real"—an objective view. The inclusion of any of the author's personal views (the "I")—indeed any evidence of the existence of the author as "eye"—undermines this illusion of scientific objectivity.[11]

I have told no "fable of rapport," but I have tried to make myself relatively invisible in this text. I wrote the text as if it were a series of pseudo-conversations in which (apparently) I did not participate. For example, in the fierce debate among the representatives of the social scientific perspectives, I implicitly present myself as a quiet, personally uninvolved listener who records the conversation accurately. Those who have participated with me in these arguments know that this self-characterization is unlikely. The quotations from discussions with OZCO employees are presented with the researcher's part of the dialogue deleted. The excerpts from studies characteristic of each perspective are taken from an intertextual conversation among cultural researchers, in which I have been an active participant. I could not and did not quote all the works by all the authors cited or all the authors whose work might be relevant.

In each of these pseudo-conversations among "others," I have tried to minimize my visibility. I have deleted or de-emphasized my own contributions to these interpersonal and intertextual interactions, refrained from describing relevant aspects of the contexts in which these interchanges took place, and omitted explanations of any specific-to-the-occasion aspects of these utterances. These, then, are not accurate transcriptions of pseudo-conversations; I edited them to make a point as persuasively as I could. As author, like most social scientists, I have been more a dramaturgist than the supposedly accurate, neutral reporter I implicitly claimed to be.

What is the alternative? Clifford suggests a full presentation of the dialogue, with information about the specific context:

> Every use of "I" presupposes a "you," and every instance of discourse is immediately linked to a specific, shared situation. No discursive meaning, then, without interlocution and context. (Clifford, 1983, p. 133)

In a related recommendation, Van Maanen argues that we should take seriously the "impressionist tales" that ethnographers tell when they gather at the bar after scholarly conferences.[12] These tales have a textual immediacy, giving listeners the feeling that "you are there" as the ethnographer gathers data and develops interpretations. An impressionist tale keeps both the ethnographer and the ethnographer's subjects or "informants" in view. The limitations in what the ethnographer can know become evident. For example, Van Maanen tells an impressionist tale about one of his first experiences riding in a police squad car. As he careens around street corners in a futile chase of clever car thieves, a shotgun slides dangerously back and forth on the front seat. You hear the dialogue as he talks with police. You experience his frustration as he copes with the dangers inherent in being a neophyte in this culture.

This kind of tale presents both the researcher and his informants as individuals. A two-way dialogue replaces the omniscient, invisible writer of a traditional ethnographic description. This structure, however, brings the writer's epistemological discomfort to the surface of the text. One moral of an impressionist tale, therefore, concerns the inherent impossibility of a researcher (the "etic" stranger from outside the culture) ever coming to fully understand the "emic" perspective of a cultural insider.

In the next section, I experiment with these ways of writing about culture. My quasi-impressionist tale is more like a transcript of a wiretapped conversation than a polished story. My tale has little emotional buildup, no crisis, and no dramatic ending. Instead, I simply present an excerpt from a dialogue with an OZCO employee, along with my unspoken reactions to the conversation.

Van Maanen's impressionist tales tacitly portray the ethnographer as hero—an awkward cultural neophyte perhaps, but astute, witty, and brave nonetheless—particularly in the realms of insight where an intellectual is expected to excel. In my impressionist tale, my own role is far from heroic, even in the realm of intellectual insight. I ask a series of questions, get answers I did not anticipate, and increasingly expose my own lack of understanding of what cultural manifestations mean to cultural members.

This lack of closure is congruent with postmodernism. Instead of attempting to resolve differences with a unifying abstraction, a dialectical synthesis, or a gripping narrative tale, a postmodern analysis proceeds in a nonlinear fashion, without a plot or closure, raising questions rather than providing answers:

> Knowledge does not grow in a linear way, through the accumulation of facts and the application of the hypothetico-deductive method, but rather resembles an upward spiral, so that each time we reevaluate a position or place we've been before, we do so from a new perspective. (Jaggar, 1983, p. 368)

The researcher spirals through multiple perspectives, looking at an issue from all sides. This examination is a process without an endpoint. Understanding is deepened and broadened, but never finalized.

This does not mean that postmodernism necessarily entails anything-goes-relativism or nihilistic social philosophizing, as some have argued. Rather, it requires a painstaking analysis of how different points of view relate to each other, how they do and do not intersect.[13] Competition among discourses (e.g., conflicting social scientific theories) becomes decentralized, a creative ferment. From this viewpoint, the cultural fights with which this book began are a healthy exploration of difference, a conceptual "chaos" that can be reconceptualized as an absence of domination in discourse that permits new understandings to emerge.

The description above is deceptive, however. Self-disclosure and modesty about lack of closure are ways of establishing rapport. When the Wizard of Oz was exposed as an ordinary man, he admitted he was a "very bad Wizard" (but insisted that he was still a "very good man"). My quasi-impressionist tale is, in a sense, a "fable of rapport" designed to reinforce my authority as an author by, paradoxically, undermining that authority with an admission of ignorance. Postmodern self-reflexivity, whereby an author reflexively deconstructs the weaknesses in his or her own argument, is similarly, and paradoxically, a way of strengthening the authority of an author. Thus, to the extent that I have admitted personal biases and preferences throughout this text, I may have enhanced my authority as author more than if I had consistently attempted to reduce my visibility and appear neutral. Admitting this, my tale has begun.

A QUASI-IMPRESSIONIST TALE

At the end of the OZCO data collection effort, I gave a dinner for Debra Meyerson and two OZCO informants, "Jane Cordova" and "Danielle Small." We had been together at social gatherings before so this personal and informal setting was not unusual. Cordova and Small had agreed to give feedback on the first draft of the OZCO description, "filling in some holes" and correcting errors. Because this was to be our last meeting about this material, my questions were unusually direct. With everyone's permission, we tape recorded our conversation. Below is a complete transcript of our discussion of the Caesarean story. (My unspoken reactions are in italics. Explanatory additions, as well as deletions or substitutions to protect anonymity, are placed in brackets.)

Martin: Tell me what you thought about that Caesarean story and—

Cordova: I wonder who [the protagonist of the story] was. Can you tell me who that was? It wasn't Karen, was it?

Martin: Is Karen the one who was promoted to [a high-ranking position]?

Cordova: Yeah. Rumor has it that [the story protagonist] was Karen, right?

Cordova wanted to know who the woman in the story was, while I wanted to know if the story was generalizable, that is, if other women executives would have received the same treatment if their pregnancies conflicted with the demands of their jobs.

Martin: This is very important. We thought that the quotes we had after that story [in the OZCO description] weren't really first rate and—well, isn't the story true? How do you interpret it?

Cordova: I used to work for Karen.

Martin: You did! Yeah, great—talk to us?

Cordova: I didn't work for her very long. I quit about four months after she was promoted.

Martin: OK. Why?

Cordova: I knew her when she was also [holding another position]. This story about the Caesarean—I don't know.

If the story was not familiar to Cordova, it might not be known to many other OZCO employees, making its status as a cultural manifestation questionable.

Martin: You've never heard it?

Cordova: No, no, I didn't. In fact, I assumed that it was not her. I thought of her and dismissed her and Danielle asked if I thought it was her.

I search for a reason why Cordova is so sure the story protagonist is not Karen.

Martin: Don't you guys know she had a baby?

Cordova: She had a baby? She didn't have a baby. When?

Martin: When? I don't know. I mean, did she change the birth of that baby for the company?

Cordova: That wasn't entirely clear. It was the first child. No one knows when they are going to come. Do you? God just says—I actually had a couple of other women in mind. Amelia was one of them.

Suddenly I think I understand why Cordova had been focusing on Karen.

Martin: It was possible that the story could have been true for a number of women?

Cordova: Yes.

Martin: That they would have all done that for the company?

Cordova: Done that? Oh, sure.

Martin: Done that for the company? [When Debra and I first heard the story] that shocked the hell out of us. I couldn't believe it.

Cordova: I'm going to call Mary Winslow and I'm going to find out if Karen had a Caesarean. I mean I am going to buy lunch for Mary or somebody.

Meyerson: It doesn't matter if it's Karen.

Cordova: It could have been . . . [Material deleted to protect anonymity.] I would be disappointed if it were Karen, but she is a driven woman. Well, I'd be disappointed if it is anybody that I knew that I at all respected. I think, I don't know what you people think, I think it's a horrible story.

I was delighted to hear, finally, an evaluative reaction to the story. Abandoning any pretense at neutrality, I decided to be even more frank about my reaction to the story.

Martin: We do too. I mean, we were horrified by the blandness of [other people's] reaction [to the story]. Tell us what you think? Because the blandness of the reactions we have to quote now are—

Cordova: I left—I don't know how interesting the story is. I left [OZCO] because of chauvinism.

I decided not to include any of the material from this conversation in the OZCO description. I was concerned that Cordova's recent resignation from OZCO might reflect an atypically negative reaction to the company and I was worried that my leading questions and the frank expression of my personal views might have biased her responses. Perhaps because of my openness, however, this conversation surfaced several usefully difficult questions about the limitations of organizational culture research.

I was looking for evidence that Cordova was familiar with the Caesarean story and I wanted to know if she shared my negative reaction to it. Cordova revealed that she had not heard the story if the woman in the story was Karen, her former boss. However, Cordova said the story could have been told about a number of other women at OZCO. Furthermore, Cordova volunteered that "I don't know what you people think, I think it is a horrible story." To this extent, Cordova's answers fit my preconceptions.

I was troubled by other aspects of her responses. For example, my concerns about other women in the company ("How many of them would have altered the timing of a baby's birth to fit the company's product introduction schedule?") were apparently not important to Cordova. She said "Oh, sure," they would have done that. Cordova's primary concern, however, was not the questionable priorities of these OZCO employees (the pregnant woman, her bosses, the president, etc.), but rather whether her friend Karen had been the woman in the story. Cordova was focused exclusively on her part of OZCO and on those employees who were her friends and acquaintances. This local focus was supplemented by

Cordova's odd reactions to the story: it was both "horrible" and (in her last, bewildering remark) not important ("I don't know how interesting the story is"). She went on, immediately thereafter, to say she had resigned from OZCO because of (male) chauvinism. Thus the story was typical, horrible, chauvinistic, and not interesting.

This conversation made me wonder about the extent to which previous organizational culture research has focused on aspects of organizational life that employees consider not interesting, that is, not vital to their concerns. Even methods that attempt to let cultural members dictate the content of a study exclude much of what they consider important. For example, Sitkin, Boehm, and I content analyzed employees' accounts of the history of a small start-up company.[14] We asked employees to "tell us the most important events that made this company what it is today." Although we coded any concern mentioned by two or more employees (over 600 variables), a substantial proportion of employees' corporate histories were idiosyncratic. For example, 19 percent of the events recounted were mentioned by only one employee and therefore not coded. Thus even though our coding system was unusually inclusive, our study excluded much of what these employees considered important.

The dinner conversation did not "fill in the holes" in the draft of the OZCO description. Instead, it revealed how much I had not understood. It made me see how (even in those cultural studies where I had tried hardest to let cultural members shape the cultural "knowledge" I wrote about) their perceptions and evaluations of what was important had been misunderstood, omitted, or unwittingly distorted. This conversation made me wonder how cultural studies might produce deeper insights if it were possible to focus more precisely on aspects of cultures that employees consider most important. To do this would entail more than redrawing the boundaries of cultural inquiry to focus on local work environments, such as relations with bosses and co-workers.[15] More deeply, it would require rethinking concepts such as "shared" values or interpretations. For example, at the dinner, apparently shared understandings eluded scrutiny by disappearing under close inspection or fragmenting into unexpected juxtapositions of disapproval ("horrible") and indifference ("not interesting"). Rather than producing closure, this conversation raised questions and suggested ways cultural inquiries might be reoriented and deepened. In this process, some of the apparent certainties produced by the use of the three perspectives were challenged fruitfully.

GIVING UP THE AUTHOR/ITY GAME

When the interaction between a researcher and an informant is presented as a two-sided dialogue, troubling issues that are suppressed in the usual one-sided style of writing about culture, can emerge. This entails more than just giving informants a place in the text to speak for themselves and to react to what a researcher has written. A postmodern ethnography could be composed of dialogues where researchers and informants join together in a collaborative attempt to figure out what is going on.[16] This venture would be a cooperative effort, a "polyphonic text," where no one voice would "have the final word, present the authoritative interpretation or the all-encompassing synthesis."[17] Instead, the participants would confront the undecidable, "oppose, overturn, and re-negotiate established hierarchies of interpretation."[18] In this kind of exploratory, open-ended dialogue, no one participant would have more author-ity than another. Such a text would not suggest a new direction for culture research. Rather, it would offer an array of understandings with a cumulative complexity that would undermine any claim to have found a unity of shared interpretations or a more powerful meta-theory.[19]

Unfortunately, such a polyphonic text is extraordinarily difficult, perhaps impossible to write. Even the most polyphonic cultural description cannot fully abnegate the authority of an author:

> Quotations are always staged by the quoter, and tend to serve merely as examples, or confirming testimonies. Looking beyond (excerpted) quotation, one might imagine a more radical polyphony that would "do the native and ethnographer in different voices." But this, too, would only displace ethnographic authority, still confirming the final virtuoso orchestration by a single author of all the discourses in his or her text. (Clifford, 1983, p. 149)

This book permits many voices to speak. However, it falls far short of being a polyphonic text. For example, in the culture fight presented in Chapter 1, in the OZCO material, in the quotations from various studies, and in this quasi-impressionist tale, I selected parts of conversations and texts to quote. All of these quotations are taken out of a larger context. I put these quotations (and not others) in a particular sequence. I used some abstractions (e.g., the three themes in the OZCO material and the three perspectives in the theoretical material) and not others. Although I claimed to let these researchers and OZCO employees "speak in their own voices," I never relinquished editorial control.

I could have included the OZCO employees more fully in the construction of this text, for example, by including their written reactions to my interpretations or by having them write a portion of the cultural description. Even if I had done this, I still would have structured the text, decided on sequence, and so on. It is difficult to imagine how to give up the author-ity game, without reducing the researcher to the role of a secretary or a publisher:

> To accept native authority is to give up the game. . . . When the "other" drops out of anthropology, becomes subject, participant, and sole author, then. . . . we will have established a hermeneutics of vulnerability and an anthropology that calls itself into question. (Visweswaran, 1988, p. 39)

This is another aporia. Cultural researchers cannot accept the author-ity of cultural members without calling into question the worth of doing cultural research—putting themselves out of business.

There is, however, a partial escape from this dilemma. Literary theory emphasizes the importance and variability of readers' responses to a text. A book does not have just one "true," presumably shared meaning (an Integration view). Nor does a book have a set of clearly conflicting meanings that reflect a person's position in a system of domination and subordination (a Differentiation view). Instead, different readers at different times will have multiple interpretations of a text's meanings, particularly if that text is composed of many voices:

> Polyphonic works are particularly open to readings not specifically intended. (Clifford, 1983, p. 141)

My intentions, therefore, need not correspond with how you, the reader, make sense of this text:

> One may approach a classic ethnography seeking simply to grasp the meanings that the researcher derives from represented cultural facts. . . . One may also read against the grain of the text's dominant voice, seeking out other half-hidden authorities, reinterpreting the descriptions, texts, and quotations gathered together by the writer. (Clifford, 1983, p. 141)

Although this book is clearly not an ethnography, there are a variety of ways it can be read: as an indictment of the homogenizing assumptions of the Integration perspective, as a new "grand theory," as a paean to ambiguity, or as a sequence of semi- or pseudo-conversations that can be interpreted in ways I have not even thought of. I lost the author-ity game twice: once when I started to write and again when you started to read. Congruence between my intended meaning and your interpretation is as elusive as the chimera of a single organizational culture, viewed the same way by all its members.

NOTES

1. Burrell and Morgan (1979).
2. Smircich (1983b).
3. Stablein and Nord (1985).
4. For example, see Calas and Smircich (1987), Letiche (1991), and Martin (1990).
5. For example, see Alvesson (in press), Gagliardi (1990), and Turner (1989).
6. See, for example, Arac (1986) and Willmott (in press).
7. Jeffcutt (1991), p. 9.
8. Lyotard (1984).
9. Recent postmodern thinking about organizational culture includes Bjorkegren (1991), Calas and Smircich (1987), Jeffcutt (1991), Letiche (1991), Linstead and Grafton-Small (1991), and Willmott (in press).
10. Gagliardi (1990), Turner (1989).
11. For variations on these themes, see Arac (1986), Clifford (1983), Clifford and Marcus (1986), and Geertz (1988).
12. Van Maanen (1988).
13. Bjorkegren (1991).
14. Martin, Sitkin, and Boehm (1985).

15. For example, Alvesson (in press) and Christensen and Kreiner (1984) stress the importance of studying localized work cultures.

16. For example, see Arac (1986), Clifford (1983), Clifford and Marcus (1986), Geertz (1988), Jeffcutt (1991), and Willmott (1991).

17. Tyler (1986), p. 126, quoted in Jeffcutt (1991), p. 16.

18. Jeffcutt (1991), p. 16.

19. Turner (1989).

References

Abolafia, M. Y. (1989). *Constructing market culture: Ambiguity and change on Wall Street*. Unpublished manuscript, Cornell University.

Abolafia, M., & Kilduff, M. (1988). Enacting market crisis: The social construction of a speculative bubble. *Administrative Science Quarterly, 33,* 177–193.

Aldrich, H. (In press). Understanding, not interpretation: Vital signs from three perspectives on organizations. In Reed, M. & Hughes, M. (Eds.), *Rethinking organizations: New directions in organizational theory and analysis.* Newbury Park, CA: Sage.

Alvesson, M. (In press). *Perspectives on organizational culture.* Cambridge: Cambridge University Press.

Alvesson, M., & Melin, L. (1987). *Major discrepancies and contradictions in organizational culture: Both in the phenomenon of culture itself and in cultural studies.* Paper presented at the International Conference on Organizational Symbolism and Corporate Culture, Milan, Italy.

Anzaldua, G. (1987). *Borderlands/La Frontera: The new Mestiza.* San Francisco: Spinsters/Aunt Lute.

Arac, J. (Ed.). (1986). *Postmodernism and politics.* Minneapolis: University of Minnesota Press.

Argyris, C., & Schon, D. (1978). Organizational learning: A theory of action perspective. Reading, MA: Addison-Wesley.

Baburoglu, O., & Gocer, A. (1991). *The impact of privatization on the organizational culture: The Sumerbank's case.* Paper presented at the International Conference on Organizational Symbolism and Corporate Culture, Copenhagen, Denmark.

Barley, S. (1983). Semiotics and the study of occupational and organizational cultures. *Administrative Science Quarterly, 28,* 393–414.

Barley, S. (1986). Technology as an occasion for structuring: Evidence from observations of CT scanners and the social order of radiology departments. *Administrative Science Quarterly, 31,* 78–108.

Barley, S. (1991). Semiotics and the study of occupational and organizational cultures. In Frost, P., Moore, L., Lundberg, C., Louis, M., & Martin, J. (Eds.), *Reframing organizational culture* (pp. 39–54). Newbury Park, CA: Sage.

Barley, S., Meyer, G., & Gash, D. (1988). Cultures of culture: Academics, practitioners, and the pragmatics of normative control. *Administrative Science Quarterly, 33,* 24–61.

Barrett, M. (1985). *Women's oppression today: Problems in Marxist feminist analysis.* London: Verso.

Barthes, R. (1975). *The pleasure of the text* (R. Miller, Trans.). New York: Hill & Wang.

Bartunek, J. (1984). Changing interpretive schemes and organizational restructuring: The example of a religious order. *Administrative Science Quarterly, 29,* 355–372.

Bartunek, J., & Moch, M. (1991). Multiple constituencies and the quality of working life intervention at FoodCom. In Frost, P., Moore, L., Louis, M., Lundberg, C., & Martin, J. (Eds.), *Reframing organizational culture* (pp. 104–114). Newbury Park, CA: Sage.

Baum, L. (1986). *The wizard of OZ.* New York: Ballantine.

Becker, H. (1982). Culture: A sociological view. *Yale Review, 71,* 513–527.

Bell, E. (1990). The bicultural life experience of career-oriented black women. *Journal of Organizational Behavior, 11,* 459–478.

Benhabib, S., & Cornell, D. (1987). *Feminism as critique: On the politics of gender.* Minneapolis: University of Minnesota Press.

Bennis, W. (1984). Transformative power and leadership. In Sergiovanni, T., & Corbally, J. (Eds.), *Leadership and organizational culture* (pp. 64–71). Urbana: University of Illinois Press.

Bennis, W., & Nanus, B. (1985). *Leadership: The strategies for taking charge.* New York: Harper & Row.

Berger, P. (1967). *The sacred canopy.* Garden City, NY: Doubleday.

Berger, P., & Luckmann, T. (1967). *The social construction of reality.* Garden City, NY: Doubleday.

Berk, S. (1985). *The gender factory: The appointment of work in American households.* New York: Plenum.

Bjorkegren, D. (1991). *Postmodernism, its enemies and defenders.* Paper presented at the International Conference on Organizational Symbolism and Corporate Culture, Copenhagen, Denmark.

Blau, P. (1955). *The dynamics of bureaucracy.* Chicago: University of Chicago Press.

Bockus, S. (1983). *Corporate values: A refutation of uniqueness theory.* Unpublished manuscript, Stanford University.

Bonini, C. (1963). *Simulation of information and decision systems in the firm.* Englewood Cliffs, NJ: Prentice-Hall.

Bromiley, P. (1985). Planning systems in large organizations: Garbage can approach to defense PPBS. In March, J., & Weissinger-Baylon, R. (Eds.), *Ambiguity and commands: Organizational perspectives on military decision making* (pp. 120–139). Marshfield, MA: Pitman.

Brown, J., & Duguid, P. (1991). Organizational learning and communities-of-practice: Toward a unified view of working, learning, and innovation. *Organizational Science, 2,* 40–57.

Brunsson, N. (1985). *The irrational organization.* New York: Wiley.

Brunsson, N. (1986). Organizing for inconsistencies: On organizational conflicts, depression, and hypocrisy as substitutes for action. *Scandinavian Journal of Management Studies,* May, 165–185.

Burrell, G., & Morgan, G. (1979). *Sociological paradigms and organizational analysis.* London: Heinemann.

Calas, M., & Smircich, L. (1987). *Post-culture: Is the organizational culture literature dominant but dead?* Paper presented at the International Conference on Organizational Symbolism and Corporate Culture, Milan, Italy.

Chandler, A., Jr. (1962). *Strategy and structure: Chapters in the history of the American industrial enterprise.* Cambridge, MA: M.I.T. Press.

Christensen, S., & Kreiner, K. (1984). *On the origin of organizational cultures.* Paper presented for the International Conference on Organizational Symbolism and Corporate Culture, Lund, Sweden.

Christian, B. (1985). *Black feminist criticism: Perspectives on black women writers.* New York: Pergamon.

Clark, B. (1972). The organizational saga in higher education. *Administrative Science Quarterly, 17,* 178–184.

Clegg, S., & Dunkerly, D. (1980). *Organization, class and control.* London: Routledge & Kegan Paul.

Clifford, J. (1983). On ethnographic authority. *Representations, 1,* 118–146.

Clifford, J., & Marcus, G. (Eds.). (1986). *Writing culture: The poetics and politics of ethnography.* Berkeley: University of California Press.

Cohen, M., & March, J. (1974). *Leadership and ambiguity: The American college president.* New York: McGraw-Hill.

Cohen, M., March, J., & Olsen, J. (1972). A garbage can model of organizational choice. *Administrative Science Quarterly, 17,* 1–25.

Cole, R. (1971). *Japanese blue collar: The changing tradition.* Berkeley: University of California Press.

Collins, P. (1986). Learning from the outsider within: The sociological significance of black feminist thought. *Social Problems, 33,* S14–S32.

Cooper, R., & Burrell, G. (1988). Modernism, postmodernism, and organizational analysis. *Organization Studies, 9,* 91–112.

Crompton, R., & Jones, G. (1984). *White-collar proletariat.* London: Macmillan.

Daft, R., & Weick, K. (1984). Toward a model of organizations as interpretation systems. *Academy of Management Review, 9,* 284–295.

Davis, S. (1984). *Managing corporate culture.* Cambridge, MA: Ballinger.

Deal, T., & Kennedy, A. (1982). *Corporate cultures: The rites and rituals of corporate life.* Reading, MA: Addison-Wesley.

Deetz, S. (1983). Critical-interpretive research in organizational communication. *Western Journal of Speech Communication, 46,* 131–149.

Dellheim, C. (1987). The creation of a company culture: Cadburys, 1861–1931. *American Historical Review, 92,* 13–44.

Denison, D. (1990). *Corporate culture and organizational effectiveness.* New York: Wiley.

Dennings, R. (1986, February 26). Prof.'s brain theory could explain the inexplicable. *Stanford Daily,* 8.

Derrida, J. (1976). *Speech and phenomenon.* Evanston, IL: Northwestern University Press.

Diamond, I., & Quinby, L. (Eds.). (1988). *Feminism and Foucault: Reflection on resistance.* Boston: Northeastern University Press.

Donaldson, L. (1989). Redirections in organizational analysis. *Australian Journal of Management, 14,* 243–254.

Du Plessis, R. B. (1985). For the Etruscans: Sexual difference and artistic production—The debate over a female aesthetic. In Eisenstein, H., & Jardine, A. (Eds.), *The future of difference* (2nd ed.) (pp. 128–156). New Brunswick, NJ: Rutgers University Press.

Dyer, G. (1982). *Patterns and assumptions: The keys to understanding organizational cultures.* Unpublished manuscript, Massachusetts Institute of Technology.

Eagleton, T. (1976). *Marxism and literary criticism.* Berkeley: University of California Press.

Eisenberg, E. (1984). Ambiguity as strategy in organizational communication. *Communication Monographs, 51*, 227–242.

Enz, C. (1988). The role of value congruity in intraorganizational power. *Administrative Science Quarterly, 33*, 284–304.

Farley, T. (1985). Lesbianism and the social function of taboo. In Eisenstein, H., & Jardine, A. (Eds.), *The future of difference* (2nd ed.) (pp. 267–273). New Brunswick, NJ: Rutgers University Press.

Feldman, M. (1983a). *Information use in policy making*. Unpublished manuscript, Stanford University.

Feldman, M. (1983b). *Policy expertise in a public bureaucracy*. Unpublished doctoral dissertation, Stanford University.

Feldman, M. (1989). *Order without design: Information processing and policy making*. Palo Alto, CA: Stanford University Press.

Feldman, M. (1991). The meanings of ambiguity: Learning from stories and metaphors. In Frost, P., Moore, L., Louis, M., Lundberg, C., & Martin, J. (Eds.), *Reframing organizational culture* (pp. 145–156). Newbury Park, CA: Sage.

Feldman, S. (1985). Culture and conformity: An essay on individual adaptation in centralized bureaucracy. *Human Relations, 38*, 341–356.

Feral, J. (1985). The powers of difference. In Eisenstein, H., & Jardine, A. (Eds.), *The future of difference* (2nd ed.) (pp. 88–94). New Brunswick, NJ: Rutgers University Press.

Ferguson, K. (1984). *The feminist case against bureaucracy*. Philadelphia: Temple University Press.

Fernandez, J. (1982). *Racism and sexism in corporate life: Changing values in American business*. Lexington, MA: Lexington Books.

Flax, J. (1987). Postmodernism and gender relations in feminist theory. *Signs, 12*, 621–643.

Flax, J. (1990). *Thinking fragments: Psychoanalysis, feminism, and postmodernism in the contemporary West*. Berkeley: University of California Press.

Foucault, M. (1977). *Discipline and punish: The birth of prison*. London: Allen Lane.

Frederick, T. (1985). *A theory of culture development and methodology for analysis*. Unpublished manuscript, Stanford University.

Friedman, S. (1983). *Cultures within cultures? An empirical assessment of an organization's subcultures using projective measures*. Paper presented at the Annual Meeting of Academy of Management, Dallas, Texas.

Frost, P., Moore, L., Louis, M., Lundberg, C., & Martin, J. (Eds.). (1991). *Reframing organizational culture*. Newbury Park, CA: Sage.

Frug, G. (1986). The ideology of bureaucracy in American law. *Harvard Law Review, 97*, 1276–1388.

Gagliardi, P. (Ed.). (1990). *Symbols and artifacts: Views of the corporate landscape*. Hawthorne, NY: Walter de Gruyter.

Gagliardi, P. (1991). *Reflections on reframing organizational culture*. Invited presentation at the International Conference on Organizational Symbolism and Corporate Culture, Copenhagen, Denmark.

Gagnier, R. (1990). Feminist post-modernism: The end of feminism or the end of theory? In Rhode, D. (Ed.), *Theoretical perspectives on sexual difference* (pp. 21–30). New Haven, CT: Yale University Press.

Geertz, C. (1973). *The interpretation of cultures*. New York: Basic Books.

Geertz, C. (1988). *Works and lives: The anthropologist as author*. Stanford, CA: Stanford University Press.

Gelpi, B. (1990). *Shelley's goddess: Maternity, language, and subjectivity.* Unpublished manuscript, Stanford University.

Gerwin, D. (1981). Relationships between structure and technology. In Nystrom, P. & Starbuck, W. (Eds.), *Handbook of organizational design: Vol. 2. Remodeling organizations and environments* (pp. 3–38). New York: Oxford University Press.

Glaser, B., & Strauss, A. (1967). *The discovery of grounded theory: Strategies for qualitative research.* Chicago: Aldine.

Golding, D. (1987). *Certainty as a symbolic artifact of management.* Paper presented at the International Conference on Organizational Symbolism and Corporate Culture, Milan, Italy.

Goodhead, G. (1985). *What do corporations believe?* Unpublished manuscript, Stanford University.

Grafton-Small, R., & Linstead, S. (1987). *Theory as artefact.* Paper presented at the International Conference on Organizational Symbolism and Corporate Culture, Milan, Italy.

Greenwood, R. & Hinings, C. (1988). Organizational design types, tracks and the dynamics of strategic change. *Organization Studies, 9,* 293–316.

Gregory, K. (1983). Native-view paradigms: Multiple cultures and culture conflicts in organizations. *Administrative Science Quarterly, 28,* 359–376.

Greiner, L. (1972). Evolution and revolution as organizations grow. *Harvard Business Review,* July/August, 37–46.

Habermas, J. (1975). *Legitimation crisis* (T. McCarthy, Trans.). Boston: Beacon Press.

Haraway, D. (1985). A manifesto for cyborgs: Science, technology, and socialist feminism in the 1980s. *Socialist Review, 15,* 65–108.

Hatch, M. (1990). The symbolics of office design. In Gagliardi, P. (Ed.), *Symbols and artifacts: Views of the corporate landscape* (pp. 129–146). Hawthorne, NY: Walter de Gruyter.

Hedberg, B. (1981). How organizations learn and unlearn. In Nystrom, P., & Starbuck, W. (Eds.), *Handbook of organizational design: Vol. 1, Adapting organizations to their environments* (pp. 3–27). Oxford: Oxford University Press.

Hernes, G. (1976). Structural change in social processes. *Annual Journal of Sociology, 82,* 513–547.

Hess, B., & Ferree, M. (Eds.). (1987). *Analyzing gender: A handbook of social science research.* Newbury Park, CA: Sage.

Hinings, B., & Greenwood, R. (1987). The normative prescription of organizations. In Zucker, L. (Ed.), *Institutional patterns and organizations* (pp. 53–70). Chicago: Ballinger.

Hochschild, A. (1983). *The managed heart.* Berkeley: University of California Press.

Hoffman, D. (1982). *Managing high technology companies.* Unpublished manuscript, Stanford University.

Huff, A. (1988). Politics and argument as a means of coping with ambiguity and change. In Pondy, L., Boland, R., Jr., & Thomas, H. (Eds.), *Managing ambiguity and change* (pp. 79–92). New York: Wiley.

Huntington, J. (1981). *Social work and general medical practice.* London: George Allen & Unwin.

Irigary, L. (1985). *Speculum de l'autre femme* [*Speculum of the other woman*]. Paris: Editions de Minuit.

Jaeger, A. (1979). *An investigation of organizational culture in a multinational context.* Unpublished doctoral dissertation, Stanford University.

Jaggar, A. (1983). *Feminist politics and human nature*. Totowa, NJ: Rowman & Allanheld.

Jamison, M. (1985). The joys of gardening: Collectivist and bureaucratic cultures in conflict. *Sociological Quarterly, 26,* 473–490.

Jardine, A. (1988). Prelude: The future of difference. In Eisenstein, H., & Jardine, A. (Eds.), *The future of difference* (pp. xxv–xxvii). New Brunswick, NJ: Rutgers University Press.

Jeffcutt, P. (1991). *Styles of representation in organizational analysis: Heroism, happy endings and the carnivalesque in the organizational symbolism literature.* Paper presented at the International Conference on Organizational Symbolism and Corporate Culture, Copenhagen, Denmark.

Jeffcutt, P. (In press). *Culture and symbolism in organizational analysis.* Newbury Park, CA: Sage.

Jelinek, M., Smircich, L., & Hirsch, P. (1983). Introduction: A code of many colors. *Administrative Science Quarterly, 28,* 331–338.

Jermier, J. (1985). When the sleeper wakes: A short story extending themes in radical organization theory. *Journal of Management, 11,* 67–80.

Jermier, J., Slocum, J., Fry, L., & Gaines, J. (1991). Organizational subcultures in a soft bureaucracy: Resistance behind the myth and facade of an official culture. *Organizational Science, 2,* 170–194.

Jonsson, S., & Lundin, R. (1977). Myths and wishful thinking as management tools. In Nystrom, P., & Starbuck, W. (Eds.), *Studies in Management Sciences: Vol. 5. Prescriptive models of organizations* (pp. 157–170). Amsterdam: North Holland.

Kanter, R. (1972). *Commitment and community.* Cambridge: Harvard University Press.

Kanter, R. (1977). *Men and women of the corporation.* New York: Anchor Press.

Kanter, R. (1984). Managing transitions in organizational culture: The case of participative management at Honeywell. In Kimberly, J., & Quinn, R. (Eds.), *Managing organizational transitions* (pp. 195–217). Homewood, IL: Irwin.

Katz, D., & Kahn, R. (1978). *The social psychology of organizations* (2nd ed.). New York: Wiley.

Keesing, R. (1981). *Cultural anthropology: A contemporary perspective.* New York: Holt, Rinehart and Winston.

Kegan, R. (1982). *The evolving self.* Cambridge: Harvard University Press.

Keohane, N. (1988). *The public and the private as categories of human experience.* Unpublished manuscript, Center for the Advanced Study of the Behavioral Sciences, Stanford, CA.

Kilmann, R. (1985). *Beyond the quick fix: Managing five tracks to organizational success.* San Francisco: Jossey-Bass.

Kimberly, J. (1979). Issues in the creation of organizations: Initiation, innovation, and institutionalization. *Academy of Management Journal, 22,* 437–457.

Kimberly, J., & Miles, R. (1980). *The organizational life cycle.* San Francisco: Jossey-Bass.

Kimberly, J., & Quinn, R. (Eds.). (1984). *Managing organizational transitions.* Homewood, IL: Irwin.

Krackhardt, D., & Kilduff, M. (1990). Friendship patterns and culture: The control of organizational diversity. *American Anthropologist, 92,* 142–154.

Kristeva, J. (1980). *Desire in language.* New York: Columbia University Press.

Kuhn, T. (1970). *The structure of scientific revolutions* (rev. ed.). Chicago: University of Chicago Press.

Kunda, G. (1991a). *Engineering culture: Control and commitment in a high-tech corporation.* Philadelphia: Temple University Press.

Kunda, G. (1991b). *Ritual and management of corporate culture: A critical perspective.* Paper presented at the International Conference on Organizational Symbolism and Corporate Culture, Copenhagen, Denmark.

Latane, B., & Darley, J. (1970). *The unresponsive bystander.* New York: Appleton.

Lawrence, P., & Lorsch, J. (1967). *Organization and environment: Managing differentiation and integration.* Boston: Graduate School of Business Administration, Harvard University.

Letiche, H. (1991). *Postmodernism goes practical.* Paper presented at the International Conference on Organizational Symbolism and Corporate Culture, Copenhagen, Denmark.

Levitt, B., & Nass, C. (1989). The lid on the garbage can: Institutional constraints on decision making in the technical core of college-text publishers. *Administrative Science Quarterly, 34,* 190–207.

Lincoln, J., & Kallberg, A. (1985). Work organization and workforce commitment: A study of plants and employees in the U.S. and Japan. *American Sociological Review, 50,* 738–760.

Linstead, S.. & Grafton-Small, R. (1991). *No visible means of support: Ethnography and the end of deconstruction.* Paper presented at the International Conference on Organizational Symbolism and Corporate Culture, Copenhagen, Denmark.

Louis, M. (1983a). Organizations as culture-bearing milieux. In Pondy, L., Frost, P., Morgan, G., & Dandridge, T. (Eds.), *Organizational symbolism* (pp. 39–54). Greenwich, CT: JAI Press.

Louis, M. (1983b). Sourcing workplace cultures: Why, when, and how? In Kilmann, R. (Ed.), *Managing corporate cultures* (pp. 126–136). San Francisco: Jossey-Bass.

Louis, M. (1985). An investigator's guide to workplace culture. In Frost, P., Moore, L., Louis, M., Lundberg, C., & Martin, J. (Eds.), *Organizational culture* (pp. 73–94). Beverly Hills, CA: Sage.

Lucas, R. (1987). Political-cultural analysis of organizations. *Academy of Management Review, 12,* 144–156.

Lyotard, J. (1984). *The postmodern condition.* Minneapolis: University of Minnesota Press.

March, J. (1976). The technology of foolishness. In March, J., & Olsen, J. (Eds.), *Ambiguity and choice in organizations* (pp. 69–81). Bergen, Norway: Universitetsforlaget.

March, J. (1978). Bounded rationality, ambiguity and the engineering of choice. *Bell Journal of Economics, 9,* 587–608.

March, J. (1981). Footnotes to organizational change. *Administrative Science Quarterly, 26,* 563–577.

March, J., & March, J. (1977). Almost random careers: the Wisconsin school superintendency, 1940–1972. *Administrative Science Quarterly, 23,* 434–453.

March, J., & Olsen, J. (Eds.). (1976). *Ambiguity and choice in organizations.* Bergen, Norway: Universitetsforlaget.

March, J., & Simon, H. (1958). *Organizations.* New York: Wiley.

Martin, J. (1982). Stories and scripts in organizational settings. In Hastorf, A., & Isen, A. (Eds.), *Cognitive social psychology* (pp. 255–305). London: Routledge.

Martin, J. (1990). Deconstructing organizational taboos: The suppression of gender conflict in organizations. *Organizational Science, 1,* 339–359.

Martin, J., Anterasian, C., & Siehl, C. (1988). *Externally espoused values and the legitimation of financial performance.* Unpublished manuscript, Stanford University.

Martin, J., & Casscells, A. (1985). *Companies where women succeed or fail.* Unpublished manuscript, Stanford University.

Martin, J., Feldman, M., Hatch, M., & Sitkin, S. (1983). The uniqueness paradox in organizational stories. *Administrative Science Quarterly, 28,* 438–453.

Martin, J., & Meyerson, D. (1988). Organizational culture and the denial, channeling and acknowledgment of ambiguity. In Pondy, L., Boland, R., Jr., & Thomas, H. (Eds.), *Managing ambiguity and change* (pp. 93–125). New York: Wiley.

Martin, J., & Powers, M. (1983). Organizational stories: More vivid and persuasive than quantitative data. In Staw, B. (Ed.), *Psychological foundations of organizational behavior* (2nd ed.) (pp. 161–168). Glenview, IL: Scott, Foresman.

Martin, J., & Siehl, C. (1983). Organizational culture and counterculture: An uneasy symbiosis. *Organizational Dynamics, 12,* 52–64.

Martin, J., Sitkin, S., & Boehm, M. (1985). Founders and the elusiveness of a cultural legacy. In Frost, P., Moore, L., Louis, M.,Lundberg, C., & Martin, J. (Eds.), *Organizational culture* (pp. 99–124). Beverly Hills, CA: Sage.

McCall, M., Jr. (1977). Making sense with nonsense: Helping frames of reference clash. In Nystrom, P., & Starbuck, W. (Eds.), *Studies in the management sciences: Vol. 5, Prescriptive models of organizations* (pp. 111–124). Amsterdam: North Holland.

McCaskey, M. (1988). The challenge of managing ambiguity and change. In Pondy, L., Boland, R., & Thomas, H. (Eds.), *Managing ambiguity and change* (pp. 1–18). New York: Wiley.

McDonald, P. (1991). The Los Angeles Olympic Organizing Committee: Developing organizational culture in the short run. In Frost, P., Moore, L., Louis, M., Lundberg, C., & Martin, J. (Eds.), *Reframing organizational culture* (pp. 26–38). Newbury Park, CA: Sage.

Meyer, A. (1982). Adapting to environmental jolts. *Administrative Science Quarterly, 27,* 515–537.

Meyer, J., & Rowan, B. (1977). Institutionalized organizations: Formal structures as a myth and ceremony. *American Journal of Sociology, 83,* 340–363.

Meyerson, D. (1989). *The social construction of ambiguity and burnout.* Unpublished doctoral dissertation. Stanford University.

Meyerson, D. (1990). Uncovering socially undesirable emotions: Experiences of ambiguity in oranizations. *American Behavioral Scientist, 33,* 296–307.

Meyerson, D. (1991a). "Normal" ambiguity?: A glimpse of an occupational culture. In Frost, P., Moore, L., Louis, M., Lundberg, C., & Martin, J. (Eds.), *Reframing organizational culture* (pp. 131–144). Newbury Park, CA: Sage.

Meyerson, D. (1991b). Acknowledging and uncovering ambiguities in cultures. In Frost, P., Moore, L., Louis, M., Lundberg, C., & Martin, J. (Eds.), *Reframing organizational culture* (pp. 254–270). Newbury Park, CA: Sage.

Meyerson, D., & Martin, J. (1987). Cultural change: An integration of three different views. *Journal of Management Studies, 24,* 623–647.

Miller, D. (1980). Toward a new contingency approach: The search for organizational gestalts. *Journal of Management Studies, 18,* 1–26.

Miller, D., & Friesen, P. (1980). Archetypes of organizational transition. *Administrative Science Quarterly, 25,* 268–299.

Miller, D., & Friesen, P. (1983). Successful and unsuccessful phases of the corporate life cycle. *Organization Studies, 4,* 339–356.

Millman, M., & Kanter, R. (1975). *Another voice: Feminist perspectives on social life and social science*. Garden City, NY: Anchor Books.

Mills, A. (1988). Organization, gender, and culture. *Organization Studies, 9,* 351–370.

Moi, T. (1985). *Sexual/textual politics: Feminist literary theory*. New York: Methuen.

Moore, S., & Myerhoff, B. (1977). Introduction. In Moore, S. & Myerhoff, B. (Eds.), *Secular ritual* (pp. 3–24). Atlantic Highlands, NJ: Humanities Press.

Moore, W. (1962). *The conduct of the corporation*. New York: Random House.

Morgan, G. (Ed.) (1983). *Beyond method: Strategies for social research*. Beverly Hills, CA: Sage.

Morgan, G., & Ramirez, R. (1984). Action learning: A holographic metaphor for guiding social change. *Human Relations, 37,* 1–28.

Morgan, R. (1977). *Going too far: The personal chronicle of a feminist*. New York: Random House.

Nadler, D. (1988). Organizational frame bending: Types of change in the complex organization. In Kilmann, R., & Covin, T. (Eds.), *Corporate transformation: Revitalizing organizations for a competitive world* (pp. 66–84). San Francisco: Jossey-Bass.

Nicholson, L. (1986). *Gender and history*. New York: Columbia University Press.

Nkomo, S. (1989). *Comments on existing research on race effects in organizations*. Paper presented at the Annual Meeting of Academy of Management, Washington, D.C.

Nord, W. (1978). Dreams of humanization and the realities of power. *Academy of Management Review, 3,* 674–679.

Olsen, F. (1983). The family and the market: A study of ideology and legal reform. *Harvard Law Review, 96,* 1497–1578.

O'Reilly, C. (1989). Corporations, culture, and commitment: Motivation and social control in organizations. In Tushman, M., O'Reilly, C., & Nadler, D. (Eds.), *Management of organizations: Strategies, tactics, and analyses* (pp. 285–303). Cambridge, MA: Ballinger.

O'Reilly, C., Chatman, J., & Caldwell, D. (1991). People and organizational culture. A Q-sort approach to assessing person-organization fit. *Academy of Management Journal, 34,* 487–516.

Ortner, S. (1974). Is female to male as nature is to culture? In Rosaldo, M., & Lamphere, L. (Eds.), *Woman, culture and society* (pp. 67–88). Stanford: Stanford University Press.

Ott, J. (1989). *The organizational culture perspective*. Pacific Grove, CA: Brooks & Cole.

Ouchi, W. (1980). Markets, bureaucracies, and clans. *Administrative Science Quarterly, 25,* 125–141.

Ouchi, W. (1981). *Theory Z: How American business can meet the Japanese challenge*. Reading, MA: Addison-Wesley.

Ouchi, W., & Jaeger, A. (1978). Type Z organization: Stability in the midst of mobility. *Academy of Management Review, 3,* 305–314.

Ouchi, W., & Wilkins, A. (1985). Organizational culture. *Annual Review of Sociology, 11,* 457–483.

Owens, C. (1983). The discourse of others: Feminists and postmodernism. In Foster, H. (Ed.), *The Anti-Aesthetic* (pp. 57–82). Port Townsend, WA: Bay Press.

Pascale, R., & Athos, A. (1981). *The art of Japanese management: Applications for American executives*. New York: Simon and Schuster.

Pennings, J., & Gresov, C. (1986). Technoeconomic and structural correlates of organizational culture: An integrative framework. *Organization Studies, 7,* 317–334.

Perrow, C. (1984). *Normal accidents*. New York: Basic Books.

Peters, T., & Waterman, R. (1982). *In search of excellence: Lessons from America's best-run companies*. New York: Harper & Row.

Pettigrew, A. (1979). On studying organizational culture. *Administrative Science Quarterly, 24,* 570–581.

Pettigrew, T., & Martin, J. (1987). Shaping the organizational context for black American inclusion. *Journal of Social Issues, 43,* 41–78.

Pfeffer, J. (1981). Management as symbolic action: The creation and maintenance of organizational paradigms. In Staw, B., & Cummings, L. (Eds.), *Research in organizational behavior, Vol. 3* (pp. 1–52). Greenwich, CT: JAI Press.

Pfeffer, J., & Salancik, G. (1978). *The external control of organizations*. New York: Harper & Row.

Pleck, J. (1985). *Working wives/working husbands*. Newbury Park, CA: Sage.

Pondy, L. (1983). The role of metaphors and myths in organization and in the facilitation of change. In Pondy, L., Frost, P., Morgan, G., & Dandridge, T. C. (Eds.), *Organizational symbolism* (pp. 157–166). Greenwich, CT: JAI Press.

Pondy, L., Frost, P., Morgan, G., & Dandridge, T. (Eds.). (1983). *Organizational symbolism*. Greenwich, CT: JAI Press.

Porras, J. (1987). *Stream analysis: A powerful way to diagnose and manage organizational change*. Reading, MA: Addison-Wesley.

Pratt, M. (1986). Interpretive strategies/strategic interpretations: On Anglo-American reader response criticism. In Arac, J. (Ed.), *Postmodernism and politics* (pp. 26–54). Minneapolis: University of Minnesota Press.

Quinn, R., & Cameron, K. (1983). Organizational life cycles and shifting criteria of effectiveness: Some preliminary evidence. *Management Science, 29,* 33–51.

Quinn, R., & McGrath, M. (1985). The transformation of organizational cultures: A competing values perspective. In Frost, P., Moore, L., Louis, M., Lundberg, C., & Martin, J. (Eds.), *Organizational culture: The meaning of life in the workplace* (pp. 315–334). Beverly Hills, CA: Sage.

Ranson, S., Hinings, B., & Greenwood, R. (1980). The structuring of organization structures. *Administrative Science Quarterly, 25,* 1–17.

Reed, M. (1985). *Redirections in organizational analysis*. London: Tavistock Publications.

Reinhardz, S. (1985). Feminist distrust: Problems of context and content in sociological work. In Berg, D., & Smith, K. (Eds.), *Exploring clinical methods for social research* (pp. 153–171). Beverly Hills, CA: Sage.

Riggs, H. (1983). *Managing high technology companies*. Belmont, CA: Lifetime Learning Publications.

Riley, P. (1983). A structurationist account of political cultures. *Administrative Science Quarterly, 28,* 414–437.

Rodgers, W. (1969). *Think*. New York: Stein & Day.

Roethlisberger, F. (1977). *The elusive phenomena*. Boston: Division of Research, Graduate School of Business, Harvard University.

Rofel, L. (1989). *Eating out of one big pot: Hegemony and resistance in a Chinese factory*. Unpublished doctoral dissertation, Stanford University.

Rogers, C. (1961). *On becoming a person: A therapist's view of psychotherapy*. Boston: Houghton Mifflin.

Rohlene, T. (1974). *For harmony and strength: Japanese white-collar organizations in anthropological perspective*. Berkeley: University of California Press.

Rosaldo, R. (1989). *Culture & truth: The remaking of social analysis*. Boston: Beacon.

Rosen, M. (1985). Breakfast at Spiro's: Dramaturgy and dominance. *Journal of Management, 11,* 31–48.

Rosen, M. (1991). Breakfast at Spiro's: Dramaturgy and dominance. In Frost, P., Moore, L., Louis, M., Lundberg, C., & Martin, J. (Eds.), *Reframing organizational culture* (pp. 77–89). Newbury Park, CA: Sage.

Rothschild-Witt, J. (1979). The collective organization: An alternative to rational-bureaucratic models. *American Sociology Review, 44,* 509–527.

Rourke, F. (1972). *Bureaucracy and foreign policy.* Baltimore: Johns Hopkins University Press.

Rousseau, D. (1989). The price of success? Security-oriented cultures and high reliability organizations. *Industrial Crisis Quarterly, 3,* 285–302.

Sabrosky, A., Thompson, J., & McPherson, K. (1982). Organized anarchies: Military bureaucracy in the 1980s. *Journal of Applied Behavioral Science, 18,* 137–153.

Saffold, G., III (1988). Culture traits, strength, and organizational performance: Moving beyond "strong" culture. *Academy of Management Review, 13,* 546–558.

Sahlins, M. (1976). *Culture and practical reason.* Chicago: University of Chicago Press.

Sathe, V. (1985). *Culture and related corporate realities: Text, cases, and readings on organizational entry, establishment, and change.* Homewood, IL: Irwin.

Schall, M. (1983). A communication rules approach to organizational culture. *Administrative Science Quarterly, 28,* 557–581.

Schein, E. (1961). *Coercive persuasion.* New York: Norton.

Schein, E. (1978). *Career dynamics: Matching individual and organizational needs.* Reading, MA: Addison-Wesley.

Schein, E. (1984). Coming to a new awareness of organizational culture. *Sloan Management Review, 25,* 3–16.

Schein, E. (1985). *Organizational culture and leadership.* San Francisco: Jossey-Bass.

Schein, E. (1991a). The role of the founder in the creation of organizational culture. In Frost, P., Moore, L., Lundberg, C., Louis, M., & Martin, J. (Eds.), *Reframing organizational culture* (pp. 14–25). Newbury Park, CA: Sage.

Schein, E. (1991b). What is culture? In Frost, P., Moore, L., Louis, M., Lundberg, C., & Martin, J. (Eds.), *Reframing organizational culture* (pp. 243–253). Newbury Park, CA: Sage.

Schneider, B. (Ed.). (1990). *Organizational climate and culture.* San Francisco: Jossey-Bass.

Schultz, M. (In press). Postmodern pictures of culture. *International Studies of Management and Organizations.*

Scott, W. (1981). *Organizations: Rational, natural, and open systems.* Englewood Cliffs, NJ: Prentice-Hall.

Selsky, J., & Wilkof, M. (1988). *Organizational culture and interorganizational relations.* Paper presented at the Annual Meeting of Academy of Management, Anaheim, CA.

Selznick, P. (1957). *Leadership and administration.* Evanston, IL: Row & Peterson.

Sergiovanni, T., & Corbally, J. (Eds.). (1984). *Leadership and organizational culture.* Urbana, IL: University of Illinois Press.

Sheldon, A. (1980). Organizational paradigms: A theory of organizational change. *Organizational Dynamics,* Winter, 61–80.

Shriver, S. (1986). The vision. In Viorst, M. (Ed.), *Making a difference: The Peace Corps at twenty-five* (pp. 15–29). New York: Weidenfeld & Nicolson.

Siehl, C. (1984). *Cultural sleight-of-hand: The illusion of consistency.* Unpublished doctoral dissertation, Stanford University.

Siehl, C. (1985). After the founder: An opportunity to manage culture. In Frost, P., Moore, L., Louis, M., Lundberg, C., & Martin, J. (Eds.), *Organizational culture* (pp. 125–140). Beverly Hills, CA: Sage.

Siehl, C., & Martin, J. (1984). The role of symbolic management: How can managers effectively transmit organizational culture? In Hunt, J., Hosking, D., Schriesheim, C., & Stewart, R. (Eds.), *Leaders and managers: International perspectives on managerial behavior and leadership* (pp. 227–239). Elmsford, NY: Pergamon.

Siehl, C., & Martin, J. (1990). Organizational culture: A key to financial performance? In Schneider, B. (Ed.), *Organizational climate and culture* (pp. 241–281). San Francisco: Jossey-Bass.

Sims, H., & Gioia, D. (1986). *The thinking organization.* San Francisco: Jossey-Bass.

Smircich, L. (1983a). Organizations as shared meanings. In Pondy, L., Frost, P., Morgan, G., & Dandridge, T. (Eds.), *Organizational symbolism* (pp. 55–65). Greenwich, CT: JAI Press.

Smircich, L. (1983b). Concepts of culture and organizational analysis. *Administrative Science Quarterly, 28,* 339–358.

Smircich, L., & Morgan, G. (1982). Leadership: The management of meaning. *Journal of Applied Behavioral Science, 18,* 257–273.

Spivak, G. (1986). *In other worlds: Essays in cultural politics.* New York: Routledge.

Spradley, J. (1979). *The ethnographic interview.* New York: Holt, Rinehart, and Winston.

Sproull, L. (1981). Beliefs in organizations. In Nystrom, P., & Starbuck, W. (Eds.), *Handbook of organizational design: Vol. 2, Remodelling organizations and their environments* (pp. 203–244). Oxford: Oxford University Press.

Sproull, L., Weiner, S., & Wolf, D. (1978). *Organizing an anarchy.* Chicago: University of Chicago Press.

Stablein, R., & Nord, W. (1985). Practical and emancipatory interests in organizational symbolism: A review and evaluation. *Journal of Management, 11,* 13–28.

Starbuck, W. (1983). Organizations as action generators. *American Sociological Review, 48,* 91–102.

Starbuck, W. (1987). Surmounting our human limitations. In Quinn, R., & Cameron, K. (Eds.), *Paradox and transformation: Toward a theory of change in organization and management* (pp. 65–80). Cambridge, MA: Ballinger.

Starbuck, W., Greve, A., & Hedberg, B. (1978). Responding to crises. *Journal of Business Administration, 9,* 111–137.

Steffy, B., & Grimes, A. (1986). A critical theory of organization science. *Academy of Management Review, 11,* 322–336.

Sternberg, R. (1985). Human intelligence: The model is the message. *Science,* December, 1111–1118.

Stinchcombe, A. (1959). Bureaucratic and craft administration of production: A comparative study. *Administrative Science Quarterly, 4,* 168–187.

Strathern, M. (1987). An awkward relationship: The case of feminism and anthropology. *Signs, 12,* 276–291.

Strober, M. (1990). Human capital theory: Implications for HR managers. *Industrial Relations, 29,* 214–239.

Sunesson, S. (1985). Outside the goal paradigm: Power and structured patterns of non-rationality. *Organization Studies, 6,* 229–246.

Swidler, A. (1979). *Organization without authority: Dilemmas of social control in free schools.* Cambridge: Harvard University Press.

Sypher, B., Applegate, J., & Sypher, H. (1985). Culture and communication in organizational contexts. In Gudykunst, W., Stewart, L., & Ting-Toomy, S. (Eds.), *Communication, culture and organizational process* (pp. 13–29). Beverly Hills, CA: Sage.

Tate, C. (Ed.). (1983). *Black women writers at work.* New York: Continuum Press.

Taylor, M. (1987, February 17). Descartes, Nietzsche, and the search for the unsayable. *New York Times Book Review.*

Thompson, J. (1967). *Organizations in action.* New York: McGraw-Hill.

Tichy, N., & DeVanna, M. (1986). *The transformational leader.* New York: Wiley.

Tom, A. (1986). *To make a life for myself: An ethnography of a job training program.* Unpublished doctoral dissertation, Stanford University.

Torbert, W. (1976). *Creating a community of inquiry.* London: Wiley.

Trice, H., & Beyer, J. (1984). Studying organizational cultures through rites and ceremonials. *Academy of Management Review, 9,* 653–669.

Trice, H., & Morand, D. (In press). Organizational subcultures and countercultures. In Miller, G. (Ed.), *Studies in organizational sociology.* Greenwich, CT: JAI Press.

Turner, B. (1986). Sociological aspects of organizational symbolism. *Organizational Studies, 7,* 101–115.

Turner, B. (Ed.). (1989). *Organizational symbolism.* Hawthorne, NY: Walter de Gruyter.

Tushman, M., & Romanelli, E. (1985). Organizational evolution: A metamorphosis model of convergence and reorientation. In Cummings, L., & Staw, B. (Eds.), *Research in organizational behavior, Vol. 7* (pp. 171–222). Greenwich, CT: JAI Press.

Tversky, A. (1977). Features of similarity. *Psychological Review, 84,* 327–352.

Tyler, S. (1986). Post-modern ethnography: From document of the occult to occult document. In Clifford, J., & Marcus, G. (Eds.), *Writing culture: The poetics and politics of ethnography* (pp. 122–140). Berkeley: University of California Press.

Van de Ven, A., & Poole, M. (1988). Paradoxical requirements for a theory of organizational change. In Quinn, R., & Cameron, K. (Eds.), *Paradox and transformation: Toward a theory of change in organization and management* (pp. 19–63). Cambridge, MA: Ballinger.

Van Maanen, J. (1986). Power in the bottle: Drinking patterns and social relations in a British police agency. In Srivasta, S. (Ed.), *Executive power* (pp. 204–239). San Francisco: Jossey-Bass.

Van Maanen, J. (1988). *Tales of the field.* Chicago: University of Chicago Press.

Van Maanen, J. (1991). The smile factory: Work at Disneyland. In Frost, P., Moore, L., Louis, M., Lundberg, C., & Martin, J. (Eds.), *Reframing organizational culture* (pp. 58–76). Newbury Park, CA: Sage.

Van Maanen, J., & Barley, S. (1984). Occupational communities: Culture and control in organizations. In Staw, B., & Cummings, L. (Eds.), *Research in organizational behavior, Vol. 6* (pp. 287–366). Greenwich, CT: JAI Press.

Van Maanen, J., & Barley, S. (1985). Cultural organization: Fragments of a theory. In Frost, P., Moore, L., Louis, M., Lundberg, C., & Martin, J. (Eds.), *Organizational culture* (pp. 31–54). Beverly Hills, CA: Sage.

Van Maanen, J., & Kunda, G. (1989). ''Real feelings'': Emotional expression and organizational culture. In Cummings, L., & Staw, B. (Eds.), *Research in organizational behavior, Vol. 11* (pp. 43–103). Greenwich, CT: JAI Press.

Venturi, R. (1977). *Complexity and contradiction in architecture.* New York: Museum of Modern Art.

Visweswaran, K. (1988). Defining feminist ethnography. *Inscriptions, 3,* 27–45.

Walter, G. (1985). Culture collisions in mergers and acquisitions. In Frost, P., Moore, L., Louis, M., Lundberg, C., & Martin, J. (Eds.), *Organizational culture* (pp. 301–314). Beverly Hills, CA: Sage.

Watzlawick, P., Weakland, J., & Fisch, R. (1974). *Change: Principles of problem formulation and problem resolution.* New York: Norton.

Webster's seventh new collegiate dictionary. (1969). Springfield, MA: Merriam-Webster.

Weedon, C. (1987). *Feminist practice and poststructuralist theory.* New York: Basil Blackwell.

Weick, K. (1976). Educational organizations as loosely coupled systems. *Administrative Science Quarterly, 21,* 1–19.

Weick, K. (1979a). *The social psychology of organizing.* Reading, MA: Addison-Wesley.

Weick, K. (1979b). *Research and training implications of interdisciplinary collaboration.* Paper presented at the Annual Meeting of the American Psychological Association, New York.

Weick, K. (1983). Contradictions in a community of scholars: The cohesion-accuracy tradeoff. *Review of Higher Education, 6,* 253–267.

Weick, K. (1985). Sources of order in underorganized systems: Themes in recent organizational theory. In Lincoln, Y. (Ed.), *Organizational theory and inquiry: The paradigm revolution* (pp. 106–136). Beverly Hills, CA: Sage.

Weick, K. (1991). The vulnerable system: An analysis of the Tenerife air disaster. In Frost, P., Moore, L., Louis, M., Lundberg, C., & Martin, J. (Eds.), *Reframing organizational culture* (pp. 117–130). Newbury Park, CA: Sage.

Weston, K., & Rofel, L. (1984). Sexuality, class, and conflict in a lesbian workplace. *Signs, 9,* 623–646.

Whitman, W. (1921). *Leaves of grass.* New York: Modern Library.

Wilkins, A. (1978). *Organizational stories as an expression of management philosophy: Implications for social control in organizations.* Unpublished doctoral dissertation, Stanford University.

Wilkins, A. (1983). Organizational stories as symbols which control the organization. In Frost, P., Moore, L., Louis, M., Lundberg, C., & Martin, J. (Eds.), *Organizational culture* (pp. 81–91). Beverly Hills, CA: Sage.

Willmott, H. (In press). Postmodernism and excellence: The de-differentiation of economy and culture. *Journal of Organizational Change Management.*

Wright, J. (1979). *On a clear day you can see General Motors.* Grosse Pointe, MI: Wright Enterprises.

Wuthnow, R., Hunter, J., Bergesen, A., & Kurzweil, E. (1984). *Cultural analysis.* Boston: Routledge & Kegan Paul.

Yanow, D. J. (1982). *Toward a symbolic theory of policy implementation: An analysis of symbols, metaphors, and myths in organizations.* Unpublished doctoral dissertation, Massachusetts Institute of Technology.

Young, E. (1989). On the naming of the rose: Interests and multiple meanings as elements of organizational culture. *Organization Studies, 10,* 187–206.

Young, E. (1991). On the naming of the rose: Interests and multiple meanings as elements of organizational culture. In Frost, P., Moore, L., Louis, M., Lundberg, C., & Martin, J. (Eds.), *Reframing organizational culture* (pp. 90–103). Newbury Park, CA: Sage.

Index

DATE DUE

DEMCO 38-297